Crisis in Russian Studies?

Nationalism (Imperialism), Racism and War

TARAS KUZIO

E-INTERNATIONAL RELATIONS PUBLISHING

E-International Relations
www.E-IR.info
Bristol, England
2020

ISBN 978-1-910814-55-0

This book is published under a Creative Commons CC BY-NC 4.0 license. You are free to:

- **Share** — copy and redistribute the material in any medium or format
- **Adapt** — remix, transform, and build upon the material

Under the following terms:

- **Attribution** — You must give appropriate credit, provide a link to the license, and indicate if changes were made. You may do so in any reasonable manner, but not in any way that suggests the licensor endorses you or your use.
- **NonCommercial** — You may not use the material for commercial purposes.

Any of the above conditions can be waived if you get permission. Please contact info@e-ir.info for any such enquiries, including for licensing and translation requests.

Other than the terms noted above, there are no restrictions placed on the use and dissemination of this book for student learning materials/scholarly use.

Production: Michael Tang
Cover Image: Triff/Shutterstock

A catalogue record for this book is available from the British Library.

E-IR Open Access

Series Editor: Stephen McGlinchey
Books Editor: Bill Kakenmaster
Editorial Assistants: Clotilde Asangna, Kai Beerlink, Alyssa Blakemore, Iñigo González, Gabriela Greilinger, Maria Markova and Leo Lin.

E-IR Open Access is a series of scholarly books presented in a format that preferences brevity and accessibility while retaining academic conventions. Each book is available in print and digital versions, and is published under a Creative Commons license. As E-International Relations is committed to open access in the fullest sense, free electronic versions of all of our books, including this one, are available on the E-International Relations website.

Find out more at: http://www.e-ir.info/publications

About E-International Relations

E-International Relations (E-IR) is the world's leading open access website for students and scholars of international politics, reaching over three million readers per year. In addition to our books, our daily publications feature expert articles, reviews and interviews – as well as student learning resources. The website is run by a non-profit organisation based in Bristol, England and staffed by an all-volunteer team of students and scholars.

http://www.e-ir.info

Abstract

The goal of this book is to launch a discussion of the crisis in Russian studies following the 2014 European crisis and Russian-Ukrainian war which has yet to be acknowledged by historians and political scientists in Russian and Eurasian studies. The book analyses the crisis through five perspectives. The first is how Western historians continue to include Ukrainians within an imperial history of 'Russia' which denies Ukrainians a separate history. The second perspective is to counter the common narrative of Crimea as 'always' having been 'Russian' which denies that Tatars are the indigenous people of Crimea – not Russians. The third perspective focuses on academic orientalist approaches to writing about Ukraine and the Russian-Ukrainian war. The fourth perspective downplays Russian nationalism (imperialism) in Vladimir Putin's Russia and completely ignores the revival of Tsarist and White émigré Russian nationalism that denies the existence of Ukraine and Ukrainians. Meanwhile, academic orientalism exaggerates the influence of Ukrainian nationalism in post-Euromaidan Ukraine. The fifth perspective counters the claim of *Putinversteher* (Putin-Understander) scholars of a 'civil war' taking place in Ukraine through extensive evidence of Russian military aggression and imperialism. Finally, these five factors taken together show Russian studies will be unable to escape its crisis if it cannot come to understand how the source of the Russian-Ukrainian war lies in Russian national identity and its attitudes towards Ukraine and Ukrainians and why therefore the chances for peace are slim.

About the author

Taras Kuzio is a Professor in the Department of Political Science at the National University of Kyiv Mohyla Academy and a Non-Resident Fellow in the Foreign Policy Institute at the School of Advanced International Studies, Johns Hopkins University, Washington DC. His previous positions were at the University of Alberta, George Washington University, and University of Toronto. He holds a PhD in political science from the University of Birmingham, England, an MA in Soviet and East European Area Studies from the University of London. He is the author and editor of seventeen books, including (with Paul D'Anieri) *The Sources of Russia's Great Power Politics: Ukraine and the Challenge to the European Order* (2018), *Putin's War Against Ukraine. Revolution, Nationalism, and Crime* (2017, 2019), *Ukraine. Democratization, Corruption and the New Russian Imperialism* (2015), *From Kuchmagate to Orange Revolution* (2009), and *Theoretical and Comparative Perspectives on Nationalism (2007)*. He is the author of five think tank monographs, including *The Crimea: Europe's Next Flashpoint?* (2010). He is a member of the editorial boards of *Demokratizatsiya: The Journal of Post-Soviet Democratization*, *Communist and Post-Communist Studies*, *Eurasian Geography and Economics*, *New Perspectives: Interdisciplinary Journal of Central and East European Politics and International Relations*, *Geopolitics, History, and International Relations* and *The Ukrainian Quarterly*. He has authored 38 book chapters and 100 scholarly articles on Ukrainian and Eurasian politics, democratic transitions, colour revolutions, nationalism, and European studies.

Contents

INTRODUCTION	1
1. WESTERN HISTORIES OF 'RUSSIA' AND UKRAINE	9
2. RACISM, CRIMEA AND CRIMEAN TATARS	36
3. ACADEMIC ORIENTALISM	66
4. RUSSIAN NATIONALISM (IMPERIALISM) AND UKRAINIAN NATIONALISM	82
5. RUSSIAN MILITARY AGGRESSION OR 'CIVIL WAR'?	106
6. CONCLUSION: IMPACT OF WAR AND PROSPECTS FOR PEACE	133
REFERENCES	151
NOTE ON INDEXING	186

Анастасія Дмитрук, Никогда мы не будем братьями!
Anastasiya Dmytruk, Never Shall We Be Brothers!
March 2014[1]

Никогда мы не будем братьями!	Never shall we be brothers!
Ни по родине, ни по матери.	Not by motherland, nor by mothers.
Духа нет у вас быть свободными —	You don't have the soul to be free -
нам не стать с вами даже сводными.	we can't even be stepbrothers.
Вы себя окрестили «старшими» —	You have christened yourselves as the 'elders',
нам бы младшими, да не вашими.	we don't mind being younger, but not yours.
Вас так много, а, жаль, безликие.	There are so many of you, though you are faceless.
Вы огромные, мы — великие.	You are huge, we - great.
А вы жмете… вы всё маетесь,	And you press ... you all toil,
своей завистью вы подавитесь.	but on your envy, you will choke.
Воля — слово вам незнакомое,	Freedom - is an unknown word to you,
вы все с детства в цепи закованы.	you have all been chained since childhood.
У вас дома «молчанье — золото»,	In your home, 'silence is golden'
а у нас жгут коктейли Молотова,	while we light up Molotov cocktails,
да, у нас в сердце кровь горячая,	yes, we have hot blood in our hearts,
что ж вы нам за «родня» незрячая?	what sort of blind 'relatives' are you to us?
А у нас всех глаза бесстрашные,	All of us have fearless eyes
без оружия мы опасные.	we are dangerous even without weapons.
Повзрослели и стали смелыми	We have grown up and become brave
все у снайперов под прицелами.	all are in the snipers' sights.
Нас каты на колени ставили —	Hangmen forced us on to our knees -
мы восстали и всё исправили.	we rebelled and fixed everything.
И зря прячутся крысы, молятся —	And in vain the rats are hiding, praying -
они кровью своей умоются.	they will wash themselves with their blood.
Вам шлют новые указания —	You are being sent new instructions -
а у нас тут огни восстания.	but here we have the fires of uprising.
У вас Царь, у нас — Демократия.	You have a Tsar, we have Democracy.
Никогда мы не будем братьями.	Never shall we be brothers.

---

[1] https://dmytruk.com.ua/nykohda-myi-ne-budem-bratyamy/ and https://www.youtube.com/watch?v=Qv97YeC563Y

Introduction

This book has six objectives. The first objective is to launch a debate about whether there is a crisis in Russian studies over finding it difficult to come to terms with the 2014 crisis and Russian-Ukrainian War. Chair of the Department of Political Science at Columbia University and Marshall Shulman Professor of Post-Soviet Politics at Columbia University Timothy Frye (2017) believes that Russian studies is thriving in political science. This book questions this claim. Indeed, it is curious that Frye (2017) neglects to mention the 2014 crisis, Crimea, Donbas or the Russian-Ukrainian War which – as this book argues – *does not* show Russian studies to be 'alive and well,' *but does* show 'low quality' of academic research in 'Russian studies.'

The legitimacy of Russian actions in Crimea are often accepted and the Ukrainian counter viewpoint not taken seriously (see Zhuk 2014). There is only one 'correct' view of the 'Russian history' of Crimea and eastern Ukraine 'which is more noble and more important than that written by 'non-historic' peoples. Russian identity is 'resting on a different level, ordained with some sort of a historic nobility' (Belafatti 2014). Only Russian feelings are to be respected, not those of subaltern subjects.

The 'last anti-Soviet revolution' in Ukraine 'destroyed the traditionally accepted Moscow-centred and Russian-focused (in fact, Russian imperialist) approaches to an analysis of recent political, social, cultural, and economic developments in the post-Soviet space' (Zhuk 2014, 207). Nevertheless, many western historians and political scientists continue to write about Russia as though nothing fundamentally has changed. This is especially true of historians who have largely ignored the emergence of independent states from the USSR in 1991 and continue to write 'Russian' history as including territory in independent Ukraine as 'Russian lands.'

The crisis in Russian studies is most evident in its treatment of Russian nationalism (imperialism). Although nationalism (imperialism) was growing in Russia during the decade prior to the 2014 crisis, the tendency among political scientists has been to downplay, minimise, or temporise it (Hale 2016, 246), with a few exceptions (see Harris 2020). Moreover, all political scientists working on Russia have ignored the rehabilitation of Tsarist Russian and White *émigré* nationalism (imperialism) (Plokhy 2017, 326–327), Putin's belief that he is the 'gatherer of Russian lands,'[1] and the impact of these two developments on Russian attitudes toward Ukraine and Ukrainians and why they are the root cause of the 2014 crisis. Many of the authors in the over 400-page volume on Russian nationalism edited by Pal Kolsto and Helge Blakkisrud (2016) talk of the rise of ethnic Russian nationalism, its competition with imperial nationalism, and how they converged in 2014 in Crimea in defence of ethnic Russians and territorial expansionism (Kolsto 2016b, 6; Alexseev 2016, 161). At the same time, there is no discussion of how Russian ethnic nationalism is synonymous with *tryedynstva russkoho naroda* (All-Russian People) where the Russian [*Russkij*] people are viewed as composed of three branches – Russians, Ukrainians and Belarusians, and how Russian ethnic and imperial nationalisms became integrated in the 'Russian spring,' in the 'New Russia' (*Novorossiya* – the Tsarist term for southeastern Ukraine) project and more generally in Russian attitudes and policies toward Ukraine since 2014 (Plokhy 2017, 335). Russian nationalism has always been deeply rooted 'in the prevolutionary past' and was never limited to only Russians, but always included Ukrainians and Belarusians (Plokhy 2017, 303–304).

Marlene Laruelle (2017a) writes that *Russkij* can also be defined as encompassing only ethnic Russians or three eastern Slavs. Western scholars often ignore this important distinction of *Russkij* (see Bacon 2015, 23; Zakem, Saunders, Antoun 2015) or downplay it by arguing that Russian ethnic nationalism only became official policy when Putin was re-elected in 2012 (Alexseev 2016, 162). Laruelle (2016c, 275) believes *Russkij* identity was already 'mainstream' by 2014. Although western political scientists debate when Russian ethnic nationalism became official policy and if it was a temporary phenomenon, none of them discuss *Russkij* as *tryedynstva russkoho naroda* and the influence of such views on Putin's policies toward Ukraine in 2014 and thereafter.

The second objective is to show how historiographies of 'Russia' can provide justification for real-life nationalist (imperialist) invasions and military aggression. This would not be the case if western historians wrote civic histories of the Russian Federation but, unfortunately, western historians continue to conflate the Russian empire and nation-state and, in so doing, depict Ukraine as 'Russian lands,' thereby denying Ukrainians a separate history. Western historians promote the Russian nation as encompassing three eastern Slavs when they should be writing about a 'modern civic nation within the borders of the Russian Federation' (Plokhy 2017, 351).

---

[1] The exception was Mark Galeotti who I am grateful for pointing out Putin's evolution after 2008 into thinking of himself as the 'gatherer of Russian lands.'

My book uses the terms imperialism, nationalism, colonialism, and racism, and integrates them into discussions and analyses of Ukrainian-Russian relations, Crimea and the Russian-Ukrainian War. Imperialism is used in this book to denote conquest by a country of foreign territory, in the case of this book, Russia's occupation of Crimea and parts of the Donbas region of eastern Ukraine.

Imperialism also denotes actions, discourse and policies, and therefore it is a better term than nationalism to describe Russia (see Rowley 2000). My book understands nationalism to mean the desire to live in an independent state which has never been a paramount objective for Russian politicians, dissidents and activists. Russian dissidents did not seek the independence of the Russian Soviet Federative Socialist Republic (SFSR) from the Soviet Union, and the Russian SFSR did not declare independence from the USSR. In the USSR, those who were described as 'Russian nationalists' were either hard-line supporters of Joseph Stalin within the Communist Party or dissidents who wanted to transform the USSR into a Russian Empire. As Alexander J. Motyl (1990, 161–173) wrote some three decades ago, Russian nationalism is therefore a 'myth.'

The third objective is to show how it is wrong to view Crimea as 'always having been Russian.' Sakwa (2016, 24) describes Russia's annexation of Crimea as 'repatriation.' An outgrowth of the narrative of Crimea 'always having been Russian' is portraying 'Russians' as the peninsula's first settlers and thereby denying Tatars their longer history and right to be described as the indigenous people of Crimea.

Colonialism and racism are integrated into my analysis of Crimea and the long-term persecution of its indigenous people, the Crimean Tatars. My book places Crimea's conquest in the 1780s by the Tsarist Russian Empire within the context of similar conquests by western European countries of North America in the early seventeenth century and Australia in the following century. Colonial rule by Russia, England/Britain and France brought genocide and ethnic cleansing of the First Nation indigenous peoples (Magocsi 2010, 691).

While western scholars are unanimous in condemning colonialism and mistreatment of First Nation indigenous peoples, those writing on Russian history adopt a different approach and usually support Russia's conquest of Crimea and what they see as justice served by its return to Russia in 2014 (see Zhuk 2014). The Tsarist Russian Empire, USSR and Putin's Russia have all undertaken – and continue to undertake – racial discrimination and ethnic cleansing of Crimean Tatars (see Coynash and Charron 2019; Skrypnyk

2019). In addition, Ukrainians in Crimea and Russian-controlled Donbas are subjected to Soviet-style Russification.

Racism toward Crimean Tatars was never confined to the far right, as it always had its supporters in the Soviet Communist Party and post-Soviet Communist Parties of the Russian Federation and Ukraine. With such a left-wing history of racism, we should not be therefore surprised at Communist China imprisoning one million Uighurs in concentration camps. In Russia and Ukraine, political forces are divided into two camps over their attitudes toward Crimean Tatars. Racists believe the fictitious Stalinist charge that Crimean Tatars collaborated with the Nazis. These political forces include Soviet and post-Soviet communists, Russian nationalist (imperialist) extreme right forces, the former Ukrainian Party of Regions and, following its disintegration, the Opposition Bloc (*Opozytsiynyy blok*) and Opposition Platform-For Life (*Opozytsiyna platforma – za zhyttya*). Political forces holding a non-racist view of Crimean Tatars include Ukrainian nationalist and democratic forces. Crimean Tatars were elected to the Ukrainian parliament by *Rukh* (Ukrainian Popular Movement for Restructuring), Our Ukraine and the Petro Poroshenko bloc. Those political forces who support Putin, the *Russkij Mir* (Russian World) and Eurasian integration hold a racist view of Crimean Tatars while those who support European integration do not.

The fourth objective is a critical literature review of academic orientalist writing about the absence of nationalism in Russia and exaggerated accounts of nationalism in Ukraine. Some, but not all, of this writing is by what I term *Putinversteher* (Putin-Understander) scholars who seek to always deflect criticism from Russian President Putin and Russia and lay blame on Ukraine, NATO, the EU, and the US.

Nationalism in Ukraine is often discussed and analysed through Soviet and contemporary Russian lenses. Ukraine has one of the lowest rates of electoral support for nationalism in Europe if we use the political science definition of nationalism. During a war that has killed upwards of 20,000 people, what are understood in Europe as nationalist parties failed to be elected in the 2014 and 2019 Ukrainian elections. If a Soviet and contemporary Russian understanding of 'nationalism' is instead used, Ukraine is overflowing with 'nationalists' because it is applied to all those who rejected the Soviet system, want Ukraine to live outside the Russian World (*Russkij Mir*) and supported the Orange and Euromaidan Revolutions.

Some western scholars seek to minimise or deny that Putin's regime is nationalistic or claim that he resorted to nationalism temporarily between 2013–14 and 2015–16. This claim flies in the face of multiple sources of evidence of nationalism (imperialism) within Putin's authoritarian regime. In making this argument, western scholars ignore how Russian nationalism under Putin exchanged the Soviet nationality concept of close but separate 'brotherly peoples' with the Tsarist Russian and White *émigré* conception of the *triyedinyy russkij narod* composed of three branches – Russians, Ukrainians, and Belarusians. It is difficult to see how an argument can be made that Putin's Russia is not nationalistic when it denies the existence of Ukraine and Belarus, and when Russian leaders and media repeatedly state that Ukrainians and Russians (and Belarusians and Russians) are 'one people.'

The fifth objective is to provide a counter-narrative of Russian military aggression to understand the Russian-Ukrainian War taking place in the Donbas region of eastern Ukraine. Russian intervention in Ukraine took place throughout the decade prior to the 2014 crisis and should be investigated not only from a purely military angle of boots on the ground, but through all aspects of Russian 'full spectrum conflict' (Jonsson and Seely 2015). Refusing to define the Russian-Ukrainian War as a 'civil war' is both a reflection of crisis in Russian studies and an outgrowth of the tendency to exaggerate the influence of Ukrainian nationalism in the Euromaidan Revolution and post-Euromaidan Ukrainian politics.

The sixth objective is to show why peace is unlikely because the choice of who Ukrainians elect is far less important than the fact that Russia's president will remain in power for a further 16 years. Although the Russian-Ukrainian War has been counter-productive and led to a reduction in Russian soft power in Ukraine, there will not be peace as long as Putin and Russian leaders continue to deny the existence of Ukraine and Ukrainians.

This book makes seven main points.

First, there are three implications arising from the manner in which histories of 'Russia' are written by western historians. The first is that Ukrainian territory is depicted as always 'Russian,' with Ukrainians inexplicably arriving from an unknown place and 'squatting' on 'Russian lands.' The second is because western histories of 'Russia' are the same or similar to official Russian views of 'Russian' history and discourse toward Ukraine and Ukrainians they have become – unwittingly – partners in Russian nationalism (imperialism) against Ukraine. Serhii Plokhy (2017, 331) writes about the link between Putin's belief in Russians and Ukrainians being 'one people' slated to live eternally in the Russian World with the Russian army annexing Crimea and invading eastern Ukraine. The third is histories of Ukraine are written in the same manner as civic histories of European nation-states with Kyiv Rus as the beginning of

Ukrainian history (Subtelny 1988, 1991, 1994a, 1994b, 2000, 2009; Magocsi 1996, 1997, 2010, 2012; Plokhy 2015, 2016). Histories with 'Kievan Russia' (Kyiv Rus) as the beginning of 'Russian history' are imperial histories which have nothing in common with European civic historiography of nation-states. Ukraine's approach is compatible with democratisation and European values, while an imperial history of Russia is synonymous with ethnic and political repression and foreign military aggression.

Second, western and Russian historians uphold Russian claims to Crimea in two ways. The first is that 'Kievan Russia' (Kyiv Rus) was a 'Russian land' and Crimea was therefore always 'Russian.' The second is that Russia has controlled Crimea since 1783 and therefore has always been 'Russian.' Both of these claims – just as in the first point – provide sustenance for Russian military aggression. Claiming that 'Kievan Russia' (Kyiv Rus) was always 'Russian' denies Ukraine its historical origins, while using the 1783 annexation to depict Crimea as 'always having been Russian' denies Crimean Tatars as Crimea's indigenous people (Sakwa 2016, 24).

Third, there was neither majority support for separatism in Crimea nor the Donbas prior to or in 2014. Opinion polls conducted in spring 2014 found no majority support for separatism in Crimea or any region of mainland Ukraine (Coynash 2019). In the eight *oblasts* of southeastern Ukraine, the highest rate of support of between 18–33% for separatism was to be found in the two *oblasts* of the Donbas. In the eight *oblasts* of southeastern Ukraine, an average of 15.4% supported separatism, and only 8.4% supported the unification of Ukraine and Russia into one state (The Views and Opinions of South-Eastern Regions Residents of Ukraine 2014).

In Crimea, a Russian invasion of sovereign Ukrainian territory was legitimised by a sham, Soviet-style referendum. In the Donbas, extremist Russian nationalists supported by a minority of the region's inhabitants took power with the assistance of Russian hybrid warfare. While separatists in South Ossetia, Abkhazia and Nagorno-Karabakh had sizeable support because the conflict was ethnically driven, the war in the Donbas has always been artificial and led by foreign actors. It is therefore flawed to describe what is taking place as a 'civil war' in the Donbas (see Kolsto 2016b, 16).

Fourth, Putin's justification for invading Crimea and eastern Ukraine (which in the latter case Russia has always denied) to defend Russian speakers was bogus. No opinion polls or international organisation reported discrimination of Russian speakers (Plokhy 2017, 339). Putin's justification 'harked back to 1938 rather than 1989' (Plokhy 2017, 339). In Crimea, 'reactive settler nationalism' (Yekelchyk 2019) exercised hegemonic control and discriminated against Crimean Tatar and Ukrainian minorities. In the Donbas, the Party of Regions and extremist Russian nationalist groups discriminated against Ukrainian speakers and the Jewish minority.

Russians and Russian speakers in Ukraine are provided with a wide range of educational, cultural, religious and media facilities. In the Donbas and Crimea, the Soviet era institutionalisation of the hegemony of the Russian language has been reinforced since 2014. In Ukraine, Russians and Russian speakers can vote for pro-Russian parties, go to Russian-language schools, watch Russian-language and pro-Russian television channels, and they can attend religious services in the Russian Orthodox Church. Putin's representative in Ukraine, Viktor Medvedchuk, is the owner of three television channels.

Fifth, since 1783, Crimean Tatars have experienced national revivals for only 33 years during what was appropriately called *korenisation* (indigenisation) in 1923–1933 in the USSR and independent Ukraine from 1991–2013. For nearly two centuries, Crimean Tatars suffered from genocide, ethnic cleansing, racism, and Islamophobia in the Tsarist Russian Empire and USSR, and since 2014 under Russian occupation, 'hybrid genocide,' as coined by Crimean Tatar journalist Ayder Muzhdabayev (Goble 2015).

Sixth, a majority of Russian speakers in Ukraine hold a civic Ukrainian not a Russian World identity and they therefore did not support the 'Russian spring' or 'New Russia' project in 2014 or since. Many western scholars were surprised at this because they held stereotypical myths of a regionally divided Ukraine (see Darden and Way 2014), did not understand Russian speaking Ukrainian patriotism, and did not take this patriotism into account when writing about the Russian-Ukrainian War. There are no differences in regional levels of patriotism among Ukrainians with 85% in the west, 83% in the south, and 82% in the east defining themselves as 'Ukrainian patriots,' and 63% in Ukraine's west, 54% in the south, and 50% in the east ready to use weapons to defend Ukraine from foreign attack (Defenders Day of Ukraine 2020). Russian military aggression is being mainly fought by Russian speaking Ukrainians who constitute the majority of the casualties (see Map 6.2). Putin is not defending but killing Russian speakers in Ukraine and driving them into becoming internally displaced persons (IDPs) and refugees.

Seventh, during the first half of the 1990s, the Russian Federation did not prioritise nation-building, and Boris Yeltsin first raised the question of formulating a 'national idea' for the new state in 1996, the same year he supported the contradictory policy of a Russian-Belarusian union (Prizel 1998). Yitzhak Brudny (1998, 261) argues that it is the absence of civic nationalism that has undermined Russia's post-Soviet political and economic transition process (see Tolz 1998a, 1998b; Kolsto 2016a, 3; Blakkisrud 2016, 260). The editor of the Russian newspaper *Vedomosti*, Maxim Trudolybov (2016), explained the different paths of Russia and Ukraine: 'The Russian body politic equates society with the state. Ukraine, with its growing number of volunteer movements, nongovernment charities and independent political parties, is occupied in framing a new civic identity.'

Ukraine is building the civic identity that has eluded Russia. Civic nationalism and patriotism are predominant in Ukraine – not ethnic nationalism (see Clem 2014; Kulyk 2014, 2016; Onuch and Hale 2018; Pop-Eleches and Robertson 2018; Kaihko 2018; Onuch and Sasse 2018; Bureiko and Moga 2019; Nedozhogina 2019). Ukrainian patriots blame Russian leaders and the Russian state for military aggression against their country – not the Russian people. Crimean Tatars and Jews would not have fled from Crimea and the Donbas, respectively, to Ukraine if it were run by extremist 'nationalists.' Russian speakers would not be fighting for Ukraine if nationalism dominated post-Euromaidan politics.

This book has six chapters. Chapter 1 analyses western, Tsarist, Soviet and contemporary Russian historiography of 'Russia,' which to varying degrees and in different forms portrays Ukraine as 'Russian land.' The second chapter discusses Crimea and why Tatars are its indigenous people and provides a survey of Russian territorial claims to the peninsula which long pre-date 2014. The third chapter critically investigates what I define as academic orientalist writing through Russian eyes of the 2014 crisis, Crimea and Russian-Ukrainian War. The fourth chapter analyses academic orientalist minimising of nationalism in Russia and exaggerating levels of nationalism in Ukraine. The fifth chapter critically engages with depictions of a 'civil war' between Ukrainians by providing a wide variety of evidence of Russian intervention prior to and since 2014 to argue that what is taking place is a Russian-Ukrainian War. The concluding chapter discusses the negative impact of the war on Russian soft power in Ukraine and analyses why there are few grounds to believe peace will be achieved during Putin's tenure of Russia.

1

Western Histories of 'Russia' and Ukraine

'It is quite true that Russian history until recently has usually been written too much from the angle of Moscow and imperial Russia, with the consequence that the special development of the Western lands and the distinctiveness and achievements of the Ukrainians have been belittled and ignored; it is also true that Ukrainian nationalist historians have contributed a large new fund of knowledge by their researches.' – B.H. Summner (1947, 224)

Western historiography of 'Russia' has always been that of a history of the Russian empire and never that of the Russian state, such as the Russian Federation since 1991. This places western historiography at odds with standard western histories of European nation-states. Western and Ukrainian histories of Ukraine are those of the nation-state, which came into existence in 1991.

This chapter focuses on Ukraine within western historiography of 'Russia' for two reasons. The first is that Russian nationalists (imperialists) have always viewed Ukrainians and Belarusians in a different manner to other nationalities in the Tsarist Empire and Soviet Union and as independent states since 1991. Ukrainians and Belarusians were viewed as two of the three branches of the *tryedynstva russkoho naroda* by Tsarist Russia; in the USSR, this was modified to the eastern Slavs being close but separate peoples.

Limited space means this book can focus on only Ukraine and not include an analysis of western historiography of Belarus. Russian attitudes to Belarus are in many ways worse than those towards Ukraine, and Russian leaders and media use 'White Russia' and 'Belarus' interchangeably.[1] President

---

[1] https://euvsdisinfo.eu/report/belarus-means-white-russia-and-white-russians-identify-themselves-as-culturally-russian/

Vladimir Putin described Belarusians as 'perhaps, the closest country to us. And ethnically the closest, both linguistically, culturally, spiritually, whatever.'[2] Putin described Belarusians and Russians as 'one people,'[3] in the same manner as he refers to Ukrainians and Russians. The second is that it is important to study western histories of 'Russia' in the context of the Russian-Ukrainian War because the myths they promote of Ukraine and Ukrainians are similar to the discourse propounded by Russian leaders.

This chapter is divided into five sections. The first defines imperialism and why it is a better description of Russian actions and policies than nationalism. Russians – like the English – have traditionally preferred to live in union states and empires and have not produced separatist movements. There is no English equivalent of the Scottish National Party (SNP) or Russian version of Ukrainian nationalist organisations. The second and third sections survey Tsarist, Soviet and western historiography of 'Russia.' The fourth section discusses how western historiography of 'Russia' ignores the origins of 'Ukrainian squatters' who came to live on what they describe from time immemorial as 'Russian lands.' The last section compares and contrasts western historiography of 'Russia' and Ukraine to demonstrate how the former continues to be that of the history of empire and the latter civic history of a nation-state.

Defining Imperialism

Imperialism is a system of unequal political and ethnic relationships between subjects and objects. Imperialists impose political control by the metropolis over colonial dependencies, which is maintained during the colonial era through military bases, political interference, media outlets, the language used by the metropolis, economic power and dependency, energy, and trade (Cohen 1996, 1–28). Some of this influence continues to remain in place in the post-colonial era, and de-colonisation is often a long, drawn-out process.

The metropolis drives colonial expansion into neighbouring territories, as in the case of Austria and Russia, and overseas in the case of Great Britain, France and the US. England's first empire was closer to home on the British mainland and Ireland. Imperialism is ultimately the domination of one nation over another. Margaret Moore (1997, 909) defines imperialism as applicable 'to any attempt by one people to dominate politically another people, especially if the latter perceive the rule to be hostile to their national identity.' The motivations for imperialism are extermination and exploitation (or a mix of the two) of the peoples who have been conquered together with loot, trade,

---

[2] https://www.bbc.com/russian/news-53929091
[3] https://spbdnevnik.ru/news/2019-12-19/vladimir-putin-russkie-i-belorusy-pochti-odin-narod

and greed (Seton-Watson 1971, 7–10).

Empires have cores where ruling elites are based and peripheries where there are outposts of the empire and peripheral elites. The absence of any independence constitutes the unequal relationship between cores and peripheries which are subordinated, coordinated, supervised and 'protected' (Motyl 1999a, 118–120). Interaction with the outside world is only via the core (Motyl 1999b, 128). Prior to 1991, non-Russian republics could only interact with the outside world through Moscow; for example, there were no direct flights into Kyiv or Tallinn, as all international flights went through Moscow. In 1991, the non-Russian nations of the USSR became independent states and were able to join the international community; nevertheless, Russia continues to view them as not possessing full sovereignty (Gretskiy 2020).

Violence often accompanies the decline of empires (Motyl 1999, 133). The USSR largely disintegrated peacefully with exceptions in Chechnya, Moldova, Azerbaijan, Georgia and Tajikistan. Ukraine resolved its Crimean separatist threat in the 1990s in a peaceful manner. Ukrainian-Russian tensions grew as Putin's Russia imperialised its memory politics and security policies and came to view Ukraine as an 'artificial' country and lost 'Russian' land. The 2014 crisis was a product of Russia unable to accept the existence of a Ukrainian state and its belief that Ukrainians are one of three branches of the *triyedinyy russkij narod*.

Colonisers are, by definition, arrogant and racially discriminatory, deeming those who have been colonised to be inferior. 'The assumption of superiority became an article of faith' Jeremy Paxman (1999, 65) writes. Nationalists in the colonies seek to regain their self-esteem after independence is achieved through new memory politics and other policies (Emerson 1967, 381, 382). Ukraine's memory politics and historiography diverged from Russia in an evolutionary fashion from the late 1980s to 2013 and in a more revolutionary manner since when four de-communisation laws adopted in 2015 laid out an extensive range of policies for the country's de-Sovietisation.

David Rowley (2000) argues it is 'inaccurate and misleading' to use the terms 'nationalism' and 'nationalist' *vis-à-vis* Russia, and it is more appropriate to use imperialism and imperialist. Rowley believes (2000, 23) that 'Russians expressed their national consciousness through the discourse of imperialism rather than the discourse of nationalism has far-reaching implications for both Russian history and nationalism theory.' I agree with Rowley (2000), and my book uses the terms imperialist and imperialism, not nationalist and nationalism, when discussing Russian policies towards Ukraine and its other neighbours.

Russian nationalists (imperialists) glorified in their multinational empire. Russians did not attempt to create a Russian nation-state in 1917 when the Tsarist Empire disintegrated, Russian dissidents and nationalists never sought independence from the USSR and the Russian SFSR did not declare independence in August 1991. After the collapse of the Tsarist Empire in 1917, no Russian equivalent of Turkish nationalist Kemal Ataturk, who created modern Turkey from the ruins of the Ottoman Empire, attempted to carve out a Russian nation-state. Indeed, the Russian Constitutional Democratic Party (*Kadets*), who politically dominated the anti-Bolshevik White movement, supported the preservation of the empire and opposed demands for federal autonomy, let alone independence for Ukraine (Rowley 2000, 28; see Procyk 1995).

The ideology that pervaded Russian discourse in the Tsarist Empire was universalist, religious and multinational, all tenets that 'ruled out nationalism' (Rowley 2000). The Tsarist and Soviet empires never promoted Russian nation-building and a Russian homeland separate to the empire or multi-national state. The Russian SFSR was the only Soviet republic not defined as a homeland for its titular nation and therefore was not given republican institutions; Soviet and Russian were one and the same in the USSR (see Kuzio 2007). The Russian SFSR only began creating republican institutions in 1990 after Yeltsin was elected Russian president.

In the former USSR no Russian dissident groups called for the secession of the Russian SFSR which is why Motyl argues it is wrong to describe Russians as 'nationalists' (Motyl 1990, 161–173). Individual Russian dissidents, such as Andrei Amalrik and Vladimir Bukovsky, who did call for independence were in a small minority. In demanding sovereignty for the Russian SFSR President Boris Yeltsin was, Rowley (2000) believes, a 'nationalist.' Nevertheless, the Russian SFSR did not declare independence in autumn 1991 from the USSR, and Russia's 'Independence Day' is based on the June 1990 Declaration of Sovereignty. Yeltsin was therefore, if anything, a reluctant 'nationalist.' In December 1991, President Yeltsin prioritised transforming the USSR into a confederal Commonwealth of Independent States (CIS) (D'Anieri, Kravchuk, Kuzio, 1999, 10–44). Ukrainian President Leonid Kravchuk prioritised Ukrainian independence.

Russian identity was greater than the Russian SFSR and has never been comfortable within the confines of the Russian Federation. In the post-Soviet era, 'Russia' has been imagined as Alexander Solzhenitsyn's Russian Union (2000) and Putin's Russian World uniting three eastern Slavs and, in some cases, northern Kazakhstan, the CIS, Belarusian-Russian union, and CIS Customs Union (since 2015 Eurasian Economic Union).

Russian and western histories of 'Russia' have submerged the existence of Ukraine and Ukrainians within a 'Russian' nationalist (imperialist) framework. Russian, Soviet, and western historians of 'Russia' also derided Ukrainian historiography as 'nationalist' because it described a history separate to that of Russia. In the aftermath of the disintegration of the former USSR such an approach became increasingly untenable because Ukrainians and the other non-Russians of the former USSR were building new states, forging new nations and writing new historiographies. It is even more untenable after the 2014 crisis and during the Russian-Ukrainian War.

Tsarist and Soviet Historiographies

What historical and disturbing legacies have Ukrainians and Russians grappled with since 1991? Russian historian Yury Afanasev complained, 'there is not, nor has there ever been a people and country with a history as falsified as ours is ...' (Velychenko 1994a, 327).

In 1934, after the *Holodomor* (Murder Famine) in Ukraine, Soviet historiography returned to Tsarist Russian nationalist (imperialist) history and produced a historiography, 'which could, for the most part, be read with approval by the tsars themselves,' Lowell Tillet wrote (1969, 4; see also Tillett 1964, 1967). Historiography served the goals of the Communist Party of the Soviet Union's nationalities policies in the elaboration and inculcation of new myths. Ukrainians were a close but separate people to Russians; they were born together, always strived to live together and were slated to always live together.

Soviet historiography accepted Ukrainians as a separate people with their own republican homeland and, after 1945, membership in the United Nations. But this was a temporary phenomenon because the 'natural' course of history would lead to the merger of eastern Slavs into a Russian speaking *Homo Sovieticus*. As Rowley (2000) points out, Tsarist nationalist (imperialist) universalism was recast as Soviet internationalism. Putin has re-constructed this as the Russian World. The end product was the same: a merger of three eastern Slavs into a Russian 'nation' in Tsarist Russia or into a Soviet man in the USSR. Twelve key elements of this Soviet 'elaborate historical myth' were (Tillett 1969, 4; see also Mazour 1975):

1. Rehabilitation of the Tsarist past;

2. Superiority of 'Great Russians' as natural leaders of the USSR (and since 2007, the Russian World);

3. There has never been ethnic hostility between Russians and non-Russians (especially between Russians and Ukrainians) now or in the past;

4. There were no conquered territories, but rather only 'unions' and 're-unions.' Communist theorists Friedrich Engels and Karl Marx, Soviet leader Vladimir Lenin and Bolshevik historians in the 1920s, such as Mikhail Pokrovskyy, had been wrong to condemn Tsarist Russian 'expansionism;'

5. These 'unions' and 're-unions' brought only positive benefits or, at a minimum, were the 'lesser of two evils.' Tsarist Russian history was no longer viewed in a negative manner and the incorporation of territories were either beneficial acts or it had been better for those peoples to be ruled by Russians rather than Poles, Austrians, Ottomans, or others (Brandenberger 1998, 878);

6. Greater centralisation was a positive development;

7. Nationalist agitation for independence was against the wishes of the people who have always sought to remain close to Russia;

8. Non-Russians were incapable of creating their own state;

9. The Russian *mission civilisatrice* was beneficial to non-Russians;

10. The *History of the USSR* was the same as that of the *'History of Russia.'* The Russian SFSR did not have a separate history to that of the USSR which could have dealt with only 'Great Russians' or Muscovites (the name for Russians before the creation of the Russian Empire in 1721);

11. Non-Russian histories were treated as regional histories of 'Russia;'

12. Russian control over Ukraine and Belarus was never perceived as 'annexation;' merely the recovery of the Tsar's patrimony. In 1947 and 1954, new theses codified the eastern Slavs as historically belonging to one 'Russian nation.' Use of the terms Russian, Rus'ian and eastern Slavic became inter-changeable;

These nationalist (imperialist) and colonialist themes in Soviet historiography and nationalities policies continue to influence contemporary Russian politics, memory politics, media and foreign policy. Russian television, which is controlled by Putin's authoritarian state, promotes the colonialist narrative of Russia having paid a heavy burden and toll to develop its neighbours (Laruelle 2014a, 328). This colonial narrative of empires being benign and a product of 'imperial amnesia' was promoted by all imperialist powers, but only in Russia does it continue in the twenty-first century to shape attitudes towards its neighbours, imagine Ukrainian territory, and guide its foreign and military policies.

In western Europe, the US, Australia and New Zealand (as discussed in chapter 2) colonialist discourse and narratives have been under attack since World War II by intellectuals and scholars. This de-colonisation of the mind has not taken place in the Russian Federation where the continued prevalence of nationalist (imperialist) narratives guides Russian foreign and security policies towards its neighbours and the broader world. Until World War II, all western historiographies were 'nationalistic' and 'equalled the Pan-Germans in their excess by the turn of the century' (Kennedy 1973, 82). Times have changed in the West, but not in Russia.

The USSR incorporated Russian nationalist (imperialist) historiography and colonialist attitudes towards Russia's neighbours, which have been preserved in slightly different forms in post-Soviet Russia and became increasingly common under Putin. In reality, none of the Tsarist, Soviet and contemporary Russian colonialist claims have anything to do with real history. In the seventeenth century, on the eve of Ukraine and Muscovy (pre-imperial name for the Russian state), signing an alliance the former was more socially and politically advanced. Muscovy had introduced serfdom in 1597; Ukraine had free Cossack peasants until the Cossack autonomous state was destroyed by Russia in 1775, only eight years before the colonial conquest of Crimea. Ukrainians associate serfdom with Russian rule because it was imposed by the Tsarist Empire in Ukraine which had been transformed into a Russian colony by 1917 (Shkandrij 2001, 82–83).

Soviet historiography restricted the collective memory and identity of each nation within the former USSR to that of an *ethnie* and geographical unit. Within southeastern Ukraine, Tsarist, and Soviet historiography reinforced a strong 'all-Russian' national component already part of popular consciousness surviving until 2014 but declining since. This channelled collective historical memory and national awareness generated by modernisation into an ethnographic regionalism 'compatible with Soviet loyalty' (Velychenko 1994b, 28). Independent Ukraine inherited identities in parts of southeastern Ukraine (especially the Donbas and Crimea), where the loyalties of the local population were multiple and loyal towards the Ukrainian SSR as a geographic unit and Russian and eastern Slavic 'brotherhood of peoples' (Velychenko 1993, 140, 160, 167, 210).

Russian historiography tailored the past to fit the present by justifying Russian rule over Ukrainian territories not in terms of conquered territories but as rule over peoples with allegedly the same history, language and cultures. There could not be, therefore, any 'oppression' of Ukrainian lands because there was allegedly cultural unity of Russians and Ukrainians. The oppressors of Ukrainians were the Poles—not the Russians.

These myths and legends formulated within Soviet historiography had gone full circle by the early 1950s. By the time of Stalin's death, further revisions of Soviet historiography made the Soviet interpretation of Ukrainian-Russian relations into a replica of that found in the Tsarist Russian Empire. The 1954 'Thesis on Re-Union' to mark the 300th anniversary of the Ukrainian-Muscovite Pereyaslav Treaty in 1654 replicated and updated much of the schema originally formulated within Tsar Nicholas I's 1833 'Official Nationality' policy of 'Orthodoxy, Autocracy, Nationality.'

By 1991, after six years of glasnost, only one Russian historian had summoned the courage to reject the 1954 'Thesis.' Mark von Hagen believes that there was 'very little attempt on the part of Russian historians to reject the imperial scheme of Russian history' in the Russian Federation even under Yeltsin.[4] Since the collapse of the former USSR, publishing houses in Moscow and St. Petersburg re-published Tsarist surveys of 'Russian' history, which increased nationalistic (imperialistic) appetites. New histories of 'Russia' do not limit themselves to only surveying Muscovy, 'Great Russians,' or the Russian Federation because they are 'in fact palimpsests of the histories of the USSR complete with the notions of "old Russian nation" and the "reunion" of Ukraine and Russia in 1654.'[5]

The propagation and digestion of these myths and legends provided negative legacies for the Russian Federation and Ukraine. They reinforced a Russian tendency to identify not with the Russian SFSR or Russian Federation – but with a union in the form of Tsarist Russia, the former USSR, CIS and Eurasian Economic Union. This impeded the development of a Russian civic national identity and national consciousness and reinforced the view that Ukrainian independence is 'temporary' and out of step with the pre-ordained destiny of the union of eastern Slavs.

---

[4] Interview with Mark von Hagen, Director of the Harriman Institute, Columbia University, 19 November 1996.
[5] Interview with Stephen Velychenko, University of Toronto, 21 November 1996.

The collapse of the former USSR left Russians rudderless when attempting to come to terms with the collapse of the Soviet state. Experts existed in Moscow on the smallest Caucasian ethnic groups and foreign countries. Yet, few Russian historians, political scientists or international relations experts had studied Ukraine or Belarus (Velychenko 1993, 191). The works of Mykhaylo Hrushevsky (1970), the doyen of Ukrainian historiography, remain unknown for many Russians. Aleksander Tsipko, the well-known Russian philosopher, believed the post-Soviet Russian leadership knew little about Ukrainian historians or culture, as reflected in the broadcasts of Russian television.

Western historians of 'Russia' have never treated Ukrainian history writing, such as Hrushevsky's 10-volume *Istoriya Ukrayiny-Rusy* (History of Ukraine-Rus) published between 1898–1937, in a serious manner. The well-known US-based historian Nicholas V. Riasanovsky (1977, 198) made only one reference to Hrushevsky when briefly discussing the Zaporozhzhyan Cossacks. Usually, when Hrushevsky was mentioned by western historians it was to deride him as someone providing a 'nationalistic viewpoint' (Billington 1970, 624). The dominant narrative in the West was that Russian nationalistic (imperialistic) historiography was 'objective' and Ukrainian historiography was 'nationalistic' in an example of academic orientalism.

Western Historiography of 'Russia'

Western historians working in conditions of academic freedom were free to pursue the study of 'Russian history' in as objective a manner as is possible. Nevertheless, western histories of imperial Russia and the former USSR traditionally portrayed it as a nation-state rather than as a multinational empire (Brown, Kaiser and Smith 1994; Plokhy 1996, 343). As Hagen found, 'Certainly, no mainstream Russian historian ever defined the empire as such; rather, they chose to write the history of Russia more or less as the history of a nation-state, or at least one in the making.'[6] Only Hugh Seton-Watson's (1967) survey of Russian history devoted some attention to the non-Russian nations of the Tsarist empire.

Western histories of 'Russia' followed the assumption laid out in the nineteenth century that nationality policy should be tailored to create a 'nation-state' from the Russian Empire. This could only be undertaken by assuming Ukrainians and Belarusians were somehow 'Russians' without a history separate to Russia. As Theodore R. Weeks argues, 'And yet the Russian Empire was not, and could not be, a nation-state. Any effort to make

---

[6] M. von Hagen, 'After the Soviet Union: Rethinking Modern Russian History', The Seventeenth Annual Philadelphia Distinguished Lecture on History, 1977, 9.

the Russian Empire into a national state was doomed to failure' (Weeks 1996, 4).

In the nineteenth century, the Tsarist Russian Empire had attempted to nationalise Ukrainians and Belarusians into an 'All-Russian People' through repression, unlike the British, French, and Germans who had nationalised their peripheries through gradual assimilationist and education policies (Plokhy 2017, 135). In the nineteenth century, dual loyalty to Ukraine and the Russian Empire, understood as a Little Russian compromise by writer Mykola Hohol (Nikolai Gogol), became untenable and the choice was left of either becoming an extremist Russian nationalist or embracing a Ukrainian identity (Plokhy 2017, 153). On both occasions, Russian repression of Ukrainians in the nineteenth century *and* military aggression against Ukraine since 2014 strengthened Ukrainian identity and damaged Russian-Ukrainian relations (Plokhy 2017, 107, 335).

Any attempt to transform the Tsarist Russian Empire into a 'nation-state' modelled on Germany and based on the core 'Russian' *(three* eastern Slavic) peoples assumed two factors (Weeks 1996, 11). First, Ukrainians and Belarusians were 'ethnographic raw material' (Weeks 1996, 46, 64)*;* that is, they were simply 'Little Russians' and 'White Russians' and not separate nations (Weeks 1996, 93). Second, the non-Slavic peoples of the Tsarist empire would agree to assimilate into a planned 'Russian nation-state' or enter into 'voluntary union' with it. This policy, supported by Tsarist officials and nearly all Russian political parties, rejected any group rights (cantons, autonomy or federalisation) for the empire (Procyk 1995).

In view of the fact 'Great Russians' constituted less than 50% of the empire's population at the turn of the twentieth century, viewing the Tsarist Empire as a potential 'nation-state' in the making where non-Russians could be somehow successfully assimilated was misguided. Why then did western historiography of 'Russia' not follow their colleagues writing on Austria-Hungary, who had little hesitation in describing it as a multinational empire rather than as a budding nation-state?

Equating the Tsarist Empire with an embryonic 'nation-state' and not recognising Ukrainians and Belarusians as separate nations meant that, as far as Russians were concerned, charges of 'Russification' were misplaced. The adoption of the 'higher' Russian language and culture by Ukrainians and Belarusians was, and continues to be, viewed as positive. In the Soviet era, Russian was the language of modernisation and the future *Homo Sovieticus.* Nation-building, as Walker Connor has stated, is, after all, also usually associated with nation destroying (Connor 1972). Ukrainian history writing about the Tsarist and Soviet regimes' Russification and de-nationalisation has always been met with a lack of understanding among Russians. The bulk of western historiography of 'Russia' had little to say about the Russification of Ukraine and this continues to be the case. Pal Kolstø's (2019) detailed and interesting discussion of what he terms 'Russian imperialist nationalism' strangely has nothing to say about Tsarist Russian nationality policy defining the three eastern Slavs as *triyedinyy russkij narod* or Russification and the banning of the Ukrainian and Belarusian languages in the Tsarist Russian Empire.

Viewing the Russian Empire as a 'nation-state' was influenced by Michael Karpovich at Harvard University, who 'shaped the post-war generation of Russian historians in North America and Europe.'[7] These historians placed their faith in modernisation theory by social scientists such as Karl Deutsch, who argued that industrialisation and urbanisation would erode national differences and homogenise populations. The application of modernisation theories to the USSR suggested that ethnic differences would be removed, nationality problems were in decline and the achievement of a *Homo Sovieticus* was a matter of time. By the early 1980s, western historians of Russia, together with the bulk of their colleagues in Sovietology, had therefore concluded that nationality problems had been resolved in the USSR. The national question was therefore largely ignored within Sovietology (Subtelny 1994). I remember only too vividly from my days as an MA student at the School of Slavonic and East European Studies (now University College London) how wrong these scholars were and how they never fully understood the origins of non-Russian nationalisms in the USSR in the late 1980s.

Two histories by Russian *émigrés* Michael Florinsky (1953) and Riasanovsky (1977) were very influential in western historiography of 'Russia.' Until the latter part of the twentieth century, these and other historians wrote about 'Kievan Russia' but were forced to change this to Kyivan Rus under the influence of Ukrainian academic centres at Harvard, the University of Toronto, and elsewhere, and due to the influence of the publication of new histories of Ukraine by North American historians (Subtelny 1988, 1991, 1994a, 1994b, 2000, 2009; Magocsi 1996, 2007, 2010, 2012). In the UK, Russophile influence continued in Russian history, and little has changed with historians continuing to use 'Kievan Russia.'

In Florinsky (1953, 18–19), Kyiv Rus is the first 'new Russian state' which covered 'the first three centuries of Russian history.' Ukraine is described as the 'fertile regions of southern Russia.' In 860, the 'Russian army' appeared at

---

[7] M. von Hagen, 'After the Soviet Union: Rethinking Modern Russian History', The Seventeenth Annual Philadelphia Distinguished Lecture on History, 1977, 9.

the gates of Constantinople, and in 1043, Prince Yaroslav organised the last 'Russian expedition' against this city. After the 'conquest of a foreign city' in 1169 by Andrey Bogolyubsky, 'the Kiev chapter of Russia's history was closed' (Florinsky 1953, 31).

After the disintegration of 'Kievan Russia' (Kyiv Rus), 'Russian history' divided into two directions 'from a common source,' which led to the 'territorial distribution of the three chief divisions of the Russian people' (Florinsky 1953, 41). In other words, 'Russians' who were united in Kyiv Rus were artificially divided into the three branches of the eastern Slavs because the unity of 'Kievan Russia' (Kiev Rus) was broken by the Mongol invasion (Riasanovsky 1977; see also Hosking 1997).

Riasanovsky (1977), in the same manner as Lionel Kochan (1974), surveys 'Russian history' from 'Kievan Russia' (Kyiv Rus) to 'Soviet Russia' as one continuous narrative. 'Kievan Russia' (Kyiv Rus) is therefore described as the 'first Russian state,' and the region is geographically coined as 'southern Russia,' which spoke the 'Old Russian language.' Therefore, 'Rus became identified with the Kievan state, and the very name came to designate the southern Russian state as distinct from the north' (Riasanovsky 1977, 27).

Although Riasanovsky (1977, 224, 229, 300, 307) admits the term 'Russian' was coined much later, he nevertheless applies it to the medieval Kyivan Rus while only briefly mentioning Ukraine during the sixteenth and seventeenth centuries. Riasanovsky's (1977) terminological confusion is evident when he discusses the division of the eastern Slavs into three nations after the disintegration of the Kyiv Rus state with Ukrainians and Belarusians seemingly accidents of history. It is not difficult to deduce from this that Ukraine is an 'artificial' construct. The eastern Slavs are really three branches of the 'All-Russian People' who could, if history and circumstances had permitted, be integrated into one nation. Ukrainians and Belarusians are therefore akin to Bavarians within a pan-Germanic nation. On a visit to Germany in 1991, then-Parliamentary Speaker and later that year President Kravchuk demanded the right to a Ukrainian-language interpreter. Members of the Russian media corps ridiculed this demand, claiming it was as ludicrous as Bavarians travelling to Moscow and demanding an interpreter to translate the Bavarian dialect of German. Tuomas Forsberg and Sirke Makinen (2019, 228) write that Russian nationalists point to the reunification of Germany in 1991 as a precedent for the 'reunification' of 'Russians,' which are divided into three nations.

When referring to the Galician-Volhynian principality and the Lithuanian-Ruthenian (Rus) principality, Riasanovsky (1977, 98, 99, 146–156) calls their inhabitants 'Russians,' and these territories the 'two south-western Russian lands' and the 'Lithuanian-Russian state' respectively. It is difficult to understand how these areas could be populated by 'Russians' and be 'Russian' when they were never part of the Muscovite state or Tsarist empire and were incorporated within 'Russia' (i.e. USSR) only in 1939 when they were annexed from Poland.

Denigrating Ukrainian History Writing

Kolstø (2000, 35) writes that western historians backed their Russian colleagues over questions such as the 'ownership' of Kyiv Rus. 'Western historians have generally accepted the Russian time perspective. True enough, certain *émigré* Ukrainian historians have always maintained that this was a theft of the history of the Ukrainian people, but most of their Western colleagues have brushed these objections aside, dismissing them as rather pathetic manifestations of Ukrainian nationalism' (Kolstø 2000, 35).

Nationalising 'Kievan Russian' (Kyiv Rus) history for Muscovites and 'Great Russians' had three consequences. First, western historians could not claim they were writing objective histories of 'Russia.' Second, they ignored pre-thirteenth century roots of Muscovy in Novgorod and Vladimir-Suzdal by focusing upon Kyiv Rus. Third, they denied a separate origin for Ukrainians, ignoring them until briefly mentioning them in the mid-seventeenth century during Hetman Bohdan Khmelnytskyy's Cossack revolt. In doing so, western historians emphasised Ukraine's ties to Russia while downplaying its non-Russian history as, for example, part of the Lithuanian-Polish Commonwealth. Western histories of 'Russia' tacitly accept the Russian nationalist (imperialist) and Soviet narratives of Ukrainian history 'culminating in union with Russia' (Yekelchyk 2004, 35) and Ukrainians merging with Russians.

Ukrainian history was marginalised and subsumed within 'Russian' imperial history in the West just as it was in the former USSR. Courses in Ukrainian history in western educational curricula were few and far between until the 1970s, when there was the creation of Ukrainian studies in the US and Canada, and only in the 1990s in the UK. The brief appearance of Ukraine at different times in history was confusing to pupils, students, and readers because Ukraine emerges in many 'Russian' history classes from nowhere to only disappear again and finally to become 'squatters' on 'Russian lands' (see Kohut 1994).

Ukrainian territories experienced long periods of existence outside the confines of the Tsarist Russian Empire and USSR. Although Ukraine and Muscovy signed the Treaty of Pereyaslav in 1654, the Ukrainian Hetmanate did not lose its autonomy until the last two decades of the eighteenth century at the same time as the Tsarist Empire conquered Crimea. Until the mid-nineteenth century, Polish cultural influences were more influential than Russian in Kyiv and central Ukraine, where the Ukrainian Greek-Catholic Church was dominant until it was banned in the 1830s. Ukraine's western regions remained outside 'Russia' until the Second World War. Roman Szporluk (1997, 88) points out that, 'It is obvious that today's Ukraine cannot be viewed simply as a part of a historic Russia or modern Soviet space; Ukraine is intimately linked not only to Russia, but also to the countries of Central Europe and the Black Sea region.'

Western Historians Writing About 'Russia'

In one of the few relatively objective histories of 'Russia,' Sumner (1947) discussed the division of the eastern Slavs into two groups after the Mongol invasion of the thirteenth century. These created the Muscovites, who intermingled with the Finns, and Ukrainians and Belarusians who came under Lithuanian-Polish influence. Sumner (1947) devotes some space in his *Survey of Russian History* to the 'Ukrainian Question,' where he discusses the strengths and weaknesses of its national movement.

The majority of western historians of 'Russia' failed to follow Sumner's (1947) lead and heed his advice, which is quoted at the beginning of this chapter. Vladimir Volkoff (1984, XIII) begins his history of Russia with the phrase, 'Russia begins with Vladimir the baptist and ends with Vladimir the apostate.' This grew into 'Holy Russia' which was only to be later artificially divided into fifteen republics. Another similarly poor use of methodology is John Lawrence's (1969) *A History of Russia.* This book, we are told in the preface, 'is a book about the Russian people, not about their neighbours.' The Kyivan era is described as 'the cradle of Russia' with its 'famous Russian black earth' and 'first Russian farmers.' 'Southern Russia' is where the 'Russians' first entered history in the seventh century, and the region where the 'Russian religion' was established. What is disturbing is that these kinds of claims found in western historiography of 'Russia' are similar to those found in Putin's discourse (see Putin 2008, 2014a, 2014b, 2015a, 2015b, 2017, 2019, 2020a, 200b, 2020c).

Nationalist (imperialist) 'Russian history' is centre stage in James H. Billington (1970, 3, 7, 8, 13). 'Russian culture,' he alleges, is a tale of three cities – Kyiv (the 'mother of Russian cities'), Moscow ('the heart'), and St. Petersburg ('the head'). We read about 'early Russians,' 'Kievan Russia' (Kyiv Rus), 'Russian soil,' 'Old Russia,' the 'Russian language,' and 'Russian theology.' Basil Dmytryshyn (1973) only refers to 'Kievan Rus' when discussing this era, but the book's very title will associate 'Kyivan Rus' with 'Russia' in the eyes of its readers.

Janet Martin (1996) follows the same logic as Dmytryshyn (1973). The entire book is defined as 'Russian history' with the Kyivan legacy transferring to Vladimir-Suzdal, Muscovy and imperial St. Petersburg. Confusingly, she states, 'In the year 980, an obscure prince landed on the northern shores of a land that became known as Rus' and later, Russia.' Her book on 'Medieval Russia' includes the Kyiv Rus era but ends at a period in time *before* the term 'Russia' was coined in the early eighteenth century.

Martin (1996) ignores evidence and the views of western and Ukrainian-based historians of Ukraine that the traditions and political culture of Vladimir-Suzdal and Muscovy were very different to those of Kyivan Rus. Martin (1996) draws upon the Russian nationalist (imperialist) school of history (for example, Sergei M. Soloviev and Vasili O. Kliuchevskyi), which claims the transfer of the Kyivan Rus legacy to be 'stages in the history of one nation.'

Martin (1996) only devotes four lines to the alternative view by Hrushevsky (1970) who wrote that the Kyivan Rus tradition was inherited by the Galician-Volhynian Principality in what is now western Ukraine. Martin (1996, 375) admits that Kyiv Rus and Muscovy were inextricably linked; nevertheless, 'Muscovy's political structures contrasted sharply with those of Kievan Rus.' Muscovite traditions radically differed from those of Kyiv Rus because these traditions were inherited by Galicia-Volhynia and not Vladimir-Suzdal. Plokhy (2015, 50) writes that the Mongols recognised two successors to Kyiv Rus which were Galicia-Volhynia, where they had little influence, and Vladimir-Suzdal, which they occupied. In 1302, the Constantinople Orthodox Patriarch recognised two metropolitans in Vladimir and Halych where Galician-Volhynian Prince Danylo was crowned King Daniel (King of the Rus).

Kochan (1974) uses 'Kievan Rus' to refer to the medieval era. But by including it within a survey of 'Russian history,' the reader is again left in no doubt as to how Kyiv Rus is part of 'Russian history' because this period represented the 'formative centuries of Russian history' (Kochan 1974, 11). After the disintegration of Kyiv Rus in 1240, the majority of Ukrainian territories became either independent in the Galician-Volhynian principality or came under Mongol rule. They then passed under Lithuanian, Polish-Lithuanian and Cossack rule. The 1654 Treaty of Pereyaslav between Ukraine and Muscovy was concluded after the Poles refused to consider the Ukrainian Cossack proposal to transform the Polish-Lithuanian commonwealth into a Polish-Lithuanian-Ruthenian (i.e. the old term for Ukrainian) Commonwealth. Ukrainian Cossack Hetman Khmelnytskyy signed the treaty on condition that Ukrainian autonomy be recognised by the Muscovite Tsar. This Ukrainian interpretation of a confederal relationship of two equal peoples, similar to the 1707 treaty between Scotland and England, has continually clashed with the Russian, Soviet and in part western view of Ukraine's submission to Muscovy and 're-union' with Russia.

Western Historiography of Russia in the Post-Soviet Era

Western historiography of Russia barely changed following the disintegration of the former USSR and creation of an independent Russian Federation. A civic history of the Russian Federation (which would equate Russian history with the nation-state that came into being in 1991) is yet to be published. British historians write as though nothing has changed and continue to use 'Kievan Russia' to this day.

An attempt to come to terms with the confusing methodology utilised by western historians of 'Russia' was provided by Simon Franklin and Jonathan Shepard (1969). Early in the book, they state, 'This book is and is not an account of the emergence of a thing called Russia. The further we pursue the thing into the past, the more misleading our modern vocabulary becomes. If we picture Russia as a state inhabited mainly by people who think of themselves as Russians—if, that is, our notion of Russia is coloured by current political or ethno-cultural geography—then most of this book is not about Russia at all, or at least not about Russia alone' (Franklin and Shepard 1969, XVII). Franklin and Shepard (1969, XVII) write, 'The story of the land of Rus could continue in one direction towards modern Russia, or in other directions towards, eventually, Ukraine or Belarus. The land of the Rus is none of these, or else it is a shared predecessor of all three.'

These two authors have therefore consciously not used the eighteenth-century terms 'Russia' or 'Russians.' Nevertheless, their book is the first volume of *Longman's History of Russia,* which the publishers do confuse with Kyiv Rus, and by placing the first volume within this series, readers will of course assume that Kyiv Rus is the first stage of 'Russian' history.

Geoffrey Hosking (1997) aims to break new ground by focusing upon how 'Rossiia obstructed the flowering of Rus' or, 'if you prefer it, how the building of an empire impeded the formation of a nation.' Yet there is little new that would differentiate it from earlier histories of 'Russia.' Hosking (1997) differentiates *Rus/Ruskij,* the people, from *Rossiiski,* the empire. By doing this, Hosking (1997, XIX) believes that one can separate the pre-imperial state and imperial Russian empire into two distinct objects of study. By differentiating these two periods, he hoped to show how the growth of the

Russian empire *(Rossiia)* obstructed the evolution of the pre-imperial Rus into a nation. Hence, 'my story concerns above all the Russians' (Hosking 1997, XIX).

The most difficult factor impeding Russian nation-building was that which Hosking (1997) does not attempt to deal with; namely, the question of Russia's *Ruskij question*. Hosking (1997) does not, for example, look to Novgorod or Muscovy as his pre-imperial object of study, either of which could be conceivably defined as the first (Great) Russian states. Instead, Hosking's (1997) study of Rus includes all three eastern Slavs. Implicit in this choice is the assumption that Kyiv Rus constituted one united entity that would have evolved into a Russian nation if its unity had not been destroyed by the Mongol invasion.

Hosking (1997) equates the *Ruskij narod* to the English and Turkish peoples and the *Rossiia* empire to the British or Ottoman empires. Hosking (1997) backs this claim by reference to the Belarusians, who, writing at that time, he believed did not seem to know who they were in the post-Soviet era (in 2020, from the vantage point of hindsight, the Belarusian revolution showed this to be untrue, if it ever was). Typically, Hosking (1997) exaggerates the alleged division of Ukrainians into the 'nationalist, Ukrainian-speaking west' and the 'pro-Russian, Russian speaking east and south' which was shown to be mythical in 2014 and which is critically discussed in chapters 4, 5 and 6.[8] Riasanovsky (1977) also speculates in a manner similar to Hosking (1997) that if the alleged unity of Kyiv Rus had been maintained it might have evolved into a single 'All-Russian People' (Riasanovsky 1977, 154).

By utilising nineteenth-century Russian nationalist (imperialist) historiography, Hosking (1997) and other western historians find it impossible to explain how 'Russians' who allegedly lived in today's Ukraine in the medieval era, were then replaced by 'Ukrainian squatters' at an undisclosed later stage. As Hosking (1997, 27), to his credit, points out: 'Ukraine's loss of its distinct national identity was more complicated than that of any other region of the empire.' The reason for bans on the Ukrainian language, Hosking (1997) believes, 'appears to have been that the national identity of Ukrainian peasants was an unusually sensitive matter for officials' (Hosking 1997, 27). Just as it continues to be for contemporary Russian leaders.

When nation-building was encouraged, as it was in Austrian-ruled western Ukraine between the late-eighteenth century and 1918, it led to the development of a Ukrainian identity. Paul R. Magocsi (1996, 456) writes,

---

[8] Geoffrey Hosking, School of Slavonic and East European Studies, University of London, 23 April 1997.

'While Ukrainianism was being suppressed in the Russian Empire, all the fundamentals that make possible a viable national life—history, ideology, language, literature, cultural organisation, education, religion and politics—were being formally established in Austrian Galicia.'

Archie Brown, Michael Kaiser, and Gerald S. Smith (1994) include no separate section devoted to any non-Russian republic of the former USSR. The authors, as is often the case with western historians, confuse and interchangeably use the terms 'Russia,' 'Russian empire' and the 'USSR' as if they were one and the same thing. They again use 'Kievan Russia' (Kyiv Rus) with everything to do with it defined as 'Russian' history. 'Russia' and 'Russians' are used instead of imperial and Soviet. We read about the 'Russian Primary Chronicle,' Kyiv as 'the Mother of Russian cities,' *Ruska Pravda* as 'Russian law,' and the Rus Church is mis-translated as the 'Russian Orthodox Church' (see Plokhy 1996, 343).

Martin Gilbert's (1993) history was reprinted in 1993 with only minor revisions to take into account the disintegration of the Soviet Union. The book spans 'Russian history' from 800 BC to the present through the prism of the standard translation of 'Russian statehood' from 'Kievan Russia' (Kyiv Rus), Vladimr-Suzdal, Muscovy, Russian Empire to USSR. Anything to do with the pre-Vladimir-Suzdal era is called 'Kievan Russia' (Kyiv Rus), and its inhabitants are 'Russians.' Similarly, John Channon and Robert Hudson (1995) include an opening chapter entitled 'The Origins of Russia.' Unfortunately, as with many western scholars, Channon and Hudson (1995) use 'Kievan Russia' and 'Kievan Rus' interchangeably, which leads one to assume they believe them to be one and the same; that is, a territory populated by 'Russians.' The history of Rus between 1054–1237 is therefore included as part of 'The Origins of Russia,' and, echoing Putin (2014a, 2014b), 'Russia' allegedly adopted Christianity in 988 in Crimea.

The Soviet state celebrated the millennium of 'Russian' Christianity in Moscow in 1988, a city that did not exist until nearly two centuries after Christianity arrived in Kyiv and six centuries after the founding of the city of Kyiv itself. Kyiv celebrated its 1,500th anniversary in 1982. In 2016, Putin unveiled a monument to Grand Prince Volodymyr in a city that never existed when he ruled Kyiv Rus. One wonders whether in taking this step one Vladimir (Putin) was influenced by another Vladimir (Volkoff 1984) who wrote *Vladimir: The Russian Viking*.

Western Historiography of 'Russia' and Ukraine

Since 1991, western historians have continued to use Russian nationalist (imperialist) historiography rather than changing and writing a civic history of the Russian Federation. This has a particularly damaging impact upon Ukraine's history and identity – especially because Russia and Ukraine have been at war since 2014. Ukrainians are ignored in western histories of 'Russia,' and, although they are the second largest minority in the Russian Federation, political science books on national minorities in Russia completely ignore them (see Prina 2016). The historian Norman Davies (1994, 41) argues: 'The best thing to do with such an embarrassing nation (Ukrainians) was to pretend that it didn't exist, and to accept the old Tsarist fiction about their being "Little Russia." In reality they were neither little nor Russian.' Ukraine was disinherited 'from any claim to historical statehood and thereby denied any future claim to independent statehood' (Szporluk 1997, 95).

David Saunders (1993, 101) writes, 'Despite Ukraine's centrality... standard works on the history of the Russian Empire and the Soviet Union say relatively little about it.' Saunders attributes this to two reasons. The first reason is that western historians derived their view of Ukrainians from Russian interpretations. The second reason is that these historians depended upon publications sanctioned by Russia and hence focused upon the Russian heartland, in another example of academic orientalism. Many western scholars of 'Russia' 'become unconsciously Great Russian centralizers' (Saunders 1993, 101) when standard western accounts of the former USSR treated the eastern Slavs as one homogenous whole. Little wonder western government leaders asked Kravchuk in 'which part of Russia was Ukraine located?'[9] Nearly three decades later, US President Donald Trump believed Ukraine (and Finland) were part of Russia (Bolton 2020).

Since 1991, western histories of 'Russia' have continued to follow the nationalist (imperialist) framework developed by Russian historians in the nineteenth century. Joseph Stein (2010), Gregory L. Freeze (2002), Abraham Ascher (2002), and Philip Longworth (2006) are four recent examples of scholars beginning the history of 'Russia' in Kyiv and after its fall, 'Russian' history moved to Vladimir-Suzdal, Muscovy, and the Russian Empire. The first chapter of Stein covers the 'early history from medieval to imperial Russia' which is called 'The era of Vladimir I.' Ascher's history of 'Russia' 'covers the entire sweep of Russian history, from the earliest settlers to the aftermath of the collapse of the Soviet Union in 1991,' beginning in Kyiv and ending in the USSR.

The USSR may have disintegrated, and Ukraine has an independent state, but historians of Russia continue to write about the territory of Ukraine as

---

[9] Former US Ambassador to Ukraine, Roman Popadiuk, American Political Science Association annual congress, Washington, DC, 28 August 1997.

'Russian lands' populated by mysterious 'squatters' with unknown origins for the last thousand years. It is impossible for these historians to ascertain who these Ukrainians are or why they do not want to be part of the Russian World.

Unexplained Origins of Ukrainian 'Squatters' on 'Russian Lands'

Because 'Russian' history is always written as beginning in Kyiv, the only explanation that can be given for Ukrainians 'squatting' on 'Russian lands' is that they are interlopers and their state is an 'artificial' construct created accidentally or by scheming outside powers who are intent on weakening Russia and dividing the 'All-Russian People.' Such a conclusion is reflected in how Ukraine is viewed by a large body of historians of 'Russia' and some political scientists who work on Russia as not a real entity, a bitterly divided country, and, let's face it, 'Russian' (see Darden and Way 2014; Charap and Colton 2017; Hahn 2018; Cohen 2019).

Western historians of 'Russia' seemingly see no need to hold scholarly interactions with western historians of Ukraine or historians working in Ukraine. Western historians of 'Russia' do not use Ukrainian sources or histories of Ukraine (see Kuzio 2001b). Academic orientalism through the use of sources and frameworks from Russia is pervasive in western writing about 'Russian' history, which leads to an imagining of Ukraine through Moscow's eyes.

With the majority of western historians of 'Russia' upholding a Russian view of 'Kievan Russia' (Kyiv Rus) as the birthplace of 'Russia,' they perhaps see no irony in President Putin unveiling a statue to Grand Prince Volodymyr in Moscow. Putin (2017) told the Valdai Club that the 'enormous Russian state' was founded in 'Kievan Russia' (Kyiv Rus) and Russians and Ukrainians are its descendants sharing 'common traditions, common mentality, common history and common culture' (Feklyunina 2016, 784). Anti-Semitic national Bolshevik Sergei Glazyev, Putin's senior adviser on Ukraine, describes Kyiv as 'our most Russian city where the whole of Russia began,' showing his belief in the 'All-Russian People' consisting of three branches.[10] The baptism of 'Kievan Russia' (Kyiv Rus) laid the 'civilised foundation which unites the peoples of Russia, Ukraine and Belarus' Putin (2014a) said.

By continuing to use nineteenth century nationalist (imperialist) theses, western historians of 'Russia' support these myths of 'Russian history' beginning in Kyiv, the closeness and unity of three eastern Slavs, and Russian title to Crimea. Laruelle (2016b) defines *Russkij* not as a form of

---

[10] *Radio Russia*, 5 March 2004.

ethnic nationalism, but as an 'imperial meaning' connecting Ukrainians to Russians and a 'ghost from the imperial past' (see also Rowley 2000). 'Seen from the Kremlin's perspective, this shared past should determine a shared future' because Russians and Ukrainians are 'one people.' Ukraine cannot be permitted to live outside the Russian World because Ukraine's 'russkii-ness' is 'embedded in a pro-Russian geopolitical position' (Laruelle 2016b).

Nineteenth-century nationalist (imperialist) 'Russian' history included four key myths:

1. Muscovy is the heir to Kyiv Rus;

2. Bringing Ukraine into the Muscovite realm was not annexation by a foreign power but the so-called 'gathering of Russian lands' (a title Putin would like to see himself go down in Russian history as);

3. Muscovites were the leading people of the eastern Slavs;

4. Muscovy's and the Russian Empire's expansion into and rule over Ukraine and Belarus aimed to rebuild the unity of Kyiv Rus.

Although it is understandable (but at the same time reprehensible) why nationalists (imperialists) such as Putin continue to use such myths, it is unclear why western historians continue to do so. Edward L. Keenan (1994, 21) writes that 'none of these axioms can withstand modern analytical scrutiny and confrontation with the sources.' This is because Muscovite rulers had no knowledge of links to Kyiv Rus and were 'only dimly aware of the history of the Kievan period, and even less interested in claiming it as their inheritance' (Keenan 1994, 22). Ivan, the Muscovite ruler who is described as the 'gatherer of Russian lands,' 'made little – almost nothing – of his Kievan ancestry' (Keenan 1994, 24; see Pritsak and Reshetar 1963); Putin is as similarly ignorant of Ukrainian history. Russian links to Kyiv Rus and Ukrainian lands had been broken for four centuries. When the Treaty of Pereyaslav was discussed in 1654, both sides used interpreters and Ukrainian (Ruthenian) Cossacks had a clear perception of Muscovites as foreign 'Others.'

Plokhy (2017, 55–104) focuses on identity questions adopted by Russia's rulers since Muscovy launched its 'gathering of Russian lands.' Russia's 'myth of origin' claiming Kyiv Rus is not merely a viewpoint in historical debates but translates into contemporary geopolitics as a claim to Ukraine. Muscovy's propagandists described the three eastern Slavs as branches of one 'All-Russian People' as do contemporary Russian leaders.

Writing nearly two decades before the Russian-Ukrainian War, Keenan (1994) warned that these myths had become embraced by most Russians, which has meant they could not accept a separate Ukrainian identity (see D'Anieri 2019). 'Should however, either government find itself motivated to "act out" any of the relevant national myths – including the "national unity" myth – unimaginable chaos could result.' Russian views of Ukraine as an artificial entity and Ukrainians as one of three parts of *tryedynstva russkoho naroda* became increasingly dominant in the Kremlin's discourse and especially after Putin's re-election in 2012 (see Zatulin 2012). What Keenan (1994) warned about happened in 2014 and thereafter.

Western Historians of 'Russia' and Ukraine

Competition between Ukraine and Russia over the legacy of Kyiv Rus did not begin in 1991, but went back as far as at least the early-nineteenth century. In 1846, *Istoria Rusov* (History of Rus/History of Ruthenians) was published of uncertain authorship. *Istoria Rusov* claimed that Kyiv Rus had been 'the first and oldest form of Ukrainian life' (Chernenko 1994, 4). The book was important in providing 'a clear sense of historical continuity for Ukraine' and, because of this, had 'an enormous impact on historians as well as on the poets, folklorists, and language enthusiasts active in the slowly emerging Ukrainian national revival' (Magocsi 2010, 383–384). *Istoria Rusov* described Ukraine as 'an independent country that only recently had come under Russian hegemony,' freedom-loving Ukrainians were contrasted with 'serfdom and slavery' in Muscovy, and Ukraine entered a period of decline in the eighteenth century after coming under Russian rule (Magocsi 2010, 19, 383–384). *Istoriya Rusov* laid the groundwork for Hrushevsky (1970) and other historians to treat Ukrainian history separately to Russian history and to claim exclusive title to Kyiv Rus (Magocsi 2010, 21).

A counter-discourse of resistance to assimilation and colonisation, and opposition to Russia's discourse of chauvinistic superiority has been prevalent in Ukrainian political writings since the early-nineteenth century (Shkandrij 2011, 283). Taras Shevchenko, Ukraine's national bard, developed narratives that condemned Tsarist tyranny and imperialism, sympathised with smaller nations subjugated by the Russian empire, attacked serfdom, and rejected Russia's 'civilising mission' (Shkandrij 2001, 134–135). This counter-discourse was also prevalent in Ukrainian underground publishing in the USSR (*samvydav* [*samizdat*]) and in the declarations and programmes of dissident groups and nationalist parties.

During the Mikhail Gorbachev era in the second half of the 1980s, Soviet historiography came under challenge in Ukraine and some other non-Russian republics (Velychenko 1991). Since 1991, Ukraine continued to replace Soviet and Russian historiography with Ukrainian national historiography (Kotsur and Kotsur 1999; Kalakura 2004). Russia and Ukraine's divergence after 1991 was based upon different views of their histories and how they should be written, taught in education, and commemorated by the state (Velychenko 1992; Kohut 1994). These changes began long before Viktor Yushchenko's election in January 2005 – even though he is usually described as Ukraine's first 'nationalist' president. Jan G. Janmaat (2000) wrote about Ukrainian historiography increasingly laying exclusive claim to Kyiv Rus in the 1990s.

The rehabilitation of Hrushevsky (Kuchma 1996) came after five decades of his denunciation by the Soviet regime as a 'German agent' and 'bourgeois nationalist.' Hrushevsky's (1970) historiography focused on the history of the Ukrainian people and was the framework used by some Ukrainian historians and western historians, such as Orest Subtelny (Kuzio 1998, 198–229). Ihor Sevcenko points out, 'There have been no serious attempts to refute Hrushevsky (1970) on the basis of facts by any historian practising the craft.'[11] One wonders whether western historians of Russia and Ukraine ever talk, have lunch together, sit on the same panels at academic conferences, or read each other's histories.

The extent to which Hrushevsky (1970) became part of the official mainstream could be seen by President Leonid Kuchma's (1996) commemorative book devoted to him. Hrushevsky (1970) was 'the founder of the revived Ukrainian state in the twentieth century, a historian of world renown' (Kuchma 1996). Hrushevsky's significance lay in his devotion to Ukraine's 'national revival,' 'the revival of its genetic memory, a deep understanding of its own history' (Kuchma 1996). Hrushevsky 'developed a concept of the historical development of the Ukrainian people, he proved that our people have its own core origins' (Kuchma 1996). Hrushevsky's (1970) *History of Ukraine-Rus* is to Kuchma (1996) 'the historical Bible of the Ukrainian people, a fundamental work.'

Subtelny (1988, 1991, 1994a, 1994b, 2000, 2009), Magocsi (1996, 1997, 2010, 2012, 2018), and Plokhy (2015) include everything that has taken place in the territory of Ukraine within their histories of Ukraine. The revival and development of Ukrainian national historiography challenged Tsarist, Soviet, and western historiographies of 'Russia' because they questioned nearly all of the assumptions found in them. Russian rule is no longer portrayed as 'progressive,' Russification and Russian imperialism are condemned, and former 'traitors' are defined as national heroes through monuments, stamps, medals, currency, and street names. Ukrainian Cossack leader Hetman Ivan

---

[11] *The Ukrainian Weekly,* 9 November 1997.

Mazepa, for example, who allied himself with the Swedes against Russia in 1709, was routinely condemned by Tsarist and Soviet historiography. His picture is used on one of the Ukrainian *hryvnya* bank notes introduced in 1996, and there are monuments to him in Kyiv and Poltava. Tsarina Catherine may be positive to Russians as a reformer-moderniser and empire builder but, to Ukrainians, she is remembered as the destroyer of the autonomous Ukrainian Hetmanate state and to Tatars as the conqueror of Crimea. The 'Tsar liberator' Alexander II banned the Ukrainian language.

When the University of Toronto published Subtelny's *Ukraine: A History* in 1988, they undoubtedly never expected it to become the most widely used textbook in an independent Ukrainian state only a few years later. Subtelny's *Ukraine: A History* (1988, 1991, 1994a, 1994b, 2000, 2009) was published in four editions in Canada and was published in Ukrainian (1991) and Russian (1994). The Ukrainian and Russian language editions were reprinted in hundreds of thousands of copies when few other non-Soviet histories of Ukraine were available in these two languages in the first half of the 1990s.

Subtelny (1988, 1991, 1994a, 1994b, 2000, 2009) was the first in 50 years to bring Ukrainian history up to the present and is therefore similar to other one-volume histories of Ukraine by Dmytro Doroshenko and Hrushevsky. All three histories were devoted to the Ukrainian people who have lived on the territory we have known since the late-nineteenth century (and more importantly since 1991) as Ukraine. Consequently Russians, Poles, and Jews, who played an important role in the history of this territory, are only given five out of 692 pages in Subtelny (1988, 1991, 1994a, 1994b, 2000, 2009).

Magocsi's (1996, 1997, 2010, 2012) *History of Ukraine*, also published by the University of Toronto, appeared in two editions in Canada and were translated into Ukrainian and Polish (2007, 2012, 2018). In contrast to Subtelny (1988, 1991, 1994a, 1994b, 2000, 2009), Magocsi (2010, 610–625) focused upon the history of all of ethnic groups and events that took place on Ukrainian territory. Magocsi (1996, 1997, 2010, 2012) follows the standard western civic historiography which traces back in time the history of territories that became nation-states in the nineteenth and twentieth centuries. Although Hrushevsky (1970) and Subtelny (1988, 1991, 1994a, 1994b, 2000, 2009) adopted people-based, while Magocsi (1996, 1997, 2010, 2012) and Plokhy (2015, 2016) adopted state-based multicultural approaches to Ukrainian history, respectively, the two approaches both claim title to Kyiv Rus (see Kuzio 2005).

Magocsi's (2010, 2012) nearly 800-page *A History of Ukraine* spans '2,500 years of Ukraine's history':

> Until now, most histories of Ukraine have been histories of the Ukrainian people. While this book also traces the evolution of Ukrainians, it tries as well to give judicious treatment to the many other peoples who developed within the borders of Ukraine, including the Greeks, the Crimean Tatars, the Poles, the Russians, the Jews, the Germans, and the Romanians. Only through an understanding of all their cultures can one hope to gain an adequate introduction to Ukrainian history. In other words, this book is not simply a history of Ukrainians, but a survey of a wide variety of developments that have taken place during the past two and a half millennia on the territory encompassed by the boundaries of the contemporary state of Ukraine.

Plokhy's (2015) history of Ukraine, published during the Russian-Ukrainian War, follows a similar approach to that of Magocsi (1996, 1997, 2010, 2012). Few western scholars have focused on national identity as the root cause of the Russian-Ukrainian War, which Plokhy (2015), a native of the Dnipropetrovsk region bordering the Donbas, focuses upon in his Epilogue. Plokhy (2015) believed the revival of a nationalistic (imperialistic) identity in Putin's Russia poses a fundamental challenge to Ukrainian nation-building because language and culture have been at the heart of Ukraine's revival since the mid-nineteenth century.

Conclusion

Until the mid-nineteenth century, most writers and historians assumed Kyiv Rus was part of 'Little Russian' (Ukrainian) history. After 1934, Soviet historiography largely reverted to its pre-Soviet roots by re-adopting nationalist (imperialist) history writing developed in the second half of the nineteenth century. In Tsarist, Soviet, and western histories of 'Russia' the medieval state of Kyiv Rus was nationalised on behalf of 'Russian' history and the birthplace of the 'Russian nation,' becoming 'Kievan Russia' (Kyiv Rus). Russian claims to Kyiv Rus and Tsarist nationality policy define the 'All-Russian People' as composed of three eastern Slavs. If Russians and Ukrainians were separate people, the history of Kyiv Rus had to belong to one of them (Plokhy 2017, 117); if they were 'one people' then 'Kievan Russia' (Kyiv Rus) was the birthplace of the 'Russian nation.' These histories ignored Ukrainians who only appeared briefly in the mid-seventeenth century as Cossacks who allied themselves with Muscovy, then again briefly in 1917, and again in 1991. Russian and western nationalist (imperialist) historiographies never made clear how Ukrainians came to be 'squatting' on 'primordially Russian lands.'

Historiographies written by Russian *émigré* historians working in the West were treated as 'objective' even though they were nationalist (imperialist), denied Ukrainians any history, and assumed Ukrainians were part of the 'All-Russian People.' Ukrainian historians, such as Hrushevsky (1970) and others, were portrayed as 'nationalists' by Russian, Soviet, and western historians. Ukrainian historiography was ignored prior to 1991 and continues to be ignored by most historians of 'Russia.'

The disintegration of the former USSR led to the revival and re-writing of civic historiographies of the Ukrainian nation-state but not in Russia. A civic Russian history of the Russian Federation would come to resemble that which is found in Ukraine and western Europe. France and Britain both have links to Rome and the Roman empire, but the histories of France and Britain are confined to the borders of the nation-states created during the past two centuries. Declaring Russia to be the heir to 'Kievan Russia' (Kyiv Rus) is as preposterous as Romania claiming it is the heir to the Roman empire. If Romania 'owns' Rome, what should be done with Italy? In this dystopian Romanian and Russian world, Italians and Ukrainians would be 'squatters' on lands that rightly belong to Romania and Russia.

Historiography, myths, and legends are important in the formation of national identities. Historiography plays an important role in creating and sustaining a national 'We,' while laying claim to earlier or first settlement in disputed territories. Former President Kuchma believed, 'History may not be limited to people's attitudes to the past. History continues in the present and has an impact on forming the future.'[12] This is clearly seen in how nationalist (imperialist) historiography underpins Russian military aggression against Ukraine (see chapters 4 and 5). Contemporary Russia's nationalist (imperialist) historiography supports Putin's views of Ukraine as an artificial state and Ukrainians and Russians as 'one people.' Western histories of 'Russia' unfortunately provide a similar picture of Ukraine and Ukrainians.

An alternative civic historiography could be used to write a national history of the Russian Federation. Teaching and writing of history are closely tied to national identity and this in turn influences a country's foreign policy toward its neighbours. The forging of a civic Russian national identity would undermine the ideology that fuels war and military aggression by Russia against Ukraine.

A Russian civic historiography based upon the Russian Federation would accomplish four tasks. First, it would support the building of a civic, inclusive Russian nation-state within the borders of the Russian Federation. Second, it would no longer include Ukrainians within 'Russian' history and would accept

---

[12] *Uryadovyy Kurier,* 13 November 1997.

Ukraine as an independent country. Third, Ukraine and Russia would be seen as separate nations. Fourthly, Russian imperialism and chauvinism fuelling Russian military aggression against Ukraine would be undermined.

The next chapter continues this discussion of western historiography of 'Russia' by focusing on Crimea, the annexation of which by Russia in 2014 was a major factor in that year's crisis. Western historians *and* Russian leaders write about Chersonesus in Crimea as the place where Grand Prince Vladimir (Volodymyr) baptised the 'first Russian state.' Therefore, its annexation in 2014 was a natural development; after all, the territory had always been 'Russian.' In his address welcoming Crimea's union with Russia, Putin (2014a) linked Crimea to a 'common history' with Ukraine in Kyiv Rus, its return to Russia in 1783, and the 'legendary city' of Sevastopol as the Black Sea Fleet base. 'Each of these places is sacred to us, these are symbols of Russian military glory and unprecedented valour,' Putin (2014a) said. Crimea was presented on Russian television as the core of the 'Russian' nation and spirit (Hutchings and Tolz 2015, 25).

2

Racism, Crimea and Crimean Tatars

'Everything in Crimea speaks of our shared history and pride. This the location of ancient Khersones, where Prince Vladimir was baptised. His spiritual feat of adopting Orthodoxy predetermined the overall basis of the culture, civilisation and human values that unite the peoples of Russia, Ukraine and Belarus.' – President Vladimir Putin (2014a).

'The Crimean Peninsula is the heartland of Russian nationhood. It was here in Khersones that Prince Vladimir adopted Orthodoxy as the official religion of the peoples of Rus.' – Richard Sakwa (2015, 12).

A large number of western historians of 'Russia' and some political scientists working on Russia supported the incorporation of Crimea into Russia based on the argument that the peninsula 'had always been Russian' (see Zhuk 2014). Many agreed with Putin that an injustice had been resolved through Crimea's 'repatriation' to Russia (Sakwa 2016, 24). This view of Crimea has its origins in western historiography of 'Russia,' which was analysed in chapter 1. Western scholarly arguments supporting a Russian Crimea are the same as those of the Russian leadership and rest on the peninsula being part of 'Kievan Russia' (Kyiv Rus) and a long period of Russian rule over Crimea since the late eighteenth century, which deny that Kyivan Rus was part of Ukrainian history and ignore the far longer Tatar history in Crimea.

This chapter disagrees with these claims. Based on a civic understanding of what constitutes the history of a nation-state, Kyiv Rus should be understood as part of Ukrainian history. This chapter argues that the Tatars are the indigenous people of Crimea.

Although Russia's invasion and annexation of Crimea has been covered in a multitude of scholarly publications, the after-effects of life under Russian occupation have not. There are very few scholarly studies of how Russia's occupation has impacted Crimean Tatars and Ukrainians (see Coynash and Charron 2019; Skrypnyk 2019). Racism towards Crimean Tatars had always existed within the Soviet Communist Party and continues within Russian nationalists. If there is very little scholarly work on the plight of Crimean Tatars, the Ukrainian minority in Crimea is totally ignored (as it is in the Donbas). Russification and Sovietisation have followed Russia's annexation of Crimea and parts of the Donbas (Violations of human rights and international crimes during the war in the Donbass 2018; Coynash and Charron 2019; Skrypnyk 2019). 50.5% of Ukrainians believe that the rights of Ukrainian speakers are infringed in Russian-occupied Crimea and the Donbas, with 18.6% disagreeing (Ukrayinska mova: shlyakh u nezalezhniy Ukrayini 2020).

This chapter is divided into five sections. The first two provide a theoretical introduction to boundaries and homelands, and a broad definition of racism based on the context of Crimea with an analysis of Russian and Ukrainian racism towards Crimean Tatars. The third section analyses genocide against Crimean Tatars and provides arguments for why they should be viewed as the indigenous people of Crimea. The fourth section surveys Russian territorial claims towards Crimea since 1991. The final section investigates Crimea under Russian occupation and how this has impacted Crimean Tatars and Ukrainians.

Boundaries and Homelands

Boundaries are important to the formation of historical, natural, cultural, political, economic and symbolic national identities. Borders are a 'manifestation of socio-spatial consciousness' (Paasi 1995, 43). Nation-building binds the inhabitants of a region to a territory and inculcates a primary loyalty to the nation-state over other forms of identity. States promote a 'We' through memory politics that can encompass landscapes, heritage, cultural products, texts, maps, and memorials. 'Boundaries make a difference. Social life is full of boundaries which give direction to existence, and which locate that existence' (Paasi 1995, 48–49). In some regions of Ukraine, such as the Donbas and Crimea, nostalgia for the former USSR and pro-Russian sentiments provided support for the Russian World and Russian-backed separatism in 2014. Nevertheless, a majority of Ukrainians expressed an allegiance to (civic or civic-ethnic) Ukraine over loyalties to the Russian World and 'New Russia.'

The 'We' formed by nation-building is differentiated from the foreign 'Other.'

Borders dramatise differences between those inside and outside the nation-state (Barth 1969). Identity is rooted in difference from neighbours (Howard, 1995, 288). Who constitutes the 'We' is made more difficult in border regions, such as the Donbas, where contestation often rests on who settled the region first and who the indigenous peoples are. Asserting who is indigenous in the Donbas is problematic because the region's history began in the late nineteenth century. Andrew Wilson (2016, 636) believes there are few indigenous locals because 'almost everyone is new – there is no real local myth of the "land of our fathers." Soviet identity put down deep roots in the Donbas because nothing much came before it.' The Donbas is therefore similar to Belarus where weak ethnic identities and pre-Soviet historical memory provided space for Alyaksandr Lukashenka to monopolise Soviet Belarusian nationalism until the 2020 revolution (Leshchenko 1998).

Russian and Ukrainian historians have put forward conflicting descriptions of who settled the Donbas first, and Russian and Ukrainian histories of the Donbas 'are mutually contradictory at almost every point' (Wilson 1995, 282). Russian historians and nationalists (imperialists) claim the Donbas was always 'Russian' and multi-national. Cossacks from the Don region of Russia are prominent in the leadership of the Luhansk People's Republic (LNR), one of two Russian proxy enclaves the Kremlin controls in the Donbas. Ukrainian historians claim that the first settlers were Ukrainian Cossack territories who migrated from what are now Zaporizhzhya and Dnipropetrovsk *oblasts*. The Ukrainian Institute of National Memory has published research showing that the Donbas region was settled by Ukrainians before the launch of nineteenth century industrialisation (Vyatrovych et al 2018).

In 1917–1918, the Ukrainian People's Republic (UNR) did not control the Donbas because it was strongly under the influence of the Bolsheviks (Velychenko 2014). The Donbas was included in the Ukrainian SSR by Soviet leader Lenin against the wishes of the local Bolsheviks who had established a quasi-independent Donetsk-Krivyy Rih Soviet Republic; the Donetsk People's Republic (DNR) (the second Donbas enclave controlled by Russia) claims to be its successor. The Donbas experienced major population changes in the 1930s and 1940s, when the *Holodomor* and Nazi occupation murdered millions of its inhabitants. After World War II, the Donbas was settled by large numbers of people from other regions of the USSR, who were sent to work in its coal mines and industrial plants. The effect of this population change was that the 'region's pre-Soviet Cossack agricultural history died with the *Holodomor*' (Wilson 2016, 636).

Following the independence of former colonies, contestation often continues with the former imperial power over a range of issues, as can be seen with

Russia and Ukraine. Michael Mann (1993, 123) writes, 'When a state no longer has arbitrary power over its own borders its sovereignty has indeed eroded.' Russia has controlled its border with Ukraine since 2014 to provide it with direct access to the region of the Donbas (DNR, LNR) it occupies. President Putin refuses to return control of the border to Ukraine until the DNR and LNR are given 'special (constitutional) status' within a federalised Ukraine.

Anthony D. Smith (1981) believes that war is one of the chief forces that has shaped ethnicity. Prolonged war strengthens national consciousness and weakens the cohesion of multi-national empires. Wars have traditionally moulded high levels of ethnic consciousness and served to harden the national space (Williams and Smith 1983). Since 2014, the Russian-Ukrainian War has produced dramatic changes in Ukrainian identity (see Kulyk 2016, 2018, 2019; Konsolidatsiya Ukrayinskoho Suspilstva: Vyklyky, Mozhlyvosti, Shlyakhy 2016; Osnovni Zasady ta Shlyakhy Formuvannya Spilnoyi Identychnosti Hromadyan Ukrayiny 2017).

Elie Kedourie (1979, 125) describe borders as 'established by power and maintained by the constant and known readiness to defend them by arms.' Wars and conflicts have often gone hand in hand with the creation of nation-states. Indeed, as Will Kymlicka (1997, 19) points out, 'The origins of virtually every state and virtually every political boundary, are tainted by conquest or other injustices.'

Nationalist struggles to control lands believed to constitute the homeland are a form of construction and interpretation of the nation-state's social space. The most bitter struggles between ethnic groups are often in border areas. Some of the most brutal fighting took place in Bosnia-Herzegovina following the disintegration of Yugoslavia. In the Tsarist Russian Empire, the extreme Russian nationalist (imperialist) 'Black Hundreds' had bases in Ukraine, and its enemies were Ukrainian and Polish nationalists and Jews (Shkandrij 2001, 166). Conflict in Northern Ireland lasted three decades from the late 1960s to late 1990s.

Williams and Smith (1983) describe eight dimensions of national territory, of which boundaries are one. Borders are not always 'natural frontiers' because they can be 'artificial' and incorporate populations of the former imperial nation who baulk at being re-defined as 'national minorities.' A good example of this would be the Russian minority in Ukraine (see Fournier 2010). Nationalism is 'always a struggle for control of land' and 'a mode of constructing and interpreting social space' (Williams and Smith 1983, 502).

Wars of independence are usually followed by 'a war for borders' (Judah 2014). A vicious Polish-Ukrainian border war took place between 1918, when the Austrian-Hungarian empire disintegrated (Magocsi 2010, 548–552) and 1947, when the Ukrainian minority in Poland was ethnically cleansed in Operation Vistula (*Akcja 'Wisła'*). Magocsi (2010, 681–682) estimates that 50,000 Poles and 20,000 Ukrainians died in the Polish-Ukrainian War. In 1991, Ukraine and Russia left the USSR in a peaceful manner without any violent conflict; nevertheless, Russia challenged Ukrainian sovereignty over the Crimea and the port of Sevastopol throughout the post-Soviet era (see the fourth section of this chapter). Ukraine and Russia signed a border treaty in 1997, but it 'brought little in the way of friendship, opposed as it was by many Russian elites,' and the treaty had 'little impact on Ukrainian-Russian relations' (D'Anieri 2019, 258). In 2014, Russia launched a war over Ukraine's southeastern borders. Western Ukrainians fought a western border war with Poland, and eastern Ukrainians are primarily fighting an eastern border war with Russia.

Williams and Smith (1983) include homeland in their different dimensions of national territory as an area of contestation. A 'historic homeland' is distinctive and unique to each national identity with nations belonging to certain territories. Nationalists seek to bring congruence to the nation and territory. Ukrainians and Crimean Tatars accepted that their homeland was the territory of the former Ukrainian SSR, including Crimea.

Russians, on the other hand, have never been reconciled with the borders of the Russian Federation because Soviet and Russian identity were one and the same in the USSR (see Kuzio 2007). Russian civic identity, confined to the Russian Federation, proved to be weak in the 1990s (Tolz 1998a, 1998b). Russian nationalists (imperialists) imagine their homeland as Solzhenitsyn's Russian Union, Putin's Russian World, the former USSR, Eurasia, CIS Customs Union (since 2015, the Eurasian Economic Union), or a mix of these. A majority of Russians (and not just their leaders) believe that Ukraine is part of the 'Russian' homeland and the Russian World.

Comparative Racism and Crimea

Martin Bulmer and John Solomos (1998, 823) write, 'Racism is an ideology defined of specific social and political relationships of dominance, subordination, and privilege.' Racism is therefore an integral part of colonialism and orientalism. As discussed in this chapter and chapter 3, the tendency to infantilise colonised people was commonplace in European colonies and continues to be found in Russia's chauvinistic belief in its cultural and racial superiority over its neighbours, particularly towards Ukraine and Belarus (Wu 2018, 15; Kuzio 2020a).

Anti-Semitism and racism have always co-existed in colonialism in what Neil MacMaster (2000) describes as the 'Africanisation' of Jews. This could be seen in Tsarist Russian nationalistic (imperialistic) groups such as the Russian Black Hundreds and in nationalist (imperialistic) groups in the contemporary era (Shekhovtsov 2017; Glazyev 2019). During the height of the race to build empires in 1875–1914, racist policies in European colonies returned to the metropolis through racist and anti-Semitic prejudices and attitudes that had built up overseas. Black people and Jews were both depicted in a negative manner. While Black people were depicted as inferior, lazy, dirty, of low intelligence, and needing of a firm hand, Jews were dangerous and a threat because they constituted a powerful and scheming group. Anti-Zionism, a camouflaged form of anti-Semitism, was a staple of Soviet propaganda and nationality policies during the last three decades of the USSR and continues to flourish in the DNR and LNR (on anti-Zionism, see Kuzio 2017c, 118–140).

Stigmatisation of the Irish in Britain replicates the manner in which Ukrainians were subjected to chauvinism in Tsarist Russia, the USSR, the Russian Federation, and Russian-occupied Crimea and Donbas (see Kuzio 2020a). Racist slurs against the Irish were similar to those made against Ukrainians. Imperialists and colonialists have traditionally disparaged the capabilities of their former colonies to lead independent states because 'natives' are supposedly in need of an 'elder brother' to guide them in the modern world.

Racial superiority of the Russian language and culture as representative of modernity were promoted by the Tsarist Empire and Soviet Union. Irish Catholics were viewed as backward because of their rural and peasant backgrounds (Laughlin 2001). The Ukrainian and Gaelic languages were backward and rural objects of derision with no place in the modern world. Russification and Anglicisation were progressive steps that gave Ukrainians and Irish access to the modern world and 'higher' Russian/Soviet and British civilisations. Post-colonial states have the means to access the modern world directly without an imperial intermediary.

The Russians and British disparaged the very concept of Ukrainians and Irish being capable of running independent states. When Ukraine and Ireland became independent states, long struggles for independence were given central place in their memory politics, education, symbolism and monuments. Heroes were uncritically praised, and foreign imperialists condemned.

Following the 2004 Orange Revolution, President Yushchenko prioritised memory politics in the *Holodomor* and nationalist groups and partisans from the 1940s, but these continued alongside Soviet historical myths, such as the

Great Patriotic War. Violent repression of the 2013–2014 Euromaidan Revolution and Russian military aggression radicalised Ukrainian memory politics and the introduction of de-communisation modelled on what had taken place earlier in central-eastern Europe and the three Baltic states (Ukrainian Parliament 2015b, Ukrainian Parliament 2015c, Ukrainian Parliament 2015d, Ukrainian Parliament 2015e). De-communisation (1) rehabilitated a myriad of Ukrainian political groups that had fought for Ukrainian independence in the twentieth century, (2) replaced Soviet and contemporary Russian bombastic celebrations of victory in the Great Patriotic War with commemoration of the tragedy and human suffering of World War II and the crime of the Holocaust, (3) opened Soviet secret services archives, and (4) banned and removed Soviet and Nazi symbols and monuments.

Kymlicka (1996, 96–99) discusses how the first settlers in conquered territories are the colonial vanguard. Immigrants arrived later in societies created by settler colonialism. When those who have been conquered fight back and demand their rights, settler colonialists dig in and increase their repression of colonised indigenous peoples. Serhy Yekelchyk's (2019) exploration of what he defines as 'reactive settler nationalism' in Crimea is a useful tool with which to integrate Russian-Crimean relations into post-colonial studies. Russian settlers in Crimea increased during the post-war era after Crimean Tatars were ethnically cleansed in 1944. Putin's 'unique imperial restoration is based on implicit approval of this particular Stalinist crime and empowerment of Russophone Crimean's as the avant-garde of Russia's resistance to the West' (Yekelchyk 2019, 323).

From the late 1980s, when Crimean Tatars began returning to Crimea in large numbers, reactive settler nationalism mobilised against the mythical threats of 'Ukrainian nationalism' and 'Tatarisation.' As in earlier European colonies, settler nationalists feared being displaced by the indigenous people – Crimean Tatars – and they mobilised 'by embracing a regional political identity linked to the imperial (post war) Soviet past' (Yekelchyk 2019, 313). Colonial settlers supported Soviet allegations and Russian nationalist (imperialist) stereotypes of Crimean Tatars, did not welcome the return of Tatars to Crimea, and never fully reconciled themselves to living in independent Ukraine. Settler colonialists took on board Soviet accusations of 'traitors,' 'bandits,' and 'uncivilised' Crimean Tatars.

Settler colonialists in Crimea mobilised against the threat to the Soviet imperial hierarchy, where the Russian language and culture were hegemonic and where Tatar and Ukrainian were provincial and slated to disappear (Fournier 2010). Settler colonialists re-invented themselves as 'disadvantaged aboriginals' (Yekelchyk 2019). The Party of Regions and its Crimean nationalist-separatist allies positioned themselves as the defenders of Russian speakers against mythical threats of 'Tatarisation' and 'Ukrainianisation.'

In the decade prior to 2014, Ukraine's regional tensions were inflamed by US and Russian political consultants. In 2005, US Republican Party strategist Paul Manafort was hired by the Party of Regions and worked in Ukraine for the next decade. In 2015, he was head of Trump's election campaign. In March 2019, Manafort was sentenced to 47 months in jail and again to another 43 months, or a total of 90 months on a variety of criminal charges.

Manafort imported to Ukraine the Republican Party's 'Southern Strategy.' Until the early 1960s, whites in the US south had largely voted for the Democratic Party because they associated President Abraham Lincoln's Republican Party with the emancipation of slaves during the US Civil War. The Republican Party's 'Southern Strategy' targeted white voters in the US south who were opposed to racial equality and voting rights for African Americans. Manafort re-formulated the Republican Party's 'Southern Strategy' from a defence of white racist privilege over African Americans into a defence of Russian settler colonialist hegemony over Ukrainians and Crimean Tatars (Motyl 2015).

Manafort's 'Southern Strategy' inflamed regional tensions by mobilising Russians and Russian speakers against enemy 'Others' – western Ukrainians, 'Ukrainian nationalists,' 'fascists,' NATO, and the Euromaidan. Pro-Russian forces in Ukraine used Soviet-era anti-fascist rhetoric as a means to portray themselves as the defenders of Russian speakers who were preventing 'civil war' and bloodshed if 'Ukrainian nationalists' took power (Osipan 2015). These pro-Russian forces included:

1. Party of Regions;
2. Communist Party of Ukraine;
3. Progressive Socialist Party;
4. Extremist Russian nationalist Donbas-based groups, such as Donbas Against Neo-Fascism and Donetsk Republic (see Na terrritorii Donetskoy oblasty deystvovaly voyennye lagerya DNR s polnym vooruzheniyem s 2009 goda 2014);
5. Odesa-based extremist Russian nationalist party *Rodina*;
6. Crimean nationalist-separatist parties Russian Unity, Russia Bloc, Soyuz, and Russian Community of the Crimea.

The Party of Regions and its Russian nationalist allies in Ukraine 'aimed at artificially escalating conflict and increasing hostility towards the rest of the country on the part of the population of the south-east regions of Ukraine'

(Osipan 2015, 133). The US Embassy in Ukraine reported that Russian support for Crimean nationalist-separatists 'increased communal tensions in Crimea,' fanning xenophobia and racism towards Ukrainians and Crimean Tatars by manipulating fears over the threats posed by the Ukrainian language and NATO to focus 'on shaping public perceptions and controlling the information space' (Ukraine: The Russia Factor in Crimea – Ukraine's "Soft Underbelly?").

One aspect of Manafort's Ukrainian 'Southern Strategy' was to increase Ukrainian nationalist *Svoboda* (Freedom) Party's popularity and, by doing so, provide the Party of Regions with 'fascist' opponents against whom it could mobilise Russian speakers. The plan was to engineer President Viktor Yanukovych to face *Svoboda* leader Oleh Tyahnybok in the second round of the 2015 presidential elections, where Russian speaking voters would be mobilised *against* the 'fascist' candidate (the 2015 election did not take place because Yanukovych fled from Kyiv, and pre-term presidential elections were held in May 2014). This tactic was a re-run of the 1999 elections, which Kuchma won against the leader of the Communist Party of Ukraine, Petro Symonenko. The Party of Regions was the main source of financing for the *Svoboda* Party as a means to take votes from other opposition parties and also to mobilise Russian speakers against a 'fascist' opponent (Jatras, 2011). The Party of Regions provided free airtime for *Svoboda* on Ukraine's popular television channel *Inter*.

While deriding 'monists,' Sakwa (2015) praises the Party of Regions for its 'comprehensive vision' of Ukraine. Anna Matveeva (2018) also mythically frames the conflict as between nationalistic 'monism' and eastern Ukrainian 'pluralism.' Kharkiv-born Borys Lozhkin (2016, 78), President Petro Poroshenko's former chief of staff, wrote that 'the facts disprove Professor Sakwa's concept.' The Party of Regions never had any interest in the equality of Ukrainian and Russian languages, a balanced and inclusive approach to Ukrainian history or respect for religious diversity. In 2012, at the height of Yanukovych's presidency, 60% of newspapers, 83% of journals, 87% of books and 72% of television programmes were in Russian. This reinforced Soviet-era hegemony of the Russian language, not equality between Ukrainian and Russian.[1]

In Russian-occupied Donbas, intolerance towards the Ukrainian language, culture, and religion makes it incomprehensible how it can be described as a sanctuary of 'multiculturalism' (Cordier 2017), which is based upon two misnomers. First, it is based on a lack of understanding of multiculturalism, which is built on tolerance of pluralism and practised in countries such as

---

[1] http://life.pravda.com.ua/society/2012/11/9/115486/

Canada (see Kymlicka 1996, 1997). Second, it is based on a biased analysis of the DNR and LNR that ignores evidence of intolerance towards and repression of Ukrainians and Jews. Describing the Donbas as a region of Russian 'Orthodox culture' reflects this pro-Russian bias and is factually wrong because the majority of Orthodox parishes in Ukraine are found in central and western Ukraine. Prior to 2014, Protestant parishes were nearly as numerous as Russian Orthodox parishes in the Donbas. Russia is also far less religious than Ukraine. Ukraine with a population (42 million), 3.4 times less than that of Russia (144 million), has 40% of the parishes of the Russian Orthodox Church. The Canadian province of Ontario would never, for example, be described as a region of 'Presbyterian culture' because a monopoly of one religious confession would not be synonymous with an understanding of tolerance of pluralism found in countries that practise multiculturalism.

The religious tolerance that exists in Ukraine stands in stark contrast to religious intolerance and monism in the Russian Federation, Crimea, and Russian-occupied Donbas, where the Ukrainian Orthodox Church-Kyiv Patriarch a (UOC-KP), Ukrainian Greek-Catholics, and Ukrainian protestants are banned or suffer discrimination and repression (Coynash 2017). After Russian occupation forces fled from the western Donetsk city of Slavyansk, the bodies of the Church of the Transfiguration pastor's two sons, Ruvim and Albert Pavenko, and two deacons, Victor Brodarsky and Vladimir Velichko, were found tortured and murdered (Peterson 2014).

The Jewish minority has fled from Russian-occupied Donbas (DNR, LNR) to Ukrainian-controlled territory after Russian proxies demanded they pay $50 to register and provide proof of properties and businesses they owned. It is rather odd that Jews had no compulsion in fleeing the allegedly 'multicultural' Russian-controlled Donbas to the 'nationalistic' and 'fascist' Ukraine, while Jews living abroad have no hesitation in travelling to Ukraine in large numbers.

Ukraine holds the largest annual gathering of Jews outside Israel with 30,000 Hasidic Jews gathering in Uman each year to celebrate the Rosh Hashanah New Year festival at the grave site of the founder of the Hasidic movement, Rebbe Nachman. In summer 2019, Ukraine was the only country outside Israel with a Jewish president (Zelenskyy) and Jewish Prime Minister (Volodymyr Hroysman). A Pew Research Centre survey found that Ukraine had the lowest (5%) proportion of people who would *not* accept Jews as citizens in their country. This is compared to nearly three-times higher numbers in Belarus (13%) and Russia (14%), and similarly high numbers in EU members Latvia (9%), Estonia (10%), Hungary (14%), Czech Republic

(19%), Poland (18%), and Romania (22%) (In some countries in Central and Eastern Europe, roughly one-in-five adults or more say they would not accept Jews as fellow citizens 2018).

Racism is a common thread running through Tsarist, Soviet and Putin's attitudes and policies towards Crimean Tatars. The Communist Party of the Soviet Union, nearly all Russian political parties, the Party of Regions, and the Communist Party of Ukraine have been racist towards Crimean Tatars. This has been undertaken in seven ways:

1. Support for Stalin's 18 May 1944 ethnic cleansing of 288,000 Crimean Tatars, 40,000 Armenians, Bulgarians, and Greeks to Uzbekistan, and the Udmurt and Mari autonomous republics in the RSFSR. Crimean Tatars were accused of having 'collaborated' with the Nazis;

2. No remorse for the suffering this ethnic cleansing inflicted upon Crimean Tatars;

3. Opposition to the return of Crimean Tatars to Crimea and the restitution of their confiscated property and other assets;

4. Claims that Crimea was always 'Russian' (Sakwa 2016, 24) and denial that Tatars are the Crimea's indigenous people;

5. Continuation of a racially constructed colonial settler superiority towards 'backward' and 'Muslim interlopers' (Yekelchyk 2019);

6. Systematic socio-economic discrimination towards Crimean Tatars who have returned to Crimea in the workplace;

7. Denial of Crimean Tatar political representation through the use of fixed quotas in the Crimean parliament.

Crimea was Always 'Russian,' So What's the Problem?

Academic orientalist and *Putinversteher* attitudes towards Crimea are common. A large body of western academics support Russia's 'natural' ownership of Crimea and see Russians, not Crimean Tatars, as the indigenous people of the region (Sakwa 2015, 2017a; Ploeg 2017, 117). Sakwa's (2015, 108) claim that the 1954 transfer of the Crimea from the Russian SFSR to the Ukrainian SSR had always been contested was undertaken using 'highly manipulative, sophisticated and fallacious argumentation put forward by Russian nationalist Sergei Baburin' (Gretsky 2020, 5).

Sergei I. Zhuk (2014) found, to his surprise, that his North American colleagues in Slavic and east European studies, and historians of Russia and the USSR refuted Ukraine's right to defend its territorial integrity. At the same time, they defended 'Russia's historical territorial rights in both Crimea and Donbas' (Zhuk 2014, 200). Zhuk (2014, 200), who is a Russian speaker from Ukraine with Russian, Ukrainian, Jewish and Greek ethnic backgrounds, was criticised for his 'pro-Ukrainian nationalistic position' when he condemned Russia's annexation of Crimea.

In a letter to *The Times* a year after Russian annexation of Crimea, Calum Paton, professor of public policy at Keele University, was adamant that Crimea was 'Russian' and, using the language of *Putinversteher* scholars, claimed that Putin was responding to NATO and EU enlargement to Soviet borders (why Soviet?) and western support for the overthrow of Yanukovych. Paton (2015) wrote:

> Crimea is part of historic Russia and was only given to Ukraine (by the same Khrushchev demonised by Boyes) as a post-Stalin — intra-USSR — symbol of change. Khrushchev was not ceding Crimea to a state independent of, let alone hostile to, the USSR. And just as the USSR's missiles in Cuba can be equated with the US's in Turkey, Putin's perspective on Ukraine is coloured by the US and EU supporting the removal of a democratically elected Ukrainian leader (however distasteful) and also supporting the expansion of Nato right up to Soviet borders, breaking a recent agreement.

Chris Kaspar de Ploeg (2017, 117) writes, 'Indeed, Crimea has been a part of Russia for 170 years, much longer than its history as a Ukrainian province.' Neil Kent (2016, 150) describes Crimea as the 'Cinderella of the Ukrainian state.' Sakwa (2015, 12) and Putin (2014a) agree that Crimea was 'the heartland of Russian nationhood.' Ukrainians do not compete with Russia over who are the indigenous people of Crimea as they believe Crimean Tatars are.

Condescending Views of Ukraine and Ukrainians

The influence of Russian nationalist (imperialist) thinking about Ukraine and Ukrainians is found among the same liberal and left-wing scholars who write about Crimea as 'always having been Russian.' Contributing editor to the left-wing *Nation* magazine, Stephen F. Cohen (2019, 17) writes that 'when the current crisis began in late 2013, Ukraine was one state, but it was not a single people or united nation. There is not one Ukraine or one "Ukrainian people" but at least two, generally situated in its Western and Eastern regions' (Cohen 2019, 22). It is a small step to transition from this mythical stereotype of Ukraine to depicting the conflict as a 'civil war' brought about by 'Ukraine's diverse history, political, social realities, and culture' (Cohen 2019, 74).

Ukraine's 'artificiality' is centre-stage in Gordon M. Hahn (2018) and Kees van der Pijl (2018). Devoting an entire chapter to the 'Stateness Problem,' Hahn (2018, 297) writes that the 'rump Ukraine' (Hahn 2018, 288) 'borders on becoming a failed state' (Hahn 2018, 297). In writing that 'contemporary Ukraine's territory was cobbled together by vicissitudes of history' and 'Ukraine's shifting and often non-existent state and borders,' Hahn (2018, 119) repeats catchphrases found in Russian nationalist discourse and Kremlin disinformation.

Pijl's (2018, 40) descent into Russian chauvinism is evident when the Ukrainian language is discussed, as he is convinced that 'all educated Ukrainians speak Russian.' If Pijl (2018) were to have written that all 'educated Indonesians' speak Dutch, he would have been condemned as a racist. Pijl (2018, 45) writes that Russian is 'the language of education and media, including internet.' Meanwhile, the Ukrainian language is 'hardly developed as a modern language' (Pijl 2018, 45).

Indigenous People of Crimea and Genocide Against Crimean Tatars

Crimea continues to be imagined by western historians of 'Russia' through the prism of Russian nationalistic (imperialistic) historiography. Western historians of 'Russia' are continuing the traditions of settler colonialism in European empires, who 'imagine 'the nature of colonised peoples and territories through the filter of an imperial lens' (Dwyer and Nettlebeck 2018, 4). The approach used and sources drawn upon contribute to academic orientalism and provide the desired history of 'Russia,' Crimea, and the 2014 crisis.

Contemporary debates on colonialism, racism, and settler colonialism are absent from western histories of 'Russia' and Crimea. This is compounded by the ignoring of Ukrainian and Crimean Tartar scholarship and their views of Crimea. It would be impermissible to write a history of any country in North or South America, Australia, or New Zealand in the same manner as histories of 'Russia' continue to be written, where European Russian settlers are depicted as the 'indigenous' people and the indigenous Crimean Tatars are excluded, minimised, or subjected to racist stereotypes. In 2017, Australian Labour opposition leader Bill Shorten reminded his fellow Australians, 'Our history didn't start when Captain Cook sailed into sight of Australia in 1770.'[2] Similarly, the history of Crimea did not begin when Tsarina Catherine's troops occupied the peninsula in 1783.

Debates about whether monuments constitute praise for racists, imperialists, and those who have committed crimes against humanity against native peoples have had limited impact upon western historians and political scientists writing 'Russian' and Crimean histories. Since before 2020, monuments to the first European to set foot in the US, Christopher Columbus, have been removed in the US. His nemesis in Crimea is Tsarina Catherine, whose imperialist army occupied Crimea in 1783. Russian leaders would never consent to the removal of monuments to Russian leaders and military officers who expanded the boundaries of the Tsarist empire and USSR.

If the approach of western scholars on 'Russian history' were used in the Americas, it would mean the histories of these countries began when European colonists arrived in the 15th and 16th centuries. The indigenous peoples could no longer be called 'First Nations' or 'Native Peoples.' Scholars and journalists no longer write that European settlers who settled Virginia in 1607 and Quebec in 1608 were the first people, while ignoring 'native peoples.'

'Russians' are described by western historians as the 'native people' of Crimea in two ways. The first manner, as discussed in Chapter 1, is by treating 'Kievan Russia' (Kyiv Rus) as the beginning of 'Russian' history with Crimea thereby always having belonged to 'Russia.' This dovetails with Putin's (2014a) views. The second manner is by stressing the importance of the 1783 annexation of Crimea.

Magocsi (2014b) believes that the only people who can claim to be indigenous to Crimea are Tatars; that is, they are the 'First Nation' because they lived there for six hundred years before the peninsula's conquest by Tsarist Russia (Magocsi 2014a). Ukrainian dissidents in the USSR, the most notable being former Soviet General Petro Grigorenko, condemned the 1944 ethnic cleansing of Crimean Tatars. Ukrainian Presidents Poroshenko and Zelenskyy support Crimean Tatars as the indigenous people in Crimea. Ukrainian legislation and nationality policies include Crimean Tatars within the Ukrainian civic nation, and plans are under discussion to add Crimean Tatar anniversaries, including the 1944 genocide, to Ukrainian official holidays (Rik diyalnosti Prezydenta Volodymyra Zelenskoho: zdobutky i prorakhunky 2020,

---

[2] https://www.theaustralian.com.au/national-affairs/update-inaccurate-plaques-says-labor-mp-linda-burney/news-story/9ec5b19253bd60b9cd651706d1865787

66). In 2016, Crimean Tatar singer Susana Jamaladinova, known as Jamala, represented Ukraine in the Eurovision song contest with the song '1944' about the genocide of her people, winning first place in the annual contest.[3]

Crimean Tatar activist Kuku agrees with Magocsi (2014a) about who the indigenous people of Crimea are. From a Russian court room, Kuku stated, 'We Crimean Tatars have always remembered and will never forget that Crimea is our land. We did not give it to Russia, nor did we sell it' Coynash 2020). 'Therefore, we – the people, did not recognise and will not recognise as legal the occupation and annexation of Crimea by Russia, neither in 1783, nor in 2014 and now' (Coynash 2020).

Russia, Europe, and Ukraine are on different sides of history on the Crimean Tatar question; the former pursues nationalistic (imperialistic) and racist policies towards Crimea and Crimean Tatars, while the latter two abide by international law and support minority rights. The Ukrainian Parliament (2015a) issued a resolution entitled 'On recognising genocide of the Crimean Tatar people.' The European and Ukrainian parliaments adopted resolutions on the 1944 ethnic cleansing of Crimean Tatars (European Parliament 2016; Ukrainian Parliament 2016b).

Magocsi (2014b) has pointed out that if length of time within a state is the criterion for deciding to whom Crimea should belong, then it should be returned to Tatars who ruled the peninsula from the thirteenth to the late-eighteenth centuries. For 330 years, the Crimean Khanate was a vassal state of the Ottoman Empire. The 'Russians' only arrived after the 1783 conquest and primarily settled there in the nineteenth century. Magocsi (1996, 2010) does not accept Russian and western imperial historiography, which claims that Crimea was populated by 'Russians' or that it was part of 'Kievan Russia' (Kyiv Rus). 'This means Slavs (including Russians) cannot be considered the indigenous inhabitants of the Ukrainian steppe and certainly not of Crimea' (Magocsi 2014b). Magocsi (2014b) continues: 'Therefore, pride of place as the population which has lived longest in Crimea goes to the Tatars.' Crimea is the historic homeland of Tatars – not Russians.

Wilson (2014, 100) calculates that Crimea, although annexed by Russia in 1783, 'was only ever truly Russian from the Crimean War of 1853-56 until 1917' and again from 1945-54; that is, it was under Russian rule for seventy-three years. The Crimea was a Soviet republic from 1921 to 1945. The Crimea was part of Soviet and independent Ukraine for a slightly shorter period of sixty years from 1954–2014; that is, only thirteen years less than it was included within 'Russia' (Wilson 2014, 100).

---

[3] https://www.youtube.com/watch?v=wNECV2h-y58

Russian Territorial Claims Towards Crimea Began in the Early 1990s

As Chapter 1 and this chapter have shown, beginning 'Russian' and Crimean history in 'Kievan Russia' (Kyiv Rus) or in 1783 is chauvinistic towards Ukrainians in the former case and racist towards Crimean Tatars in the latter case. Putin's nationalistic (imperialistic) views of Ukraine, Ukrainians, and Crimea long pre-dated 2014, but have been largely ignored in the bulk of western writings about the crisis. Claiming Crimea as always part of 'Russian' history gained prominence after the launch of the Russian World in 2007, and the 1,020th and 1,025th anniversaries of the adoption of Christianity by Kyiv Rus in 2008 and 2013, respectively. In 2013, Putin and Russian Orthodox Church Patriarch Kirill travelled to Ukraine to participate in celebrations organised by Medvedchuk, President Yanukovych, and the Ukrainian Orthodox Church (Ukrainian branch of the Russian Orthodox Church) (see chapter 5). Although Kyiv Rus had developed ties to Constantinople, it accepted Christianity at a time when the centre of Christianity was Rome and prior to the 1054 split.

Between 1991–2013, Russia *de facto* did not recognise Ukrainian sovereignty over Crimea and Sevastopol. Russia *de jure* recognised Ukrainian sovereignty over Crimea and Sevastopol in the 1994 Budapest Memorandum signed by Russia, the US, and the UK in exchange for Ukraine giving up nuclear weapons, the 1997 Ukraine-Russia treaty recognising their border, the 1997 twenty-year 'temporary' Black Sea Fleet basing agreement, the 1998 Crimean constitution, and the 2004 Treaty Between the Russian Federation and Ukraine on Cooperation in the Use of the Sea of Azov and the Kerch Strait. These five documents were flouted by Russia in 2014 when it invaded and annexed Crimea and in 2018 when, in an act of state piracy, the Russian Black Sea Fleet rammed Ukrainian naval ships in the Sea of Azov and imprisoned Ukrainian seamen. In May 2019, the Hamburg-based UN International Tribunal for the Law of the Sea ruled in favour of Ukraine and demanded that Russia release the illegally imprisoned ships and seamen.

In the 1990s, Moscow Mayor Yuriy Luzhkov was a prominent agitator for the non-recognition of Ukrainian sovereignty over Crimea and the port of Sevastopol, as were Russian political parties and political technologists (political consultants who work on negative aspects of election campaigns) at the Russian presidency. On many occasions, both houses of the Russian parliament have voted in support of territorial claims towards Crimea and the port of Sevastopol. Russian intelligence services in the Black Sea Fleet based in Crimea under the twenty-year 'temporary' agreement signed in 1997 undertook covert activity in support of Russian separatist groups. Crimean media fanned exaggerated claims of the threat of 'Ukrainianisation' to

Russian speakers and racism towards Crimean Tatars.

Russia's rhetoric and covert action towards Crimea have changed in two ways under President Putin. The first change concerns Putin's cooperation with his Russian nationalist parliament, which the president controlled through the United Russia party and an array of satellites political parties, such as the national-Bolshevik *Rodina* (Motherland). Under Yeltsin, the president did not officially support parliament's territorial claims towards Crimea and Sevastopol. A second change concerns marginal nationalist ideologues who had been defeated in the 1993 failed Russian parliamentary *coup d'état*, but whose strident views on Ukraine became influential and received support at the presidential level.

In 2014, Putin's alliance with 'brown' (fascist), 'white' (monarchist and Orthodox fundamentalist), and 'red' (Communist) political forces was evident in his 'New Russia' project for southeastern Ukraine (Laruelle 2016a). The Russian nationalist (imperialist) *Zavtra* and Sovietophile *Sovetskaya Rossiya* newspapers converged on 'New Russia' in what Plokhy (2017, 342) describes as a joint project of Russian intelligence and 'Russian nationalists.' Putin and 'brown-white-red' extremist political forces supported 'conservative,' eastern Slavic, and 'Orthodox' civilisation values, using the same arguments and colourful and threatening language portraying Russia at the centre of a messianic Russian World civilisation at war with the West (O'Loughlin, Toal and Kolosov 2016, 753). These political forces not only supported the dismemberment of Ukraine (through, for example, the 'New Russia' project), but also enthusiastically embraced the annexation of Crimea.

The Russian-Crimean-Ukrainian triangle of conflict has gone through four stages since 1991. In the first half of the 1990s, Crimean separatism threatened Ukraine's independence, but was subdued using peaceful means. From the second half of the 1990s until the 2004 Orange Revolution, a period of stabilisation took hold after Russian nationalist-separatists were marginalised and pro-Ukrainian forces took control of Crimea. Following the 2006 Ukrainian and Crimean parliamentary elections, the Party of Regions and Crimean Russian nationalist-separatists took power in Crimea. The final stage, beginning with Russian occupation in 2014, witnesses Crimea undergoing Russification, Sovietisation, and repression of Crimean Tatar history, language, culture, and religion.

Separatism and State Building: 1990–1995

In the early 1990s, Ukraine began its 'quadruple transition' of state and nation-building, democratisation and marketisation (Kuzio 2001a). A weak

Ukrainian state and strong pro-Russian separatist movement made Ukrainian control over Crimea tenuous. In 1991, to take the wind out of Crimean separatist sails, Parliamentary Chairman Kravchuk backed the holding of a Crimean referendum over whether Crimea's status should be changed from an *oblast* to an autonomous republic inside the Ukrainian SSR. Kent (2016, 145) ignores Ukrainian sovereignty over Crimea at that time and confusingly describes the referendum as leading to the 're-establishment of the Crimean Soviet Socialist Republic.' Following the Crimean referendum, the number of Soviet republics did not increase from fifteen to sixteen.

Defining the contours of Crimean autonomy plagued Kyiv-Crimean relations until the adoption of a Crimean constitution in 1998. Although Ukraine remained a unitary state, Crimean autonomy was an exception because it was the only region of the country with an ethnic Russian majority. There were two key dates during this period. In May 1992, the Crimean parliament voted to secede from Ukraine, but then backtracked after being promised greater autonomy. In 1994, Crimea held parliamentary and presidential elections and elected separatist leader Yuri Meshkov, defeating Kyiv's favourite candidate, former first secretary of the Crimean branch of the Communist Party during the Soviet Union, Mykola Bahrov. Meshkov's presidency proved to be short-lived as President Kuchma annulled the Crimean presidency a year later. Eastern Ukrainian Kuchma adopted a more hard-line stance towards Crimean nationalist-separatists than had his 'western Ukrainian nationalist' predecessor Kravchuk.

Marginalisation of Separatists: 1995–2004

From 1995 until the 2004 Orange Revolution, Russian nationalist-separatist groups in Crimea were marginalised, which provided the political space for Kyiv and Crimea to complete their negotiations and establish a new constitutional relationship. A crucial event was the adoption of a Crimean constitution in October 1998, which recognised Crimea as part of Ukraine. The Ukrainian parliament ratified the constitution three months later, opening the way for both houses of the Russian parliament to ratify the 1997 Ukrainian-Russian treaty. With the adoption of these domestic and international legislative acts, the Russia-Crimea-Ukraine triangular relationship was stabilised.

Crimea was ruled by the Communist Party of Ukraine and pro-presidential NDP (People's Democratic Party) until the end of Kuchma's presidency in 2004. At that time, Russian nationalist-separatists received little active support from Russia. President Yeltsin was incapacitated in the second half of the 1990s, while from 2000 Putin consolidated his power domestically and flirted with the West's anti-terrorist campaign. Importantly, Russian nationalism (imperialism) had not yet become the driving force of Putin's regime.

Another important factor was that Kuchma, an eastern Ukrainian military-industrial plant director, had good relations with Yeltsin and Putin. The exception was the autumn 2003 crisis, when Russian security forces attempted to occupy the Ukrainian island of Tuzla off the eastern Crimean coast. Good Russian-Ukrainian relations remained in place despite Ukraine outlining its goal of NATO membership in July 2002, twice seeking MAPs (Membership Action Plans) from NATO in 2002 and 2004 and Prime Minister Yanukovych's government sending the third largest military contingent to US-led coalition forces in Iraq.

With Russian Assistance, Crimean Nationalist-Separatists Return from the Margins

Following the Orange Revolution and Yushchenko's election as president, three factors changed in the Russian-Crimean-Ukrainian triangle of conflict. The first was the rise of the Party of Regions, a leftist, populist, and Sovietophile political party led by oligarchs and supported by former Communist Party of Ukraine voters. After Kuchma left office, the Party of Regions was able to establish a monopoly of power over southeastern Ukraine by absorbing, co-opting, or destroying other centrist parties. The process of the co-option of the Communist Party of Ukraine, which shared the stronghold of Donetsk with the Party of Regions, had begun when Yanukovych was Donetsk Governor, and they remained allies through to the Euromaidan Revolution (Kuzio 2015a).

From 2005–2006, the marginalisation of the NDP and co-option of the Communist Party of Ukraine opened a political vacuum in Crimea, which the Party of Regions exploited. The Party of Regions, Crimean Russian nationalist-separatists, and Russian leaders were united in their conviction that 'colour revolutions' were 'used by the West in contestation with Russia' as western-backed conspiracies to install anti-Russian nationalists into power in Eurasia (Delcour and Wolczuk 2015, 467). Putin had twice visited Ukraine during the first and second rounds of the 2004 elections to support Yanukovych; US President George W. Bush did not visit Ukraine until 2008.

In 2005, the Party of Regions and the United Russia party signed a cooperation agreement. During the 2006 Crimean parliamentary elections, Russian political technologist Konstantin Zatulin, director of the (pro-Putin) Institute for CIS Countries, brokered the creation of the 'For Yanukovych bloc' between the Party of Regions, the nationalist-separatist Russia bloc, and the Russian Community of the Crimea. The 'For Yanukovych' bloc elected 44 deputies, enabling them to install Russian Community of the Crimea leader Sergei Tsekov as the Crimean Parliament's First Deputy Chairperson. The 44 'For Yanukovych' deputies aligned with nine Communist, seven People's Opposition Bloc of Natalia Vitrenko (leader of the extreme left Progressive Socialist Party), and four Medvedchuk-controlled Opposition Bloc *Ne Tak* (Not Like This) deputies, giving pro-Russian forces 64 out of 100 deputies in the Crimean parliament, practically a constitutional majority. Pro-Ukrainian forces were limited to 26 deputies from the Serhiy Kunitsyn bloc (representing the Kuchma-era NDP), Bloc of Yulia Tymoshenko (BYuT), and Crimean Tatars. The remaining ten deputies were independents.

The US Embassy in Ukraine believed the Party of Regions had given the Russia bloc excessive political prominence by forming a single electoral list that had given them seats they would not have won on their own (Ukraine: The Russia Factor in Crimea – Ukraine's "Soft Underbelly?" 2006; Ukraine: Crimea Update – Less Tense Than in 2006: Interethnic, Russia, Land Factors Remain Central 2007). The Party of Regions was willing to bring Crimean nationalist-separatists out of marginalisation because this was the only manner in which they could spread their influence into Crimea, which was a new territory for the Donetsk oligarchic clan. Crimean Russian nationalist-separatists acted as Russian proxies in 2014 during the invasion and annexation of Crimea, and most Party of Regions deputies defected to United Russia.

Between 2006-2014, the Party of Regions and Russian intelligence squeezed Ukrainian political forces out of the Crimean parliament. This and many other examples of the Party of Regions' authoritarianism makes it very odd that western *Putinversteher* scholars portray the Party of Regions as a pluralistic force (Sakwa 2015, 2017a). Party of Regions and Russian strategies dovetailed during this period. The former wished to stay in power indefinitely by undermining their Ukrainian opponents, while Russia viewed pro-western Ukrainian political forces as Russophobes and 'Ukrainian nationalists.'

In the 2010 Crimean elections, widespread abuse of state-administrative resources ensured that the Party of Regions doubled its deputies to 80. Another 13 pro-Russian deputies were elected from the Communist Party of Ukraine, *Soyuz* (Union) and Russian Unity, a Crimean neo-fascist Party of Russian Unity led by Sergei Aksyonov. Pro-Ukrainian forces were reduced to only five deputies elected by the Crimean Tatar-*Rukh* bloc. Two deputies were elected by Serhiy Tihipko's *Silna Ukrayina* (Strong Ukraine) party, which merged with the Party of Regions in 2011.

Putin's and Russia's hostility to Ukrainian sovereignty, territorial integrity, and

Yushchenko's pro-western foreign policy grew exponentially in Crimea after 2005. Russia expanded its covert operations in Crimea, Donbas, and Odesa, infiltrated the Party of Regions and other pro-Russian forces, and provided paramilitary training for Donbas extremist groups who played an active role in 2014 (see chapter 5), while Russian television and media propaganda became more bellicose. After two Russian diplomats were expelled from Ukraine for espionage in summer 2009, President Dmitri Medvedev (2009) sent an undiplomatic and strongly critical open letter to Yushchenko demanding a raft of changes to Ukrainian domestic and foreign policies (D'Anieri 2019, 147).

Putin's evolution into a nationalist (imperialist) towards southeastern Ukraine rested on long-standing Russian nationalistic views. Russian nationalist dissidents (Russian Patriots 1971; Joo 2008), well-known dissident and nationalist writer Solzhenitsyn (1990), and Russian nationalists (imperialists) have long contested Ukraine's sovereignty over southeastern Ukraine on historic and linguistic-cultural grounds (Kuzio 2017c, 33–84). A large proportion of Russian opposition groups and parties support Solzhenitsyn's call for a Russian Union of the three eastern Slavs and northern Kazakhstan (see Verkhovskyj 2014). The Russian Union which Solzhenitsyn called for in 1990 to replace the USSR is strikingly similar to the Russian World Putin created in 2007. Solzhenitsyn and Putin came to a consensus on nationalist (imperialist) questions (Horvath 2011; Coalson 2014).

Western studies of 'Russian nationalism' have ignored the evolution away from the Soviet formulation of close, but different Russians and Ukrainians to Tsarist Russian and White *émigré* views of Russians and Ukrainians as 'one people' (see Kolsto and Blakkisrud 2016), with a few exceptions (see Bacon 2015, 34; Kuzio 2017d; Belton 2020, 427). Trudolybov (2016) points out, 'Even those Russians who are not supporters of Mr. Putin often deny their Ukrainian neighbours a separate identity and do not recognise Ukrainian "otherness."' Trudolybov (2016) adds, 'The "one people" phrase has long been an irritant for many Ukrainians, in large part because Mr. Putin has used it so often.'

Between 2007–2011, nationalist (imperialist) views of Ukraine and Ukrainians gained ground among Russian leaders and the Russian opposition. During this period, Putin began to think of himself as the 'gatherer of Russian lands.' Putin (2008) told the NATO-Russia Council in Bucharest that Ukraine was an 'artificial state' and questioned Ukraine's right to its southeastern regions.

Since then, Putin has repeatedly made nationalist (imperialist) claims to 'Russian' southeastern Ukraine, called the region 'New Russia' and *Prichernomorie* (Black Sea Coast Lands), and without any foundation claimed that it is populated by 'Russians' (Socor 2020a). It is not difficult to find examples of Putin's nationalism (imperialism) towards Ukraine; that is, if one treats Ukraine as a separate country from Russia and if one wants to accept his discourse as nationalistic (imperialistic) (Putin 2014a, 2014b, 2015a, 2015b, 2017, 2019, 20230a, 2020b). Unfortunately, many political scientists working on Russia do not want to do so, or they downplay what this author sees as evidence (see chapter 4).

A month after the annexation of Crimea, Putin (2014b) said, talking about southeastern Ukraine, 'These territories were given to Ukraine in the 1920s by the Soviet government. Why? Who knows? They were won by Potyomkin and Catherine the Great in a series of well-known wars. The centre of that territory was Novorossiysk, so the region is called New Russia. Russia lost these territories for various reasons, but the people remained.' In his annual press conference in December 2019, Putin said that *Prichernomorie* 'never had anything to do with Ukraine' (Socor 2020a). 'When the Soviet Union was created, ancestral Russian territories (such as) all of the *Prichernomorie* and Russia's western lands, that never had anything to do with Ukraine, were turned over to Ukraine' (Socor 2020a). Putin's (2020a) views are becoming increasingly bellicose, as when he said: 'When creating the USSR, the right to leave was prescribed but without a procedure for this. If a republic which became part of the USSR received a huge amount of Russian lands, then it would leave the USSR with what it had received.'

Putin's discourse in the six years prior to 2014, and especially during the 'Russian spring,' sent signals to Russian nationalists (imperialists) and pro-Russian groups in Crimea and the Donbas that Russian leaders no longer upheld Ukraine's territorial status quo, while large areas of Ukraine are 'Russian' and were wrongly included in Ukraine by Soviet leaders. In spring 2014, these views 'were now widely disseminated in the government-controlled press and by Russian leaders' (D'Anieri 2019, 235). Although Russians had always argued that Crimea and Sevastopol were wrongly included in Ukraine, the addition of 'New Russia' as another mistake made by Soviet leaders was an outgrowth of the growing influence of Tsarist and White *émigré* nationalistic (imperialistic) views of Ukraine and Ukrainians (see Wolkonsky 1920; Bregy and Obolensky 1940).

In August 2008, Russia invaded Georgia, and its armed forces nearly reached Tbilisi, only forty kilometres from the southeastern border of the frozen conflict zone of South Ossetia. Russia's invasion of Georgia was a trial run for its invasion of Crimea six years later (Plokhy 2017, 337). The launch of the EU's Eastern Partnership a year after the invasion of Georgia gave the possibility of integration (but not membership) to Ukraine, Georgia, and Moldova into the

EU (Armenia pulled out in 2013 while Belarus and Azerbaijan have never been enthusiastic). Putin was hostile to the EU initiative and henceforth viewed 'EU enlargement' in the same negative manner as Russia had traditionally viewed NATO enlargement. The first reason is because Russia is opposed to the enlargement of western influence into what the Kremlin considers its exclusive sphere of influence in Eurasia (Gretskiy 2020). The second reason is the belief Ukraine signing an Association Agreement with the EU would constitute a permanent break of that country with the Russian World (D'Anieri 2019, 210). It made no difference the EU was offering Ukraine integration without membership because Russia was not focused upon trade or economics but on identity and culture.

Russia's Annexation of Crimea

Yanukovych's election in 2010 re-configured the Russian-Ukrainian relationship of imperial power and dependency to that which the Kremlin believes constitutes 'normality;' that is, how the Kremlin has developed the Russian-Belarusian relationship. In the first year of his presidency, President Yanukovych implemented all of Medvedev's (2009) demands. These included Ukraine adopting the Russian view of the 1933 famine as an all-Soviet tragedy rather than a genocide directed against Ukraine. Minister of Education Dmytro Tabachnyk expanded Soviet and Russian historical myths in Ukrainian education, and new state anniversaries were created that imported Putin's cult of the Great Patriotic War. The Black Sea Fleet basing agreement in Sevastopol was extended to 2042–2047. Ukraine adopted an ephemeral 'non-bloc' foreign policy which dropped the goal of NATO membership. Despite these numerous concessions, Russia refused to change the 2009 gas contract, and Ukraine continued to pay the highest gas price in Europe. Paul D'Anieri (2019) writes how these tough Russian policies towards Ukraine have been commonplace since 1991 and reflect the Kremlin's disdain towards Ukrainian independence.

Why did Belarus under Lukashenka receive Russian gas subsidies, but Yanukovych did not? Lukashenka has always been fully servile to Russia, and Belarus is a Russian dependency and a member of every Russian-led integration project in Eurasia. Yanukovych continued to balance between Europe and Eurasia, still supporting an Association Agreement with the EU, which became increasingly untenable and collapsed into disarray in the Euromaidan Revolution (Kuzio 2017a). Ukraine would have received Russian gas subsidies if Putin's plan to re-elect Yanukovych in 2015 had gone ahead and if Ukraine had joined the Eurasian Economic Union. The Euromaidan put paid to Putin's plans, and he took revenge for his second humiliation (the first being in 2004) by invading and annexing Crimea (see Hosaka 2018). A bloodless annexation was assisted by Yanukovych who during his presidency *de facto* turned Crimea over to Russia. Russia's FSB (Federal Security Service) returned to the Black Sea Fleet (see Table 5.1). Russian influence increased in Ukraine's military, SBU (Security Service of Ukraine), and the government as Russian citizens were appointed to important positions (Kuzio 2012).

During and after the Euromaidan, Russia used the post-revolutionary chaos in Kyiv to invade and annex Crimea. Ukraine's leadership responded passively, neither giving the order to its security forces to strategically retreat or defend their bases. The West was shocked by Russia's actions but advised Ukraine not to resist in order to not provoke an all-out Russian-Ukrainian war.

The results of the Crimean parliamentary election held during Russia's occupation in 2014 reflected those commonly found in Putin's authoritarian system. Ukrainian and Crimean political parties and civic organisations were banned. In the 2014 Crimean elections, 70 deputies were elected by United Russia and another 5 by Vladimir Zhirinovsky's LDPRF (Liberal Democratic Party of the Russian Federation), a fake nationalist party that has always been controlled by the Kremlin. The artificiality of the election results was obvious, as neither of these two parties had existed in Crimea prior to 2014. Many former Party of Regions deputies from the Crimean parliament were re-elected as United Russian deputies. In late 2014, Crimean Prime Minister Aksyonov's neo-fascist Russian Unity party was absorbed by Putin's United Russia.

In March 2014, Russia held a sham referendum that voted for 'union' with Russia. The annexation of Crimea, illegal under Ukrainian and international law, made a mockery of Russia as a 'guarantor' of Ukrainian sovereignty in the Budapest Memorandum and destroyed any trust in Russian promises. The claim of 97% support in the referendum was 'reminiscent of Soviet-era elections' (Plokhy 2017, 337) and was not recognised by any international organisation.

Actual support for a union with Russia was much lower. A leak from the (surely misnamed) Russian 'Human Rights Council' showed that the official turnout of 83% was bogus, and the real turnout had been 30% and, of those, only 15% backed a union with Russia. The leaked report said: 'In Crimea, according to various indicators, 50–60% voted for unification with Russia with a voter turnout of 30–50%.' This gave a range of between 15% and 30% voting for Crimea's union with Russia. The turnout in Sevastopol, according to the 'Human Rights Council' was higher at 50–80% (Gregory 2014).

Some western scholars of Russia took the referendum results at face value because of their subjective belief that Crimea has 'always been Russian.' Kent (2016, 157) claims that the referendum 'was joyfully received by most Crimeans.' Kent (2016, 160), believing that popular sentiment in Crimea is 'Russian' writes, 'There is no doubt that the majority of the population of Crimea supported joining the Russian Federation.' Sakwa (2015, 112) claims, without providing any evidence, that Crimean Tatars 'welcomed the reunification with Russia' because 'Crimean Tatars are ready to be loyal citizens of Russia.' Both of these claims have no basis in empirical data and, rather, reflect the authors' subjective biases.

Russia's July 2020 referendum endorsing changes to its constitution to extend Putin in office until 2036 also made changing Crimea's status in the future impossible. An additional paragraph was installed between paragraphs 2 and 3 of Article 67 which states, 'The Russian Federation ensures protection of its sovereignty and territorial integrity. Actions (excluding delimitation, demarcation and re-demarcation of the state border of the Russian Federation with bordering states) aimed at removing a part of the Russian Federation's territory, as well as calls to such actions, are not permitted.' Russian Senator Andriy Klishas admitted 'this was written so that nobody could seriously insert an amendment into legislation according to which Crimea would be handed to Ukraine.' 'It was done so that not one state body, including the President or parliament, or the government, could seriously hold negotiations, for example, on the return of Crimea to Ukraine' (Coynash 2020b).

The July 2020 constitutional change means that relations between the West and Russia will continue to remain cold for a long time to come because some of the US, Canadian, and EU sanctions against Russia are linked to its illegal annexation of Crimea. In 2014, only 17% of Russians accepted Ukraine's borders, while the remainder believed that Ukraine should be a smaller country (Alexseev and Hale 2016, 196). There is no domestic opposition to Crimea's annexation, with 85% of Russians supporting Crimea's annexation and only 10% opposing it (Crimea: Five Years 2019). Additionally, 56% of Russians support the separation of the Donbas from Ukraine into an independent state or the region joining Russia (Crimea: Five Years 2019). 70% of Russians support their government's policy of issuing Russian passports to residents of Russian-occupied Donbas, which would make them Russian citizens and provide Russia with a legal fig leaf to intervene on their behalf (Crimea: Five Years 2019).

Minority Rights in Russian-Occupied Crimea

Exaggerated complaints of 'Ukrainianisation' and 'Islamicisation' in Crimea were never reflected in the very low number of Ukrainian and Crimean Tatar schools and media outlets that existed when the peninsula was part of Ukraine. Following Russia's occupation, Ukrainian educational facilities and media publications have all been closed, while Crimean Tatar education and media outlets have been drastically reduced in number.

The Russian Federation, Party of Regions, and its Crimean nationalist-separatist allies mobilised, agitated, and used inflammatory rhetoric and a massive information warfare campaign alleging discrimination against Russian speakers. That this was a myth could be seen by Ukrainians always ascribing low levels of importance to language issues and low levels of grievances over alleged discrimination against Russian speakers. In Donetsk and Luhansk, 9.4 and 12.7% of Ukrainians, respectively, were anxious at the imposition of one language. 59% in Donetsk and 80% in southeastern Ukraine did not believe that there was discrimination against Russian speakers (Kulyk 2018, 20; Giuliano 2018). Only 5% of Ukrainians younger than 29 had witnessed discrimination of languages (Zarembo 2017, 19). A 2020 poll found only 10.1% of Ukrainians who had witnessed infringements of the Russian language and 52.2% who had not (Ukrayinska mova: shlyakh u nezalezhniy Ukrayini 2020). Nevertheless, in 2014, a high 89% of Russian citizens were convinced that the rights of Russian speakers were being infringed in neighbouring states (Pain 2016, 71).

In spring 2014, the UN High Commissioner for Human Rights (UNHCHR) and the Council of Europe reported no attacks on Russian speakers anywhere in Ukraine, despite Putin using this bogus myth as justification for Russia's invasion and annexation of Crimea. Only 5% of Ukrainians believe that Russia intervened in Crimea and Donbas because of the violation of the rights of Russian speakers. Eight to ten times as many Ukrainians believe that Russia's intervention was to prevent Ukraine from leaving Russia's sphere of influence (46.2%), Russia's inability to accept Ukraine as an independent state (42.5%), and Russian opposition to Ukraine's European integration (42.3%) (Perspektyvy Ukrayinsko-Rosiyskykh Vidnosyn 2015).

In spring 2014, the Council of Europe did not find credible claims of Russian speakers being threatened in Crimea (Ukraine: ad hoc visit of the Advisory Committee on the Framework Convention for the Protection of National Minorities 2014). The Council of Europe was, however, concerned 'about the safety and enjoyment of cultural, education and language rights of all national minorities in Crimea, including in particular the numerically smaller ones such as the Karaim and Krimchak as well as persons belonging to the Ukrainian community who are in a minority situation in Crimea' (Ad hoc Report on the situation of national minorities in Ukraine adopted on 1 April 2014). Also, in spring 2014, inter-ethnic relations did not deteriorate in Crimea (In Crimea serious human rights violations and attacks on minorities and journalists require urgent action 2014). Since then, only Ukrainians and Crimean Tatars have been subjected to political repression, and ethnic and religious discrimination.

Exaggerated claims about 'Ukrainian nationalism' and the threat it posed to Russian speakers were a central theme in Russia's information warfare during and after the Euromaidan, which inflamed rhetoric. Ukrainian nationalism has always had low levels of support among Ukrainians, and it played a minor role in the Euromaidan (Onuch and Sasse 2018). Opinion polls have consistently shown that Ukrainians hold negative attitudes towards Russian leaders and largely positive attitudes towards Russian citizens; this is even the case in western Ukraine (Despite Concerns About Governance, Ukrainians Want to Remain One Country 2014). These polls provide evidence of Ukrainian patriotism, not ethnic nationalism.

Some western scholars paint a fairy-tale picture of life for Tatars in Crimea that could have been prepared by political technologists working for the Kremlin. Pijl (2018, 40) describes Russian policies towards Crimean Tatars in glowing terms based on the 'spirit of Soviet nationality policy' and 'internationalism and autonomy,' which continue to be used in the Russian Federation. Pijl (2018, 40) is obviously unaware of the plight of Ukrainians in the Russian Federation, who have no rights whatsoever because he contrasts Russia's supposedly positive nationality policies with anti-Russian and 'ethnic' policies in Ukraine. The Russian Federation comes out worse than Ukraine in any comparison of minority rights. Russian speakers and ethnic Russians in Ukraine have a wide array of cultural, linguistic, and religious rights, while the second largest minority in Russia – Ukrainians – have none. Ukrainians in the Donbas and Ukrainians and Tatars in Crimea suffered from a wide range of discriminatory policies prior to 2014, and their plight has massively deteriorated during Russia's occupation (Motyl 2015; Lukanov 2018; Coynash and Charron 2019; Skrypnyk 2019).

Sakwa (2015, 21, 38, 59, 206, 249, 279) has taken the mythologising of Ukrainian regionalism and nationalism to a new level in his dichotomy between Ukrainian 'monism' and 'pluralism,' a framework he never applies to Russia or Russian-controlled territories. Sakwa's (2015) mythical framework is unable to explain why the bulk of the fighting against Russian military aggression is being undertaken by Russian-speaking eastern Ukrainians (Hunter 2018, 94; Kaihko 2018; Aliyev 2019, 2020). Why would Russian speakers fight and die for Ukraine if they were living under a tyranny ruled by 'western Ukrainian nationalists' and neo-Nazis? Five leading volunteer battalions were composed of eastern Ukrainians (Donbas, Dnipro-1, Dnipro-2, Aydar, Azov) and the highest rates of casualties of security forces are found in Dnipropetrovsk *oblast* (see the map at 6.2).

Ukrainians and Tatars accounted for 36% of Crimea's population in Ukraine's 2001 census, and many of them were opposed to Russia's annexation. Some Ukrainians and Russians holding a Ukrainian civic identity in Crimea opposed Russia's annexation (Nedozhogina 2019, 1086). One of these was the Russian film director Oleg Sentsov, who was sentenced in 2015 to twenty years imprisonment on trumped up charges of plotting terrorist acts. He was released four years later in a prisoner exchange with Russia and has remained a virulent critic of Russia's occupation of Crimea.

Political repression of Crimean Tatars and repression of their culture and language is on-going in occupied Crimea (Coynash and Charron 2019; Skrypnyk 2019). The UN Educational, Scientific and Cultural Organisation (UNESCO) has reported on systematic violations by Russia of cultural, educational, media freedom, and human rights of Crimean Tatars and Ukrainians as well as endangering Crimean Tatar and Ukrainian cultural heritage sites (Follow-up of the situation in the Autonomous Republic of Crimea Ukraine 2019). Russia has imprisoned Crimean Tatar activists, closed down Crimean Tatar institutions (such as the unofficial parliament *Majlis*), persecuted Crimean Tatar culture, and imprisoned and deported Tatar leaders (Coynash and Charron 2019; Skrypnyk 2019). Official 'self-defence' forces (in reality, death squads) have abducted and most likely murdered up to 18 Crimean Tatar activists (Situation of human rights in the temporarily occupied Autonomous Republic of Crimea and the city of Sevastopol (Ukraine) 2014). Twenty thousand Crimean Tatars have fled from Russian-occupied Crimea to Ukraine (see Magocsi 2014a, 2014b; Williams 2015). Crimean Tatar activist Emir-Usein Kuku told a Russian court that sentenced him to twelve years on false charges of 'terrorism': 'Does it not strike you as strange that in the 23 years Crimea was under Ukrainian rule, there were no 'extremists' nor 'terrorists,' and no 'acts of terrorism,' but as soon as Russia arrived with its FSB, there was suddenly all of that?' (Coynash 2020a).

Widespread evidence of systematic human rights abuses and ethnic discrimination in Russian-occupied Crimea and Donbas is of course ignored by *Putinversteher* scholars (see Violations of human rights and international crimes during the war in the Donbass 2018; Coynash and Charron 2019; Skrypnyk 2019). In June 2018, Ukraine presented a large volume of evidence ('Memorial') to the UN's International Court of Justice in The Hague, Netherlands documenting Russia's violation of the International Convention on the Elimination of All Forms of Racial Discrimination (Ukraine versus Russia 2018, 2019). A second part of the 'Memorial' dealt with Russia's violation of the International Convention of the Suppression of the Financing of Terrorism. The 447-page 'Memorial' stated, 'The Russian Federation is responsible for a brazen and comprehensive assault on human rights and international law in the territory of Ukraine' (Ukraine versus Russia 2018). In particular:

> In Crimea, the Russian Federation acts overtly and directly. There, in Ukrainian territory that Russia unlawfully occupies, Russia maintains its domination through a policy of racial discrimination and cultural erasure directed against those ethnic communities that dared to oppose its purported annexation of the peninsula. It has methodically trampled the political and civil rights of these communities: disappearing, torturing, and murdering Crimean Tatar and Ukrainian activists; subjecting others to arbitrary searches and detention; and banning the *Mejlis*, the representative institution that has been a bulwark for the rights of the Crimean Tatar people since they returned from Stalin's ruthless exile. Russia is also choking off the cultural expression that these communities need if they are to preserve and perpetuate their distinct identities: banning or disrupting cultural gatherings; suppressing the media outlets serving Crimean Tatar and Ukrainian audiences; and restricting opportunities for children from those communities to be educated in their native languages. These well-documented and widely condemned actions violate international law (Ukraine versus Russia 2018).

Conclusion

Russian nationalists (imperialists) view Crimea as always having been 'Russian' in two ways. The first is through the myth of Crimea being part of 'Kievan Russia' (Kyiv Rus) and the birthplace of the 'All-Russian People,' while the second is through justifying its 1783 annexation by the Tsarist Russian empire. The former denies Kyiv Rus as part of Ukrainian history and includes Ukrainians as one of three branches of the 'All-Russian People.' The latter denies Crimean Tatars as the indigenous people of Crimea. Past genocide and ethnic and religious persecution of Crimean Tatars in the Tsarist empire, USSR, and especially since 2014 in occupied Crimea are often ignored.

In their belief that Crimea has always been 'Russian' (whether since Kyiv Rus or after 1783), western historians of 'Russia' and some political scientists writing about Russia viewed the March 2014 sham referendum as genuine, even though it has never been internationally recognised. Yet, no opinion poll conducted prior to 2014 gave majority support for separatism in Crimea, making it highly likely the March 2014 referendum was a sham.

Academic orientalism, as found in western writing about Crimea, has already been critically discussed in this book. It is beyond doubt that most western historians of 'Russia' see Crimea as 'always having been Russian' and therefore have not criticised Russia's 2014 invasion and annexation. Academic orientalism is, however, a far bigger problem in Russian studies than in Crimea and in the next chapter, this will be shown through my critical review of western writing on the 2014 crisis and Russian-Ukrainian War. This will show how Moscow's viewpoint is often found in western writing of the 2014 crisis and Russian-Ukrainian War because of the selective use of sources made by historians and political scientists.

3

Academic Orientalism

This book uses the term academic orientalism to describe how western historians of 'Russia' and some political scientists with expertise on Russia selectively use sources when writing about Ukraine and other non-Russian countries of the former USSR. Using sources mainly published in Russia is both lazy and biased. Academic orientalism is lazy because we live in an Internet era where sources from Ukraine are available online and in the Russian language; therefore, scholars do not necessarily need a command of Ukrainian. Publications, sociological polls, think tank publications, and official web sites – which as this book shows are available online – are largely ignored by most western scholars of Russia who have written about Ukraine, Crimea, Donbas, and Ukrainian-Russian relations.

Until World War II, orientalism was reflected in western scholars writing about overseas colonies through the eyes of London, Paris, and other imperial metropolitan cities. Today, academic orientalism is reflected in western scholars writing about Ukraine through the eyes of Moscow. Academic orientalism is biased because it produces a subjective, Russo-centric outlook on Ukrainian-Russian relations. This form of academic orientalism is taken one step further when western scholars writing about Ukrainian-Russian relations cite Russian leaders *ad infinitum*, but rarely cite Ukrainian politicians. Sakwa (2015), for example, never once cites Poroshenko, but quotes Putin 31 times. Gerard Toal (2017) cites Putin and Prime Minister Medvedev on 44 occasions and Poroshenko only once – fewer than his two citations for Soviet President Gorbachev. Samuel Charap and Timothy J. Colton's (2017) work is full of citations of Russian leaders with only four of Poroshenko.

Changes in Ukrainian historiography since 1991 and identity since 2014 have been recognised to some degree among historians in North America (but not in the UK and western Europe) and to varying degrees among political scientists. Academic orientalism remains an issue within Russian studies, whose political scientists are usually the gatekeepers in most western academic centres on post-communist Europe and Eurasia. One example of academic orientalism on Ukraine is that of political scientist Sakwa (2015), an expert on Russian politics. The only Ukrainian source used by Sakwa (2015) was the English-language *Kyiv Post*. This is because 'the author has no intention of delving into the Ukrainian material comprehensively' (Kravchenko 2016). Writing a book on the Russian-Ukrainian War 'had no impact on his [Sakwa's] preconceived notions and interpretation of Russia, Eastern Europe, and the world order' (Kravchenko 2016). Other examples of academic orientalism are given throughout this chapter.

This chapter is divided into five sections. The first section applies Edward Said's (1994, 1995) concept of orientalism to western writing on the 2014 crisis and the Russian-Ukrainian War. The second section uses orientalism to analyse how the Russian-Ukrainian War is imagined through a biased use of sources. The third section discusses manipulation of opinion polls, and the fourth section discusses non-scholarly review processes and analyses. The final section is a critical discussion of four conspiracies of the Euromaidan Revolution: first, that it was a US-backed operation to install western Ukrainian nationalists in power; second, that Ukrainian nationalists murdered protestors during the Euromaidan; third, that the May 2014 fire in Odesa was organised by Ukrainian nationalists; and fourth, that Ukraine's military strategy (in the same manner as the country as a whole) is controlled by the US and NATO.

Academic Orientalism

Said's (1994, 1995) description of western nationalist (imperialist) imagining of the Orient is found in Russian nationalist (imperialist) imagining of Ukraine and in the imagining of Ukraine by western historians and some political scientists. The Orient and Ukraine are treated as passive, subaltern subjects of the world order who are denied the dignity of choosing their own destiny.

The imaging of European colonies and Russia's neighbours was – and remains – a relationship of power, domination, and hegemony that allegedly benefitted the lives of those who were ruled over. This is a relationship of the strong over the weak, best served by a great power awarded a sphere of influence to maintain order over subaltern people incapable of ruling themselves. Such views were found in British imaginings of Ireland and Polish and Russian imaginings of Ukraine (see Kuzio 2020a). Ukraine was imagined in Polish and Russian literature as *terra incognita*, an empty land where chaos reigned and where there was a need for the imposition of order by more 'civilised' peoples.

Said's (1995, 7, 15) orientalism is reflected in the relationship of power and cultural hegemony in western writing of 'Russian' history, Crimea, and the Russia-Ukraine crisis. Said (1994, 96) points out, 'Almost all colonial schemes begin with an assumption of native backwardness and general inadequacy to be independent, "equal," and fit.' To legitimise colonial rule, the colonies of European empires, Irish, and Ukrainians were treated as backward, ignorant, barbarians, dangers to civilisation, children, gullible, devoid of energy, cunning, dishonest, treacherous, liars, and cheats (Said 1995, 35, 38–40, 39–40, 59, 228, 232, 328).

In the Russian-Ukrainian 'colonizer-colonised' relationship, 'Russia endures disobedience from these leaders in the way adults endure naughty children' (Minchenia, Tornquist-Plewa and Yurchuk 2018, 225). When Lukashenka and Yanukovych have behaved in support of Russia's interests, they were encouraged and pardoned. When they did not, they were castigated as 'traitors' and 'Russophobes.' Russian nationalism (imperialism) is presented as benevolence that conserves 'Russian feelings of superiority over its neighbours and endorsing among the Russians the ruling logistics of dominance' (Minchenia, Tornquist-Plewa and Yurchuk 2018, 226). Igor Gretskiy (2020, 19) writes, 'What the Kremlin wants from the Ukrainian government is the public demonstration of compliance with Moscow's preponderance.' When this did not take place in 2004 or 2014, the Kremlin became angry and retaliated against Ukraine. Russian political technologist Gleb Pavlovsky described 2004 as 'Putin's 9/11' (Krastev 2005; Belton 2020, 271). Would Hiroshima or Nagasaki be the best way to describe 2014 for Putin?

Western imperialists brought 'civilisation' to 'backward peoples' who were unable to rule themselves. The colonies are 'a subject race, dominated by a race that knows them and what is good for them better than they could possibly know themselves' (Said 1995, 35). Colonial rule was justified in the name of progress by a more 'civilised' people.

There is a long history of Russian national identity, which claims moral superiority over a 'degenerate West.' Solzhenitsyn complained about a 'degenerate West' during his western exile in the 1970s and 1980s. Russian nationalists (imperialists) believe that Tsarist Russian and Soviet rule were beneficial to Ukraine and other peoples, and therefore that life in the Russian World would be better than in the EU. Eurasianism claims that Russia's values are superior to European values, rejects western political models and embraces the Mongol-Tatar-Eurasian heritage.

The origins of Putin's 'neo-revisionism' are found in long-term Russian inferiority complexes, where nothing negative is found in Russia's past. The most extreme example of this is the rehabilitation of Stalin (Kuzio 2017b). A cult of Stalin during Putin's presidency has made him the second most popular historical figure in Russia (Tsar Nicholas II came first).

Laruelle (2020b, 345) denies that a full-blown Stalinist cult is emerging in Russia, instead describing it as an 'ambivalent rehabilitation of Stalin by some segments of the Russian political elites.' Cohen (2019) also denies that there is a cult of Stalin in Russia. Putin's cult of Stalin has led to high numbers of Russians holding a positive view of Stalin. By 2019, 52% of Russians held a positive view of Stalin, compared to only 16% of Ukrainians. In contrast to Russians, nearly three-quarters of Ukrainians (72%) believed, 'Stalin is a cruel, inhuman tyrant, guilty of the destruction of millions of innocent people' (Stavlennya Naselennya Ukrayny do Postati Stalina 2019).

In 2019, the Russian Levada Centre, the last remaining independent think tank and polling organisation in Russia, wrote:

> There is no significant age differentiation in relation to views of the leader – in all age cohorts and generational groups, a positive perception of Stalin now dominates over a negative one, although 18–24-year-olds in Russia are generally more indifferent than others. At the same time, the dynamic trend of opinions between 2012 to 2019, even in the youngest age group, indicates acceptance of the norm of the older generations with young people beginning to express positive assessments more often to avoid answering questions about the leader. Support for the positive image of Stalin and the romanticisation of the Soviet era are characteristic not only of respondents with communist views, but also of supporters of other political parties (Stavlennya Naselennya Ukrayny do Postati Stalina 2019).

Academic orientalism describes European colonies and Ukraine as artificial entities, regionally divided and weak states with immature rulers. European depictions of cunning colonial peoples are similar to Russian depictions of sly (*khytryy*) Ukrainians, who excel at intrigue, lying, and deception. Left to themselves, colonial peoples and Ukrainians would produce instability and threaten 'civilised' order (Said 1995, 328–367). From the nineteenth century to the present day, Russian scholarship, literature, novelists, travelogues, military expeditions, judges, pilgrims, and bureaucrats have written about Ukrainians as disorganised, uncivilised, despotic, backward, and bloodthirsty people (see Riabchuk 2016).

Russian nationalists (imperialists) imagine Ukraine as an artificial, failed, and divided state, whose ruling elites have sold their souls to the West (see chapter 4). Being incapable of their own initiative, Ukrainians are manipulated by the West to pursue 'Russophobic' policies and 'anti-Russian conspiracies' (Belafatti 2014). Ukraine is viewed as a puppet state of the West because, as Said (1994, 1995) observed, colonists always imagine those they conquer to be passive subaltern subjects unable of becoming active subjects (Belafatti 2014).

Ukraine's artificiality is allegedly compounded by its lack of history. European colonies and Ukraine are marginalised as 'un-historic peoples' in what Said (1994, 1995) describes as a western-imposed, racist hierarchy. European and Russian identities hold greater significance than that of the subaltern subjects in the Orient or Ukraine.

Western writing on post-communist countries has been written from 'a distorted, hierarchical and, ultimately, orientalist (if not outright racist) perspective on the small countries of Eastern Europe' (Belafatti 2014). Condescending mentalities have long shaped how the West views central-eastern Europe and the former USSR. In the mid-twentieth century, Hans Kohn (Kuzio 2002) wrote about 'good' western and 'bad' eastern nationalisms and Said (1994, 1995) wrote about colonial imagining of the Middle East.

Liberals, Realists, and Nationalists (Imperialists)

Since the nineteenth century, hegemonic imperial ideologies in cultures have been part of European and Russian imaginings of the territories over which they ruled. There was little dissent then in western Europe and there is little dissent now in Russia over the right of certain races to rule over others (Said 1994, 62). British and Russian liberals (e.g. John Stuart Mill, Pyotr Struve, Pyotr Stolypin, Russian liberal *Kadets* in 1917, and the White army) supported the building of empires and a racist hierarchy of peoples (Said 1994, 96, 129; Procyk 1995).

Mill opposed Irish and Indian independence (Smart 1992, 529) because he believed some countries were not ready to take this step (Said 1994, 96, 97). European countries such as Britain had a 'schizophrenic adherence to both racism and liberalism' (Weight 2000, 437). Russian intellectuals have 'granted the empire the role of a Western "civilizing" power with license to repress national resistance in the name of modernization and social reform' (Shkandrij 2001, 103).

Russian liberalism has always ended at the Russian-Ukrainian border. The concept of Russians and Ukrainians as 'one people' harks back to Struve, a member of the liberal *Kadets* and after 1917, the anti-Bolshevik Whites. 'In 2014, Putin brought about the reincarnation of Struve's ideas at the highest levels of Russian politics' (Plokhy 2017, 341). The phrase 'Russian Westernisers' is an oxymoron, as they had always been suspicious of any Ukrainian movement (Plokhy 2017, 115). In the nineteenth century, a leading Russian 'Westerniser,' Vissarrion Belinsky, criticised Ukrainians such as Shevchenko for seeking independence for Ukraine because a union with Russia gave them an opportunity to overcome their earlier 'semi-barbaric way of life' (Shkandrij 2001, 121). Similar colonial racism typified British views of Ireland (see Kuzio 2020a). Belinsky wrote, 'Oh those *khokhly*! [a racist term for Ukrainians]. They are just dumb sheep, but they liberalise in the name of dumplings with pig fat!' (Plokhy 2017, 116). Ukrainians are stereotyped as eaters of lard (pig fat [*salo*]) just as Irish are of potatoes.

There were a small number of exceptions, such as Aleksandr Herzen, the father of Russian populism and socialism, as well as Russian dissidents Bukovsky and Amalrik. Writing in January 1859 in *The Bell* published in London, Herzen described the suffering inflicted upon Ukrainians by 'Muscovites' and asked why Russians were surprised that Ukrainians do not wish to be either Poles or Russians: 'As I see it, the question is to be decided very simply. In that case, Ukraine should be recognised as a free and independent country' (Plokhy 2017, 128). Herzen had let the cat out of the bag.

During the Cold War, the Russian diaspora in the West was dominated by the National Alliance of Russian Solidarists (NTS), which continued supporting Tsarist Russian and White *émigré* views of Ukraine and Ukrainians. *Émigré* Eurasiasnists who, like NTS, emerged from the younger generation of White *émigrés*, came around to supporting Stalin's national Bolshevism. NTS's monopoly was challenged beginning in the 1970s with the arrival in the West of exiled democratic Russian dissidents, such as Bukovsky. Russian democrats were not anti-Ukrainian, but they rarely commented on nationality questions in the USSR. Ukrainian dissidents and nationalists had good relations with Jewish dissidents and non-Russian nationalists.

In the post-Soviet era, most Russian liberals evolved into nationalists during the 1990s. Alexei Navalnyi (2012a, 2012b) began talking of Russians and Ukrainians as 'one people' at the same time as Putin (see Laruelle 2014b, 281). In 2014, Navalnyi said, 'I don't see any kind of difference at all between Russians and Ukrainians' (Dolgov 2014; Bukkvoll 2016, 270). It is therefore strange that nearly all western political scientists working on Russia have ignored how many parts of the Russian opposition have taken Putin's chauvinism towards Ukrainians on board. At the same time, it is wrong for scholars to describe opposition politicians such as Navalnyi as professing 'liberal nationalism' because there is nothing liberal in Navalnyi's attitudes towards Ukraine (see Kolsto 2014; Laruelle 2014b; Hale 2016).

There are a few exceptions that could be described as Russian liberals. Grigory Yavlinsky, leader of the *Yabloko* party, believes that Crimea has a right to self-determination, but he opposed the use of Russian troops to achieve this (see Bacon 2015). Boris Nemtsov (who was assassinated in February 2015) and Garry Kasparov opposed the annexation of Crimea and Sevastopol. In the 1990s, Nemtsov had different views and supported the integration of the three eastern Slavs and Russian 'economic expansion' (rather than military aggression) into 'Crimea, beginning in Sevastopol.'

On Crimea, there is no such thing as Russian 'liberalism.' Nemtsov supported Moscow Mayor Yuri Luzhkov's claims to the port of Sevastopol, describing it as a 'Russian city acquired with Russian blood.'[1] The Communist Party of the Russian Federation (KPRF), LDPRF, Just Russia, Other Russia (successor to the National Bolshevik Party led by Eduard Limonov), and exiled oligarch Mikhail Khodorkovsky have supported Crimea's annexation. Russia's most popular opposition leader, Navalnyi, has said on many occasions that Crimea will not be returned to Ukraine (see Dolgov 2014).

Russian and European imperialists believed that they possessed 'inalienable' rights to Eurasia and the Middle East, respectively. Russia is viewed as possessing a 'hierarchical superior position' in Crimea, Ukraine, and Eurasia, which Ukrainians have no right to question. Ukrainians should accept their place in 'an order of things in which Russia' dominates (Belafatti 2014).

The 2014 Russia-Ukraine crisis has brought together the western left- and right-wing realists (Mearsheimer 2014; Menon & Rumer 2015), who agree that Ukraine is naturally part of Russia's sphere of influence, and non-Russians in Eurasia 'are denied the dignity of actors in the process' with no right to choose their alignment (Belafatti 2014). Such views permeate realist proposals about how Eurasia should be configured by Russia and the West in a new grand bargain[2] – over the heads of Ukrainians, just as this was undertaken in 1945 over eastern Europe in the Yalta Agreement signed by the

---

[1] *Tass*, 20–21 January 1997.
[2] https://www.theatlantic.com/international/archive/2014/08/a-24-step-plan-to-resolve-the-ukraine-crisis/379121/; https://www.europeanleadershipnetwork.org/group-statement/easlg-twelve-steps-toward-greater-security-in-ukraine-and-the-euro-atlantic-region/; https://www.defensepriorities.org/explainers/saying-no-to-nato-options-for-ukrainian-neutrality

victorious allied powers.³

Left-wing critics and right-wing realists *both* deny agency to Ukraine and small countries to determine their future, believing that the fate of countries such as Ukraine should be decided by the great powers. Bizarrely, therefore, left-wing scholars became fans of populist nationalist Trump (Cohen 2019). In seeking Trump's election, 'Russia wanted the deal clinched by the great powers and imposed on Ukraine' (Charap and Colton 2017, 131).

Downplaying Russian and exaggerating Ukrainian nationalism lays blame on Kyiv for the Donbas War. Just as the West is blamed for democracy promotion and fomenting colour revolutions, and as NATO and EU enlargement are blamed for leading to the crisis, so too are Ukrainian leaders blamed for fighting, rather than negotiating. While Putin presumably shares little to no responsibility, President Poroshenko was blamed for unleashing a war after he was elected in May 2014, rather than seeking compromise.

Hahn (2018, 253, 264) blames the Ukrainian authorities for launching an 'unnecessary war' accompanied by war crimes, human rights abuses, and a 'dehumanising' discourse. Pijl (2018, 8) compares Ukraine's military actions from April 2014 as similar to those conducted by Georgia, which launched an 'invasion' of South Ossetia in 2008. Pijl (2018) is obviously unaware that countries cannot 'invade' their own territories.

Imaging the War Through Russian Sources

The crisis in relations between Russia and the West following Russia's annexation of Crimea and military aggression in eastern Ukraine has led to a large number of publications and the proliferation of poor scholarship. Scholars have written about the crisis from the vantage point of their field of speciality, whether Russian and Eurasian area studies, international relations, realism, and security studies. Other have added chapters on Ukraine to books that were already in production.

The Euromaidan, Russia's annexation of Crimea, and Russian hybrid warfare in eastern Ukraine have led to the publication of over 500 scholarly and think tank books, journal articles, and papers (for a partial bibliography see Kuzio 2017c, 363-399). Western scholarship on the crisis is not dominated by a pro-Ukrainian perspective or an official Ukrainian interpretation of the conflict. Claims to this effect rest upon stereotypes that exaggerate the influence of

---

³   https://www.theatlantic.com/international/archive/2014/09/response-boisto-peace-plan-ukraine-russia-us/379428/

the Ukrainian 'nationalist' diaspora (see Matveeva 2017, 276; Molchanov 2018, 73, 227; Sakwa, 2015, 257). The Harvard Ukrainian Research Institute and Canadian Institute of Ukrainian Studies (CIUS) do not traditionally cover politics and international relations and have largely ignored Crimea and the Russian-Ukrainian War. *Harvard Ukrainian Studies* and the *East-West/Journal of Ukrainian Studies* have published no articles on the 2014 crisis, Crimea, or Donbas War.[4]

Scholars of Russian politics have continued to claim expertise on the non-Russian countries that emerged as independent states after 1991. In the Soviet era, travel was restricted beyond Moscow to sensitive republics, such as Ukraine, but this is not the case today. The Internet also provides scholars with widely available primary sources from Ukraine, many of which are in Russian. The official websites of the Ukrainian president, parliament, and government are available in Ukrainian and Russian.[5] The majority of Ukrainian media have Russian-language pages or are published in both Russian and Ukrainian. Three of Ukraine's five weekly political magazines are published in Russian: *Fokus*, *Korrespondent*, and *Novoye Vremya*, and two are published in Ukrainian: *Kray* and *Ukrayinskyy Tyzhden*.

MA and PhD students are instructed to use primary sources and undertake fieldwork in pursuing their research. This advice is ignored by scholars of Russia writing on Ukraine (Sakwa 2015, 2017a; Toal 2017; Charap and Colton 2017), who rely heavily on secondary sources and quotes from official Russian sources.

While citing sources from Russia on 75 occasions, Sakwa's 16 Ukrainian sources are all from the English-language *Kyiv Post*. One wonders whether external reviewers would provide positive reviews of a manuscript about a hypothetical Ukrainian invasion of Russia if it only used sources from the English-language *Moscow News*. Mark Galeotti's (2016) study of hybrid warfare uses no Ukrainian sources from a country that has experienced the greatest impact of Russian hybrid warfare and which has published many studies of hybrid warfare (see Russia's 'Hybrid' War – Challenge and Threat for Europe 2016; Horbulin 2017).

The overwhelming majority of western authors writing about the crisis and war have never travelled to Ukraine. One Ukrainian expert notes, 'Many people participate in the discussions about the Donbas. Far fewer of them actually

---

[4] https://www.husj.harvard.edu/ and https://www.ewjus.com/
[5] The official Russian-language pages of the websites of the Ukrainian president: http://www.president.gov.ua/ru; parliament: http://iportal.rada.gov.ua/ru; and government: http://www.kmu.gov.ua/control/ru.

went there. The lack of real experts on the region is noticeable' (Maiorova 2017, 83). While many scholars may not wish to follow in the footsteps of this author in travelling to the Donbas warzone, this does not excuse the absence of fieldwork research in Kyiv, and southeastern Ukraine. Few western publications on the crisis include interviews with Ukrainian officials, civil society activists, and security forces in Kyiv, and in southeastern Ukraine.

Anna Matveeva (2018) travelled to Russian-controlled Donbas enclaves and to Moscow, where she conducted interviews in the course of her fieldwork, and her book provides a bottom-up view of the Donbas War. This could have been more balanced if similar fieldwork had been undertaken in Kyiv and southeastern Ukraine, including in Ukrainian-controlled Donbas. Seemingly, academic orientalism does not believe that the Ukrainian viewpoint is worthy of study or citation.

Interviews in southeastern Ukraine would have illuminated the views of Russian speakers, traditionally wrongly stereotyped as 'pro-Russian' by Western scholars and journalists writing about Ukraine. The failure of Putin's 'New Russia' project in Ukraine's eight southeastern *oblasts* brings out the importance of interviews with primary sources on the ground (see O'Loughlin, Toal, and Kolosov 2016; Kuzio 2019a). Ukrainian opinion polls available on the Internet are useful for researchers; however, nothing is more illuminating than talking to people in the midst of a conflict because, throughout history, wars have sped up the crystallisation of national identity (Smith 1981). By not doing fieldwork, scholars ignore an intellectually rewarding opportunity to research a crucial moment in the remaking of Ukrainian national identity and Russian-Ukrainian relations.

Manipulating Opinion Polls

Manipulation of polling data to provide 'evidence' for pre-conceived views that seek to prove that there is support for pro-Russian separatism in Crimea. In 1991, 93% of Crimeans did not vote for a 'separate Crimean republic,' but rather for upgrading their *oblast* into an autonomous republic of Soviet Ukraine (Pijl 2018, 87). In writing that Crimea 'never reconciled itself with its place in an independent Ukraine,' Pijl (2018, 40) aims to prove that Crimea eagerly awaited its 'liberation' and return to Russia in 2014. This unscholarly claim has no relationship to historical facts.

Presenting Crimea's annexation as a 'return to normality' has been undertaken by some western scholars misusing sociological data to make the case that a majority of the peninsula's population have always supported separatism. This was never the case. In his desperation to find sociological data showing a majority of Crimeans supporting separatism, Sakwa (2017a, 155) writes, 'Already in 2008 the Razumkov Centre for Economic and Political Studies (hereafter Razumkov Centre) 'polling agency' found that 63.8 percent of Crimean's wished to secede from Ukraine to join Russia.' Sakwa's manipulation of Razumkov Centre polling data to portray majority support in Crimea for separatism is cited by other *Putinversteher* scholars, Ploeg (2017), Pijl (2018, 40), and Hahn (2018, 235). Sakwa's (2017a, 157) description of Crimea's annexation as 'democratic secession' is based on opinion polls that do not exist. In a rare moment of doubt, Sakwa (2017a, 157) concedes that it was also 'imperial annexation' because Russia had not reached an 'agreement with the country from which the territory seceded.' Elsewhere Sakwa (2017b, 10) admits that there was no majority support for separatism in Crimea or the Donbas.

The Razumkov Centre (AR Krym: Lyudy, Problemy, Perspektyvy 2008, 19-22) explained that the polling data cited by Sakwa (2017a, 157) show a disorientation of Crimeans over the status of their autonomous republic, which meant 'supporting at times mutually exclusive alternatives.' Half (50.1%) chose 'at least one of the options, which involves the Crimea leaving Ukraine, and one of the other alternatives that will allow it to stay in the future within Ukraine.' The Razumkov Centre concluded that 'half of the Crimeans, depending on circumstances, can support both the separation of Crimea from Ukraine as well as the opposite scenario' (AR Krym: Lyudy, Problemy, Perspektyvy 2008).

This was not an endorsement of pro-Russian separatism that Sakwa (2017a) claimed; rather it reflected confused identities that were commonplace in post-Soviet states, such as in Ukraine during the 1990s. Prior to 2014, no opinion poll had ever given majority support for separatism in Crimea, and certainly nothing of the magnitude that Russia claimed in its March 2014 referendum. Typically, polls gave support for a Crimean independent state and union with Russia, both wrongly conflated under the label of 'separatism,' with approximately 40% support. Not a single opinion poll prior to 2014 gave over 50% support for 'separatism' in Crimea.

Non-Scholarly External Review Process and Unscholarly Analysis

Factual errors in much of the writing about the Russian-Ukrainian War are a product of poor, ideologically driven scholarship that should have been flagged by external reviewers. Pijl's (2018) book cannot, for example, be described as academic when it includes citations from Wikipedia and conspiracy theories from Putin's propaganda television channel *Russia Today*.

A similarly curious case of the absence of a diligent external review process is that of Boris Kagarlitsky, Radhika Desai, and Alan Freeman (2018), whose book compiled proceedings from a conference held in May 2014 in what was then Russian occupied Crimea. Indeed, why would established western scholars attend such a conference three months after Putin annexed Ukrainian territory? One wonders how the external reviewers used by Routledge allowed this to slip through.

It is suspicious that *Putinversteher* scholars provide endorsements on the outside covers of each other's books, leading one to wonder if they were the 'blind reviewers' for Pijl (2018) and Kagarlitsky, Desai, and Freeman (2018). They cite one another liberally, especially Sakwa (2015).

Poor knowledge about Ukraine leads to numerous mistakes in books about the crisis and again leads one to ask about the low quality of the external review process. Hahn (2018) includes so many mistakes that it would require a separate chapter to discuss them. Just some of them include (Hahn 2018, 118, 165, 249) western Ukraine described as 'Catholic,' when four of its seven *oblasts* are Orthodox, *chesno* translated as garlic and honesty, when the Ukrainian word for garlic is *chisnyk*. Not only has Hahn (2018) never visited Ukraine, he most likely has never studied a map of Ukraine as he describes Chernihiv as a 'western region,' when it is located in northeastern Ukraine. Hahn's determination to pigeonhole all 'Ukrainian nationalists' as coming from western Ukraine is most likely why he has geographically placed Chernihiv in Ukraine's west. Doing so is because many of these scholars cannot accept the existence of Russian-speaking Ukrainian and Jewish patriotism in eastern Ukraine.

Claiming that western and central Ukraine are the poorest regions of the country ignores Kyiv, which is the wealthiest city in Ukraine (Hahn 2018, 121). To prove his point that Ukraine is an artificial construct, Hahn artificially lowers the proportion of the population that is ethnic Ukrainian. Current figures show that 92% of the population declare themselves to be ethnically Ukrainian, while only 6% are ethnic Russians (among 18–29-year-old, only 2%).

Pijl (2018, 25) ignores the fact that the *Holodomor* has been accepted as an act of genocide by every Ukrainian president except Yanukovych (Kuzio, 2017b). During Kuchma's presidency, the Party of Regions upheld the official position of the *Holodomor* as a genocide, only adopting the Russian position after 2005–2006 and especially during Yanukovych's presidency in 2010–2014. Throughout his book, Pijl (2018, 40) portrays eastern Ukrainian politicians as pro-federalist, which is factually inaccurate; no president, including eastern Ukrainians Kuchma and Yanukovych, and no political party, including the Party of Regions and Communist Party of Ukraine, has supported federalism.

In downplaying Yanukovych's plunder of Ukraine, Pijl (2018, 83) writes that he sent his 'private possessions' to Russia before fleeing Kyiv. In fact, as security camera footage at his palace showed, a huge amount of stolen loot, such as gold bars, art, and other valuables were taken with him when he fled Kyiv in February 2014. While downplaying Yanukovych's looting of Ukraine, Putin is presented as a president who placed 'limits on oligarchic enrichment' (Pijl 2018, 158), a statement which has no relationship to the kleptocracy that Russia has become on his watch (see Dawisha 2014; Belton 2020; Sakwa 2017b, 19, 22).

In Love with Conspiracy Theories

Academic orientalist writing about the Donbas War loves conspiracies (see Ploeg 2017, 36–68), which could have been taken from Russian information war templates. There are four key conspiracies.

The first is that the Euromaidan was a US-backed conspiracy by 'Ukrainian nationalists,' who dominated the ranks of protestors and who continue to influence Ukrainian politics heavily. Hahn (2018, 285) writes that the 'deep political paralysis' in Ukraine is 'driven by the ultranationalist and neo-fascist wings of the Ukrainian polity.' Ukrainian nationalists dominate post-Euromaidan Ukrainian politics (Sakwa 2015, 99, 320; Cohen 2019, 61, 84, 91, 126, 144. 180, 181; Pijl 2018, 1, 5).

An 'extraordinary level of repression in post-Euromaidan Ukraine' was allegedly the norm (Ploeg 2017, 176). 'Galicia-based Ukrainianness' and the 'inordinate influence' of the Ukrainian diaspora were omnipresent (Molchanov 2018, 73). Cohen's (2019, 44, 144) claim of 'pro-Yanukovych' parties being banned is complete fiction. The Opposition Bloc and Opposition Platform-For Life, two successors to the Party of Regions, have participated in every election held since 2014. D'Anieri (2018) has analysed how the loss of 16% of Ukrainian voters in Russian-occupied areas of Ukraine is one of the reasons for the reduction in the pro-Russian vote, not because Ukrainian polls manipulate Ukrainian views of Russians (Petro 2016, 2018).

Matveeva (2018, 53) wrongly claims that President Yushchenko closed Russian language television broadcasts, claiming there was 'no Russian permitted until the 2012 language law was passed.' Ukraine's most popular television channel *Inter* has always broadcasted primarily in Russian, including under Presidents Yushchenko, Poroshenko, and Zelenskyy. Far more Russian-language print media are published in Ukraine than are Ukrainian-language print media. Medvedchuk, Putin's representative in Ukraine, owns three television channels – NewsOne, 112, and Zik, and exerts a high level of influence over *Inter* through his political allies in Opposition Platform-For Life.

Seeking to claim that Ukrainianisation took place, Matveeva (2016, 27) writes that Yushchenko's presidency 'dealt a decisive blow to Russian language in Donbas.' That this is untrue is beyond question, because there were few Ukrainian-language schools in this region prior to 2014. What is bizarre is that Matveeva's accusation is based on a citation from an undated article in *RusBalt News Agency*, which was closed down in October 2013 by the Russian government, and from an undated interview with Alexei Volynets. Presumably official Ukrainian statistics and opinion polls would not have backed up her claim and hence were never used.

The second conspiracy is that the snipers who killed Euromaidan protestors were Ukrainian nationalists, not *Berkut* special forces from the Ministry of Interior. Russia later re-modelled this conspiracy theory by claiming that Georgian snipers, organised by former Georgian President Mikhail Saakashvili, killed the protestors.[6]

This conspiracy theory was developed by Ivan Katchanovski (2016), who is the only source cited by all *Putinversteher* scholars for this alleged false flag operation on the Euromaidan. Katchanovski's (2016) work reflects that of a political technologist more than that of a scholar through his highly selective compilation of sources gleaned from conspiratorial corners of the Internet and YouTube. That the conspiracy is bogus can be seen in the six imprisoned *Berkut* officers whom Russia sought in the December 2019 prisoner exchange (see chapter 6).

Katchanovski (2016) is cited by all *Putinversteher* scholars (Sakwa (2015, 320; Hahn 2018, 199; Ploeg 2017, 38, 41; Pijl 2018, 80; Cohen 2019, 144, 179). Ploeg (2018, 174–176) cites Katchanovski (2016) on thirty occasions, some of them being very long quotations. David Lane (2018, 146) praises the 'detailed research of Ivan Katchanovski' (2016). Hahn (2018, 200-201) writes that there is 'no evidence' of police shootings, and that security forces 'seemed to demonstrate some restraint,' downplaying human rights abuses by the security forces and Party of Regions vigilantes. One particularly brutal kidnapping in the Euromaidan is described as a 'faked' abduction (Hahn 2018, 218).

---

[6] https://euvsdisinfo.eu/report/georgian-snipers-admitted-that-they-shot-euromaidan-protesters-in-2014/

Proof that the killings were undertaken by *Berkut* has been shown by journalists (Harding 2014), 3D research (Schwartz 2018; Chornokondratenko and Williams 2018), and academic studies (see bibliography in Kuzio 2017c, 363–367). There is little dispute among the broad mainstream of scholars, experts, and policymakers that Yanukovych's vigilantes and *Berkut* riot police killed and wounded Euromaidan protestors.

The third conspiracy is that 'Ukrainian nationalists' are to blame for the 2 May 2014 fire in Odesa, which killed 48 protestors, 42 of whom were pro-Russian activists. The Odesa fire was planned by Kyiv using 'Ukrainian nationalists' who were 'disguised as civilians and pretending to be "separatists" who fired at Ukrainians' (Hahn 2018, 109, 260, 262; Pijl 2018, 109; Ploeg 2017, 129). Sakwa's (2015, 97–99) main source of information for this conspiracy is the Russian Ministry of Foreign Affairs' White Book (he uses no Ukrainian sources). This unsurprisingly exaggerates the number of deaths into the hundreds as a 'massacre' with 'beatings' and 'rapes' committed by 'Ukrainian nationalists' to the chants of 'Glory to Ukraine.'

This conspiracy ignores the presence of nationalists (imperialists) and neo-Nazis from Russia and the Trans-Dniestr region, who were active in Odesa from February 2014. Russian neo-Nazi leader Anton Raevskyj, who called for violent attacks against Ukrainians and Jews in Odesa, was expelled from Ukraine on 29 March 2014.

Fieldwork and interviews in Odesa were never undertaken, and Ukrainian sources were ignored. The extensive work of Odesa journalists and video footage was used by this author to compile 'The Odesa Conflict on 2 May 2014: A Chronology of What Took Place' (see Table 11.1. in Kuzio 2017c, 334–337). In Odesa, the first deaths on 2 May 2014 were of pro-Ukrainian protestors. *Both* sides were shooting at each other from and into the Trade Union building. *Both* sides threw Molotov cocktails from inside and into the building, which set fire to the building. Of the 48 people who died, six died from gunshot wounds, 34 from smoke inhalation and burns, and eight from jumping from the fire to their deaths.

The fourth conspiracy is that US and NATO lead Ukraine's military strategy. Ploeg (2017, 226) writes, 'It seems reasonable to suggest that Ukraine's war strategy is heavily influenced by Washington.' US 'directed regime change' in Kyiv by 'neo-conservatives in the US government and NATO' worked through 'fascists,' 'nationalists,' 'Blackwater' mercenaries, the CIA, and the FBI (Pijl, 2018, 30, 69, 105). Perhaps Pijl (2018) and his external reviewers at Manchester University Press were unaware that, in 2014, the US was led by Democratic President Barack Obama, who was not a neo-conservative and neither supported democracy promotion nor NATO and EU enlargement.

Pijl's (2018) purpose is to deflect blame for the shooting down of MH17 from Russia to Ukraine and the West. Pijl (2018, 29) discusses MH17 as part of a Western conspiracy of the EU Eastern Partnership (which he describes as the 'Atlantic project'), where Ukraine would be transformed into an 'advance post for NATO' (Pijl 2018, 147). Ukraine would be used 'to destabilise the Putin presidency' (Pijl 2018, 76).

Conclusion

A large number of scholarly articles, think tank papers, and books have been published on the 2014 Russia-Ukraine crisis, Russia's annexation of Crimea, and Russian military aggression against Ukraine. Many of these are excellent. They are cited in this book and can be found in the references. There is a large number of scholarly articles based on ground-breaking research, often conducted by a new generation of political scientists.

Academic orientalist imagining of Ukraine is, however, evident in scholars mainly using sources from Russia when writing on the Russia-Ukrainian crisis. The roots of academic orientalism lie in Western histories of 'Russia' and Crimea, political scientists who work on Russia acting as 'gatekeepers' to Russian and Eurasian studies in the western world, and western journalists continuing to cover the entire former USSR from Moscow. Academic orientalist views of Ukraine are fleshed out in the next chapter, in which nationalism in Ukraine and Russia is discussed. Orientalism always depicts nationalism in colonies in a negative manner and the nationalism of the imperialist hegemon in a favourable light. In the same manner, contemporary academic orientalism – as shown in the next chapter – exaggerates the influence and cruelty of Ukrainian nationalism and downplays the existence and nationalist (imperialist) drive of Russian nationalism.

4

Russian Nationalism (Imperialism) and Ukrainian Nationalism

'The result of this entire situation is so-called Belarusian separatism. They are Russian people, it is Russian land there, but during the last century these people were 'reformatted' and stopped seeing themselves as Russian people. We need to dwell on the reasons to revive our historical memory of not simply being fraternal nations but of one people composed of Belarusians, Ukrainians and Russians. And if we unite, we will prosper without these revolutions led by duped kids who grew up in post-Soviet times and were tricked by liberal ideology into thinking they are not Russians but simply anti-Russian, and to prove this they need to fight their Russian brothers.'– Russian Television in 2020 on the Belarusian 'Slipper' Revolution.[1]

European orientalism portrayed the 'White Man's Burden' as the bringing of 'civilisation' and enlightenment to colonies. Meanwhile, the nationalisms of colonial peoples were depicted in highly negative ways, and their national liberation struggles were considered 'treacherous' and acts of 'terrorism.'

An orientalist view of 'good' and 'bad' nationalisms (imperialism) is used by Western scholars when writing about the Russian-Ukrainian War. With a few exceptions (see Harris 2020), Russian nationalist involvement in the war is dismissed, completely ignored (see Clarke 2014, 50; Matveeva 2018, 182, 218, 221, 223, 224, 277), or downplayed as a temporary phenomenon (Kolsto

---

[1] Pervyi Kanal (Russian Television, First Channel), 10 August 2020. https://www.youtube.com/watch?v=RpM9FqRCgA8&t=2424. Reported by https://euvsdisinfo.eu/report/belarusians-ukrainians-russians-are-one-nation/

2016a, 6; Hale 2016, 246; Laruelle 2020a). Russian nationalists (imperialists), anti-Semites, and xenophobes, such as Aleksandr Dugin (2014), Vladyslav Surkov (2020), and Glazyev (2020), were leading figures in the 2014 'Russian spring' and 'New Russia' project (see Likhachev 2016; Laruelle 2016a; Shekhovtsov 2017). Russian chauvinistic views of Ukraine and Ukrainians did not end in 2015–2016, and therefore it is unclear how Putin's regime became less nationalistic after this date (Hale 2016; Laruelle 2020a). Since 2014, the Russian regime has become more nationalistic and chauvinistic, while nationalism in Ukraine has become more civic, and yet some western writing on Ukraine and Russia since 2014 gives the opposite impression.

This chapter is divided into five sections. The first section surveys how Russian nationalism (imperialism) is downplayed, minimised, or described as a temporary phenomenon. The second section analyses how western writing exaggerates the influence and evil nature of Ukrainian nationalism. The third section provides a historical comparison of why both Stalin and Putin had obsessions towards Ukraine and Ukrainians. The final two sections provide evidence of the rehabilitation of Tsarist and White *émigré* nationalism (imperialism), and how this influences chauvinistic views of Ukraine and Ukrainians in official discourse, diplomatic relations, military aggression, and Russian information warfare.

In Search of Russian Nationalism (Imperialism)

Downplaying the influence of Russian nationalism (imperialism) in the USSR and contemporary Russia is not a recent phenomenon (see Gessen 2017, 52, 77–78), but rather existed long before the 2014 crisis in Russia's inability to come to terms with an independent Ukraine going back to 1991 (D'Anieri 2019). Russians have always 'felt Ukraine was an intrinsic part of Russia,' which is deeply rooted in Russian identity (D'Anieri 2019, 2). The Russian-Ukrainian crisis is 'deeper than is commonly understood' because of a 'profound normative disagreement and conflicts of interest' (D'Anieri 2019, 2).

Marginal nationalism became mainstream nationalism in Russia in the 2000s when the 'emergence of a virulent nationalist opposition movement took the mainstream hostage' (Clover 2016, 287). In downplaying nationalism in Russia's political system, scholars ignore the hyper-nationalism (imperialism) underpinning Russia's authoritarian political system, including in the United Russia Party, as well as nationalist party projects that have received state support, such as the LDPR and *Rodina*.

Matveeva (2018) sidesteps the political affiliations of the Russian leaders of Donbas separatists in spring 2014 because to do so would show that Russian neo-Nazis and other similar extremists were in charge and therefore what was taking place could not be described as a 'civil war' (Kolsto 2016b, 16). Matveeva (2018, 224) disagrees with Laruelle's (2016) analysis of the Russian nationalist (imperialist) alliance during the 'Russian spring' between 'brown' (fascist), 'white' (monarchist and Orthodox fundamentalist), and 'red' (Communist) politicians. At the same time, Matveeva (2018, 97) herself writes that volunteers from Russia consisted of 'nationalists, monarchists, spiritual heirs of 'White Russia,' ultra-leftists, National Bolsheviks, and Communists.'

Matveeva (2018) makes no mention of the presence of the neo-Nazi RNE (Russian National Unity) Party although there are many photographs of their military activities in eastern Ukraine and their taking up leadership positions in the 2014 'Russian spring' (Shekhovtsov 2014). Pavel Gubarev, Donetsk 'People's Governor' in spring 2014, is one of Matveeva's (2018, 182) sources of information, and she describes him as one of the 'uprising's original ideologues.' Gubarev's colleagues, Alexander Borodai and Alexander Prokhanov, edit the fascist, Stalinist, and nationalist (imperialist) newspaper *Zavtra* (Tomorrow), which began as the *Den* (The Day) newspaper in 1990. Prokhanov supported the August 1991 hardline anti-Gorbachev coup and wrote its manifesto, 'A Word to the People.' *Den* supported the 1993 hardline coup against Yeltsin. National Bolshevik anti-Semite Glazyev is a long-time contributor to *Zavtra*.

Borodai is quoted by Matveeva (2018, 218) as saying that Russian leaders provided the 'organizational, ideological' support to the 'Russian spring.' In late February 2014, Russian intelligence assisted the neo-Nazi RNE Party to establish a branch in Donetsk (Likhachev 2016, 22). Not coincidentally, on 1 March 2014, the day pro-Russian uprisings were organised by Russian intelligence in 11 cities in southeastern Ukraine, the Donetsk Republic Party installed former RNE Party member Gubarev as 'People's Governor' (Na terrritorii Donetskoy oblasty deystvovaly voyennye lagerya DNR s polnym voorozheniyem s 2009 goda 2014).

Local journalists reported the arrival of Russian neo-Nazis in spring 2014 in the Donbas.[2] A Ukrainian blogger from Donetsk wrote: 'The skinheads dressed uniformly were clearly not local. Here shaved heads and bomber jackets have long gone out of fashion with those on the right' (Coynash 2014). The Black Hundreds organisation, RNE Party, Other Russia and its Interbrigades (Donbass), Girkin's Russian Imperial Movement (labelled by the

---

[2] See, Shekhovtsov, A. (2014). 'Neo-Nazi Russian National Unity in Eastern Ukraine,' *Shekhovtsov blog*, 14 August. http://anton-shekhovtsov.blogspot.com/2014/08/neo-nazi-russian-national-unity-in.html

US as a terrorist organisation in April 2020), Shield of Moscow, Russian Orthodox Army, and Rusich participated in the Donbas conflict from its inception.

Eurasianist and neo-fascist Dugin, a professor at Moscow State University and adviser to State Duma speaker Sergei Naryshkin, strongly backed the 'uprisings,' describing them as a 'sacrificial awakening of Russia' and a 'magnificent uprising of the Russian soul' against 'petty, crude nationalism of Galicia' (Fitzpatrick 2014). In June 2014, Dugin (2014) called for Ukrainians to be 'killed, killed, killed' in what can only be called an extreme example of racism and Russian chauvinism.

Vyacheslav Likhachev (2016, 22), Ukraine's pre-eminent authority on anti-Semitism and xenophobia in Ukraine, writes that 'Russian nationalists were far more prominent than Ukrainian nationalists at the beginning of the conflict.' Likhachev (2016, 22) argues, 'It is hardly likely, however, that the Kremlin-inspired 'separatist' rebellion in the Donbas would have played out in the way it did had Russian extreme nationalists not taken part.' The three 'most visible' leaders of the DNR at its inception were Russian citizens 'with varying degrees of connection to the intelligence services of Russia' (Bowen 2019, 329).

Academic orientalism describes Russian nationalists (imperialists) as 'patriots' and western-style 'conservatives' – only Ukrainians are 'nationalists.' Borodai is described by Matveeva (2018, 95) as a 'Russian conservative thinker.' Gubarev's and Borodai's membership in the neo-Nazi RNE Party is ignored (see Shekhovtsov 2014) and instead they are described as 'patriots' and 'conservatives.' Remarkably, Matveeva (2018, 221, 223) cannot find any evidence of extreme-right nationalism in Borodai. Laruelle (2020a, 126) writes that 'the Putin regime still embodies a moderate centrist conservatism.' Petro (2018) talks of a 'conservative turn' in Russian foreign policy (see also Sakwa, 2020b, 276–277; Robinson 2020, 284–285, 287, 289, 293, 299).

If British conservatives annexed part of Ireland and denied the existence of Irish people, they could no longer be called conservatives. Similarly, Putin's regime's annexation of Crimea and denial of the existence of Ukraine and Ukrainians has nothing to do with conservatism.

Sakwa (2017a) and Matveeva (2018) only find 'militarised patriotism' (Sakwa 2017,119) or elites divided into 'westerners' and 'patriots' (Matveeva 2018, 277). Following his 2012 re-election, Putin spoke of 'Russian identity discourse' (Sakwa 2017a, 189), while his 'conservative values' are not the same as a nationalist agenda (Sakwa 2017a, 125). Western political scientists working on Russia have a very flexible definition of conservatism. Putin was not dependent upon Russian nationalism, 'and it is debatable whether the word is even applicable to him,' Sakwa (2017a, 125) writes.

Sakwa (2017a) is simply unable to ever use the term 'nationalist' when discussing Russian politicians, while at the same time undertaking orientalist somersaults to downplay Russia's support for populist-nationalists and neo-Nazis in Europe. Russia's European allies are described as 'anti-systemic forces,' 'radical left,' 'movements of the far right,' 'European populists,' 'traditional sovereigntists, peaceniks, anti-imperialists, critics of globalization,' 'populists of left and right,' and 'values coalition' (Sakwa 2017a, 275, 276, 60,75). Sakwa (2020a) writes that, 'Anton Shekhovtsov (2017) is mistaken to argue that Russia's links to right-wing national populist movements are rooted in philosophical anti-Westernism and an instinct to subvert the liberal democratic consensus in the West. In fact, the alignment is situational and contingent on the impasse in Russo-Western relations and thus is susceptible to modification if the situation changes.' Russian support for fascists, neo-Nazis, Trotskyists, Stalinists, and racists in Europe and the US are ignored or excused (Shekhovtsov 2018), as are the hundreds of members of Europe's extreme right and extreme left who have joined Russian proxy forces in the Donbas.

Sakwa (2017a, 159) writes that 'the genie of Russian nationalism was firmly back in the bottle' by 2016. Kolstø (2016) and Laruelle (2017a) write that the nationalist rhetoric of 2014 was novel and subsequently declined, while Henry Hale (2016) also believes Putin was only a nationalist in 2014, not prior to the annexation of the Crimea or since 2015. Laruelle (2020a, 126) concurs, writing that by 2016, Putin's regime had 'circled back to a more classic and pragmatic conservative vision. Conservatism again. Laruelle (2020b, 348) describes Putin's regime as nationalistic only between 2013-2016 and 'since then has been curtailing any type of ideological inflation and has adopted a low profile, focusing on much more pragmatic and Realpolitik agendas at home and abroad.' 'Putin is not a natural nationalist' and '[w]e do not see the man and the regime as defined by principled ideological nationalism' (Chaisty and Whitefield 2015, 157, 162). Putin is not an ideologue because he remains rational and pragmatic (Sakwa 2015, 2017) and therefore not a Russian nationalist.

Rehabilitating White Émigrés *and Fascists*

Putin's rehabilitation of the White *émigré* movement and reburial of its officers and philosophers in Russia is not a sign of conservatism, but of nationalism (imperialism). It is not a coincidence that these reburials took place at the same time as the formation of the Russian World Foundation (April 2007) and unification of the Russian Orthodox Church with the *émigré* Russian Orthodox Church (May 2007). Putin personally paid for the re-burial in Russia of White *émigré* nationalists (imperialists) and fascists Ivan Ilyin, Ivan Shmelev, and General Anton Deniken. All three deny the existence of a Ukrainian nation. Ilyin's chauvinistic views of Ukraine and Ukrainians are typical of Russian White *émigrés* (see Wolkonsky 1920; Bregy and Obolensky 1940). As Plokhy (2017, 327) writes, 'Russia was taking back its long-lost children and reconnecting with their ideas' (Belton 2020, 259–260, 268, 272–273, 324, 326–329, 385, 427).

Putin is 'particularly impressed' with Ilyin whom Timothy Snyder (2018) defines as a fascist. Putin first cited Ilyin in an address to the Russian State Duma in 2006 (Plokhy 2017, 327; Belton 2020, 259, 272–273). Putin has recommended Ilyin to be read by his governors, former senior adviser Surkov, and Prime Minister Medvedev. Ilyin's publications will be used in the Russian state programme, inculcating 'patriotism' and 'conservative values' in Russian children (Sukhankin 2020). Ilyin was integrated into Putin's ideology during his re-election campaign in 2012 and influenced Putin's re-thinking of himself as the 'gatherer of Russian lands' and as bringing Ukraine back into the Russian World (Snyder 2018; Plokhy 2017, 332).

Laruelle (2017b) downplays the importance of Ilyin's ideology, writing that he did not *always* propagate fascism and Putin *only* quoted him five times. It is difficult to understand how our concerns are supposed to be ameliorated because Putin cited a Russian nationalist (imperialist) and fascist sympathiser *only* five times. Putin not only cited Ilyin, but also asked Russian journalists whether they had read Deniken's diaries, especially the parts where 'Deniken discusses Great and Little Russia, Ukraine' (Plokhy 2017, 326). Deniken wrote in his diaries, 'No Russian, reactionary or democrat, republican or authoritarian, will ever allow Ukraine to be torn away' (Plokhy 2017, 326). Putin evidently agrees with Ilyin, Deniken, and other White *émigrés* about the non-existence of a Ukrainian nation.

If we apply Laruelle's (2017a) logic to Organisation of Ukrainian nationalist (OUN) leader Stepan Bandera, he could also be described as not always having been a fascist because he spent 1941–1944 in the Sachsenhausen concentration camp. Bandera's two brothers, Vasyl and Aleksandr, were incarcerated in Auschwitz where they were murdered in 1941. President Poroshenko never cited Bandera, nor ever offered to pay for the re-burial of Bandera in Ukraine. Ilyin was re-buried in Russia, while Bandera remains buried in Germany.

One can only find a 'crisis' in Russian nationalism (Horvath 2015) or believe that Putin 'lost' nationalist support (Kolsto 2016; Hale 2016) by ignoring unanimous support by Russian politicians and nationalist parties for Tsarist Russian and White Russian *émigré* nationalist (imperialist) and fascist views, discourse, and policies towards Ukraine and Ukrainians. Russian nationalism (imperialism) might possibly be a force for good in Russia (Tuminez 1997; Laruelle 2017a), but it has shown itself to be an evil force in underpinning Russian military aggression against Ukraine and denying the existence of Ukrainians.

Academic Orientalism and Ukrainian Nationalism

Orientalism portrayed as beneficial and generous the imperialism of colonial powers and condemned the liberating nationalism of those peoples it occupied or controlled. In scholarly studies of the Russian-Ukrainian crisis, the downplaying of nationalism (imperialism) in Russia takes place at the same time as an exaggeration of the influence and terrible evils of 'Ukrainian nationalism' (for an example see Amar 2019 and Kuzio 2019b).

Over the last three centuries, Ukrainians seeking a future for their country outside the Tsarist empire, USSR, and Russian World have been castigated with different names —'Mazepinists' (followers of Hetman Mazepa, who allied Cossack Ukraine with Sweden and were defeated by Russia in 1709), 'Petlurites' (followers of Symon Petlura, who commanded the army of the 1917–1921 Ukrainian People's Republic), 'Banderites' (followers of OUN leader Bandera in the 1940s and 1950s), 'traitors,' 'agents of Western imperialism,' and 'fascists' – during the nineteenth and twentieth centuries (Kuzio 2017c, 85–117). A Soviet document from 30 August 1990 signed by the KGB Chairman and Minister of Interior provided instructions on how to foment 'anti-nationalist' propaganda to discredit the democratic opposition (Chraibi 2020). The then-KGB's 'anti-nationalist' rhetoric is the same as that which continues to be used in Putin's Russia.

The Soviet definition of 'nationalism' is applied to all Ukrainians who seek a destiny for their country outside the Russian World (Sakwa 2015, 2017a; Matveeva 2018; Cohen 2019). In the USSR, the term 'bourgeois nationalist' was applied to Ukrainians holding national communist, liberal, or nationalistic views. Soviet Communist Party of Ukraine First Secretary Petro Shelest, a national communist, was deposed in 1971 after being accused of 'nationalist deviationism.' Sakwa (2015, 257) claims that 'radicalized Ukrainian nationalist elites' were in control of the Ukrainian parliament. Hahn's (2018, 290) claim of 'nationalists, ultranationalists, and neo-fascist parties' winning 44.6% of the vote in the 2014 elections can only be made by assigning the 'nationalist' label to all Ukrainian parliamentary political forces who were not pro-Russian.

Criticism of 'Ukrainian nationalism' is an outgrowth of the Western histories of 'Russia,' as discussed in chapter 1. Whereas the vitriolic language is lifted by *Putinversteher* scholars from Russian information warfare to describe the 'grandchildren of those whose slaughtered Poles, Jews, and communists during the Nazi invasion and occupation' (Hahn 2018, 122, 129, 166, 218, 228, 246, 285, 288, 290, 293, 295).

A majority of Western scholars believe that nationalism did not dominate the Euromaidan, and in post-Euromaidan Ukraine, nationalism is civic and inclusive (Clem 2014, 231; Kulyk 2014, 2016; Onuch and Hale 2018; Pop-Eleches and Robertson 2018; Kaihko 2018; Bureiko and Moga 2019). Civic patriotism is evident in a high proportion of Ukrainians holding negative views of Russian leaders, but not of the Russian people. Volodymyr Kulyk (2014, 120–121) writes about 'the deeply inclusive nature of modern Ukrainian anti-imperial nationalism, the most obvious proof of which is the support it enjoys among Ukrainian Jews or even among Jews who have preserved their ties to the country since leaving Ukraine.' Ukrainian civic identity was found in Crimea, where some of those opposed to Russia's annexation were ethnic Russians (Nedozhogina 2019, 1086).

Ukrainian attitudes to Russian citizens and Russian leaders exhibit patriotism, not ethnic nationalism. Between 70–80% of Ukrainians hold negative views of Russian leaders, while only 20–25% hold negative views of Russian citizens (Kermch 2017). If Ukraine were so dominated by extreme nationalism, as *Putinversteher* scholars claim, then the country's far right would be winning elections, and a majority of Ukrainians would hold negative ethnic nationalist views of Russian citizens.

Stalin and Putin's Obsession with Ukraine

The Tsarist Russian Empire sought to block and repress the re-emergence of Ukrainian national identity. The Ukrainian and Belarusian languages were banned in the Tsarist Russian Empire (Saunders 1995a, 1995b). 'Ukrainian nationalism' was viewed as a threat to forging an 'All-Russian People' based on the three eastern Slavs and undermined Russian foundational myths to ownership of Kyiv Rus (Kuzio 2005). Tsarist Russian policies were 'an all-out attack on the Ukrainophile movement and its current and potential members' (Plokhy 2017, 146). Tsarist Russia denied the existence of the Ukrainian language and claimed there had never been a Ukrainian state, that Ukrainians had no history and that they were 'Russians.' Contemporary Russian information warfare propagates the same claims.

In July 1863, Minister of Interior Petr Valuev prohibited public education and religious texts in the Ukrainian language. Of the 33 Ukrainian-language publications that existed in 1863, only one survived. By the early 1870s, the system was cracking, and 32 Ukrainian-language publications re-appeared. In May 1876, the 'liberal' Tsar Aleksandr II issued the Ems Edict which was far more severe and 'was intended to arrest the development of Ukrainian literature at all levels' (Plokhy 2017, 145). The scale of Tsarist repression of the Ukrainian language was not seen in the USSR; even during the dark days of Stalinist repression, where the Ukrainian language was recognised and used in official publications. In the Tsarist Empire, the restrictions on the Ukrainian language:

1. Banned the import of all Ukrainian-language publications;
2. Banned the printing of religious and grammar books in Ukrainian;
3. Banned the publishing of books for 'common people' and intellectual elites;
4. Removed Ukrainian-language publications from libraries;
5. Banned theatre performances, songs, poetry and readings in Ukrainian;
6. Politically repressed Ukrainophile intellectuals.

Tsarist Russian policies backfired by assisting in turning 'Little Russians' into Ukrainians and, in Austrian-ruled Galicia, these policies helped to defeat the Russophile movement. The institutionalisation of the Ukrainophile movement in Galicia gave it the means to provide assistance (such as education and publications) to Ukrainophiles in the Tsarist Empire. Ukrainian historian Hrushevsky was forced to work in Galicia, where he was chair of Ukrainian history at Lviv University and a leading member of the Shevchenko Scientific Society and National Democratic Party. In 1898, he began publishing his 10-volume *History of Ukraine-Rus* with the final volume published in 1937. Ukrainophile activities in Galicia could only be transferred to Ukraine after the 1905 Russian Revolution. In 1917, as a member of the Party of Socialist Revolutionaries, Hrushevsky became president of the left-wing Ukrainian People's Republic (UNR). In 1924, he moved to the Ukrainian SSR during the Soviet policy of Ukrainianisation and died in suspicious circumstances in 1934, a year after the *Holodomor*.

Tsarist obsession with Ukraine was replicated in Stalin's USSR and Putin's Russia. Anne Applebaum (2017, 149, 155, 159) discusses the origins of (Soviet secret police) Chekist Ukrainophobia in the early 1930s during the *Holodomor* and mass arrest of Ukrainian national communists, educators, and cultural elites, which took place amid a frenzied search for 'Petlurite counter-revolutionaries' allied to external enemies of the Soviet Union. Stalin and Putin both raised and continue to raise fears of 'losing' Ukraine. Paranoia about Ukrainian nationalism 'was taught to every successive generation of secret policemen, from the OGPU to the NKVD to the KGB, as well as every successive generation of party leader. Perhaps it even helped mould the thinking of post-Soviet elites, long after the USSR ceased to exist' (Applebaum 2017, 161). Soviet leader Nikita Khrushchev talked of Stalin's plans to deport all Ukrainians in his famous speech in 1956. This did not go ahead because, Khrushchev told the congress of the Communist Party of the Soviet Union, 'there were too many of them and there was no place to which to deport them' (Medvedev and Medvedev 1976, 58).

Mikhail Zygar (2016) reveals that Putin has always been obsessed and frustrated with Ukraine. Zygar (2016, 85) writes that Putin was obsessed with Ukraine from the first day of his presidency saying, 'We must do something, or we'll lose it' (Zygar 2016, 258; Belton 2020, 385). When somebody mentions Ukraine in front of Putin, 'he flies into a fury; the words at the end of his sentences are replaced by Russian expletives. For him, everything the Ukrainian government does is a crime' (Zygar 2016, 4).

His obsession with Ukraine is because Putin views the Russian World as unifying the three eastern Slavs that allegedly belong to a common and 'fraternal' Slavic and Russian Orthodox 'civilisation' stretching from 'Kievan Russia' (Kyiv Rus) to the present day. Putin's (2014a) speech to the State *Duma* and Federation Council welcoming Crimea's accession to the Russian Federation elaborated the myth of 'Russian' civilisation beginning in Kyiv. Putin (2014a) believes:

> Everything in Crimea speaks of our shared history and pride. This the location of ancient Khersones, where Prince Vladimir was baptised. His spiritual feat of adopting Orthodoxy predetermined the overall basis of the culture, civilisation and human values that unite the peoples of Russia, Ukraine and Belarus. The graves of Russian soldiers whose bravery brought Crimea into the Russian empire are also in Crimea. This is also Sevastopol – a legendary city with an outstanding history, a fortress that serves as the birthplace of Russia's Black Sea Fleet. Crimea is Balaklava and Kerch, Malakhov Kurgan and Sapun Ridge. Each one of these places is dear to our hearts, symbolising Russian military glory and outstanding valour (on the Russian myth of Sevastopol see Plokhy 2000).

Although many Western scholars are unable to find it, Putin (2008, 2014a, 2014b, 2015a, 2015b, 2017, 2019, 2020a, 2020b, 2020c) has never hidden his nationalistic (imperialistic) views on Ukraine and Ukrainians. Putin (2014a) legitimised the annexation of Crimea and made territorial claims towards 'New Russia.' 'After the revolution, the Bolsheviks, for a number of reasons – may God judge them – added large sections of the historical South of Russia to the Republic of Ukraine. This was done with no consideration for the ethnic make-up of the population, and today these areas form the southeast of Ukraine. Then, in 1954, a decision was made to transfer Crimean Region to Ukraine, along with Sevastopol, despite the fact that it was a federal city.' Putin (2014a) believes that 'this decision was treated as a formality of sorts because the territory was transferred within the boundaries of a single state. Back then, it was impossible to imagine that Ukraine and Russia may split up and become two separate states.'

Russian Nationalist (Imperialist) Imagining of Ukraine and Ukrainians

Russia's long-term inability to come to terms with an independent Ukraine and Ukrainians as a separate people became patently obvious when Putin's regime rehabilitated Tsarist Russian and White *émigré* views of Ukraine and Ukrainians (see Wolkonsky 1920; Bregy and Obolensky 1940). Igor Torbakov (2020) traces the continued influence of Tsarist 'liberal' and White movement supporter Struve's view of what constitutes an 'All-Russian People' to contemporary Russian leaders.

In the USSR, there was a Ukrainian lobby in Moscow, while under Putin there is no such thing (Zygar 2016, 87). In the USSR, Soviet nationality policy defined Ukrainians and Russians as close, but nevertheless separate peoples; this no longer remains the case in Putin's Russia. In the USSR, Ukraine and the Ukrainian language 'always had robust defenders at the very top. Under Putin, however, the idea of Ukrainian national statehood was discouraged' (Zygar 2016, 87) and the Ukrainian language is disparaged as a Russian dialect that was artificially made into a language in the USSR.[3]

Rehabilitation of Tsarist Russian and White *émigré* views are to be found in Russian television programmes, where humour is used to mock Ukraine and Ukrainians in a manner 'typical in colonizer-colonized relationships' (Minchenia, Tornquist-Plewa and Yurchuk 2018, 225; D'Anieri 2019, 25). Russia and Russians are cast as superior, modern, and advanced, while Ukraine and Ukrainians are imagined as backward, uneducated, 'or at least unsophisticated, lazy, unreliable, cunning, and prone to thievery.' These kinds of Russian attitudes towards Ukraine and Ukrainians 'are widely shared across the Russian elite and populace' (Minchenia, Tornquist-Plewa and Yurchuk 2018, 25; see Gretskiy 2020, 21).

---

[3] https://euvsdisinfo.eu/report/ukrainian-literary-language-is-an-artificial-language-created-by-the-soviet-authorities/

Tsarist Russian and White *émigré* nationalism (imperialism) viewed Ukraine as 'Little Russia' and Ukrainians as one of three branches of the 'All-Russian People.' Contemporary Russian leaders agree. Surkov (2020), Putin's senior adviser and architect of Russian policies towards Ukraine between 2014–2020, has said, 'There is no Ukraine. There is Ukrainian-ness.' 'That is, it is a specific disorder of the mind, sudden passion for ethnography, taken to its extremes' (Surkov 2020). Surkov (2020) believes that Ukraine is 'a muddle instead of a state... there is no nation.'

Russian nationalist (imperialist) views of Ukraine crystalised during the decade before the 2014 crisis. During the 2004 presidential elections, tens of Russian political technologists operated in Ukraine working for Yanukovych's election campaign (Kuzio 2010). They produced a number of election posters designed to scare Russian speakers about the possible electoral victory of 'fascist' Yushchenko, whom they claimed was married to Kateryna Chumacenko, a 'CIA agent' (because she had worked at one time in the US White House), and who allegedly grew up in the 'Ukrainian nationalist' diaspora. In fact, neither of the Yushchenkos is western Ukrainian: Viktor Yushchenko's family is from Sumy *oblast* in northeastern Ukraine and Kateryna Yushchenko's father is from Kharkiv *oblast* (he was one of a few survivors of the *Holodomor* in his family) and her mother is from Kyiv *oblast*.

One of the 2004 election posters, reproduced on page 94, top right, imagines Ukraine in typical Russian nationalism (imperialism) discourse as divided into three parts. 'Galicia' is entitled 'First Class' (that is, the top of the pack), while central Ukraine ('Little Russia') is 'Second Class.' 'New Russia' in southeastern Ukraine was of course 'Third Class' (which has a striking resemblance to Putin's 'New Russia') with the aim of showing Russian speakers living in this region at the bottom of the hierarchy. The poster's captions extort Russian speakers to open their eyes at the impending threat to themselves from a 'nationalist' Yushchenko victory, which would lead to the domination of Russian-speaking Ukrainians by Galicia. Russian leaders and Western *Putinversteher* scholars believe that Galician 'nationalism' has ruled Ukraine since the Euromaidan.

Text to figure 4.1: 'Yes! This is how THEIR Ukraine looks. Ukrainians open your eyes!' Note: During Ukraine's 2004 presidential elections, Russian political technologists led by Vladimir Granovsky aimed to inflame regional divisions in Ukraine. Source: The author obtained a copy of this poster when he was an election observer in Ukraine's 2004 elections for the National Democratic Institute. The image is a scan of this poster.

4.1. Poster Prepared by Russian Political Technologists for Viktor Yanukovych's 2004 Election Campaign

4.2. Map of Russian Nationalist (Imperialist) Imagining of Ukraine

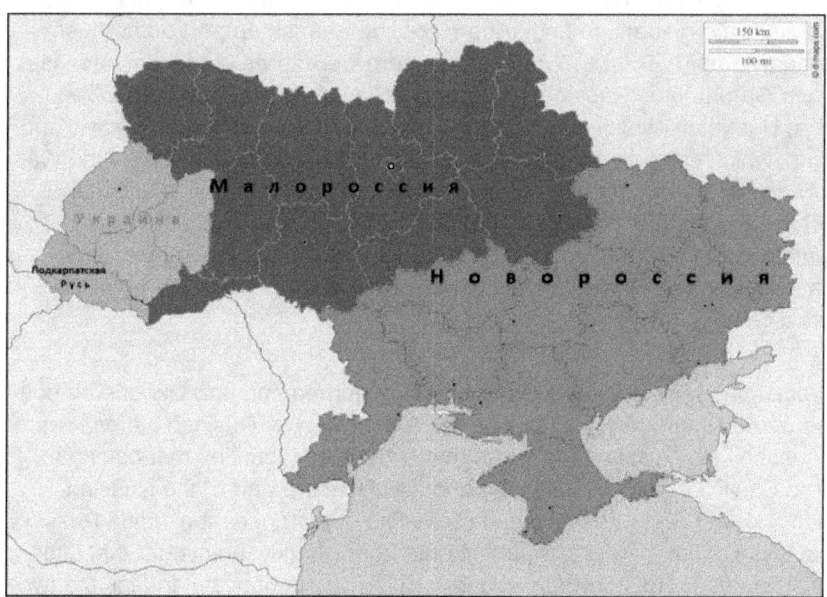

Note: In image 4.2, how Russian nationalists (imperialists) have historically imagined Ukrainian territory, a viewpoint which became rehabilitated under Putin and official policy in 2014 and since. From right to left: 'New Russia' (southeastern Ukraine in red), 'Little Russia' (central Ukraine in blue), 'Ukraine' (Galicia in orange), 'Sub-Carpathian Rus' (green). Source: This map is from the author's archives and was given to the author by a Ukrainian historian from Donetsk who is an internally displaced person living in Kyiv. The map of Ukraine in the upper 2004 election poster is remarkably similar to the traditional Russian nationalist imagining of Ukraine below it.

Historically and in the contemporary era, Russian nationalists (imperialists) have believed that Ukraine is composed of Crimea, 'New Russia,' Ukraine ('Little Russia'), and 'Galicia' (western Ukraine). Crimea has always been 'Russian,' and its fate was decided in 2014. Western Ukraine lived for long periods outside Russian control, is Russophobic, and does not belong inside the Russian World. Russian nationalists (imperialists) believe that 'Galicia' should go its own way, while the rest of the country becomes part of or aligns with Russia. Russian *nationalist (imperialist)* Girkin supports Russia (which he conflates with the USSR) returning to its 1939 borders; that is, without western Ukraine (Bidder 2015).

In some Russian nationalist (imperialist) maps of Ukraine, Trans-Carpathia (in the above map 'Sub-Carpathian Rus') is separated from 'Galicia' based on the claim that 'Carpatho-Russians' live in this territory. The Trans-Carpathian region experienced a different and repressive history under Hungary to that which Galicia experienced under the more liberal Austrian part of the Austro-Hungarian Empire. Prior to World War I, there were three competing identities in Trans-Carpathia – 'Russian' (i.e. eastern Slavic), which sought union with Russia, Ukrainian, which wanted to join Ukraine in an independent state, and Rusyns, which considered itself a fourth eastern Slavic people. By World War II, only the latter two identities remained. Ukrainianisation took place in the USSR, and today the majority of the eastern Slavic population of Trans-Carpathia holds a Ukrainian identity. A Rusyn revival has taken place since the late 1980s. But 'Russian' identity has not existed in Trans-Carpathia for nearly a century.

The remaining territories of 'New Russia'/Prichernomorie and Ukraine on both banks of the Dnipro river ('Little Russia') are viewed by Russian *nationalists (imperialists)* as 'Russian' regions with pro-Russian identities that belong to eastern Slavic Orthodox civilisation and are therefore part of the Russian World. Sakwa (2015) has little understanding of the concept of 'Little Russia.' Volodymyr Kravchenko (2016), a historian from Kharkiv, points out that Little Russianism does not contradict modern Ukrainian identity, but in fact 'the two are partially intertwined and interdependent.'

The 'natural' union of 'Ukraine' and Russia has been blocked by western Ukrainian 'nationalists,' who came to power during the 'illegal Euromaidan putsch' and are in cahoots with Ukrainian oligarchs and the West. The West's goal is to prevent the formation of a powerful Russian-Ukrainian union. Putin (2020b) has said that Russia could regain its status as 'a global rival' to western powers by 'integration' with Ukraine. 'Some like dividing Ukraine and Russia. They believe it's a very important goal,' Putin (2020b) has complained, 'Since any integration of Russia and Ukraine, along with their capacities and competitive advantages, would spell the emergence of a rival – a global rival for both Europe and the world.'

Contemporary Russian Nationalist (Imperialist) Imagining of Ukraine and Ukrainians

It is a major omission that the factors behind why Moscow is so obsessed with Ukraine are not analysed in the numerous publications on Russian information warfare. This is surprising in view of the great deal of attention that Russian information warfare devotes to Ukraine and Ukrainians.

Of the 8,223 disinformation cases that the EU database has collected since January 2015, 3,329 (40%) are on Ukraine and Ukrainians.[4] This figure is higher than the 2,825 disinformation cases collected for the entire EU, which contains 27 countries. The EU's *Disinformation Review* notes, 'Ukraine has a special place within the disinformation (un)reality,'[5] and 'Ukraine is by far the most misrepresented country in the Russian media.[6] A Ukrainian study collected nearly 400 pages of examples of Russian disinformation on Ukraine and Ukrainians (Zolotukhin 2018).

During the Euromaidan and since, Russia's information warfare has gone into overdrive when covering Ukraine. 'Almost five years into the conflict between Russia and Ukraine, the Kremlin's use of the information weapon against Ukraine has not decreased; Ukraine still stands out as the most misrepresented country in pro-Kremlin media.'[7] This coverage can only be explained by Moscow's Jekyll-and-Hyde view of Ukraine as including people hostile to Russia and, at the same time, 'good' Ukrainians who believe that they and Russians are 'one people.' How can the annexation of Crimea be justified as 'returning' to Russia if Ukraine does not exist and Russians and

---

[4]   https://euvsdisinfo.eu/ukraine-will-turn-into-a-banana-republic-ukrainian-elections-on-russian-tv/?highlight=ukraine%20land%20of%20fascists
[5]   https://euvsdisinfo.eu/what-didnt-happen-in-2017/?highlight=What%20didn%26%23039%3Bt%20happen%20in%202017%3F
[6]   https://euvsdisinfo.eu/ukraine-under-information-fire/
[7]   https://euvsdisinfo.eu/ukraine-under-information-fire/?highlight=ukraine

Ukrainians are one people? While denigrating Ukraine at a level that would make Soviet Communist Party ideologues blush, Russian leaders continue to claim that they hold warm feelings towards Ukrainians, who are the closest people to them (Putin 2015b). With the Donbas War in full swing, the Russian Information Agency, Novosti, asked on 13 September 2014, if Ukrainians were now 'lost brothers' or a 'Nazi people.' Russia's propaganda barrage has led to Russians viewing Ukraine as second to the US in being hostile to Russia.

The roots of Russia's information warfare against Ukraine and Ukrainians lie in Tsarist Russian and White *émigré* nationalism (imperialism), Soviet propaganda, and more recent inventions. Many of the key themes on Ukraine and Ukrainians used by *Putinversteher* scholars are simply lifted from Kremlin's talking points (compare them with Lavrov 2014).

'Operation Infektion,' launched in February 2014 and continued through the present day, has targeted nine themes with the greatest focus on 'Ukraine as a failed state or unreliable partner' (Nimmo, Francois, Eib, Ronzaud, Ferreira, Hernon, and Kostelancik 2020). Zolotukhin (2018) presents ten themes in Russian information warfare towards Ukraine and Ukrainians:

1. Ties to ISIS;
2. War crimes committed in the Donbas and disinterest in the Minsk peace process;
3. Ukrainians behind the downing of Flight MH17;
4. Ukraine as a NATO forward base and puppet state of the West;
5. EU integration as not bringing any benefits to Ukraine, which lacks the capacity to undertake reforms;
6. Crimea is Russian;
7. Western military assistance to Ukraine drives Ukrainian aggressive nationalism;
8. Russian fabrications on the rulings of international courts;
9. Ukraine as a failed state; and
10. Russia as a 'schizophrenic occupier.'

The following are this author's ten narratives of Russian information warfare towards Ukraine and Ukrainians, followed by a short description of each:

1. Ukraine is an artificial country and bankrupt state;
2. Ukrainians are not a separate people to Russians and Russians and Ukrainians are 'one people;'
3. The Ukrainian language is artificial and a dialect of Russian;
4. The Ukrainian nation was created as an Austrian conspiracy to divide the 'All-Russian People;'

5. Ukraine is a puppet state controlled by the West;
6. Ukrainians are belittled, ridiculed, and dehumanised;
7. Ukraine's reforms and European integration will fail;
8. Ukraine is run by 'fascists' and 'Nazi's;'
9. Anti-Zionism (Soviet camouflaged anti-Semitism) is used to attack Jewish-Ukrainian oligarchs; and
10. Distracting attention from accusations made against Russia.

First, Ukraine is an artificial country and a failed, bankrupt state. Putin (2008) raised this in his 2008 speech to the NATO-Russia Council at the Bucharest NATO summit. Ukraine as a failed state is one of the most common themes in Russian information warfare and appears in many different guises (Zolotukhin 2018, 302–358). Political collapse in 2014 required Russian intervention, Ukrainian authorities are incapable of dealing with their problems, Ukraine is not a real state and will not survive without trade with Russia, western neighbours put forward territorial claims on western Ukraine, while the east is naturally aligned with Russia, and Ukraine was artificially created with 'Russian' lands. Ukraine is a land of perennial instability and revolution where extremists run amok, Russian speakers are persecuted, and pro-Russian politicians and media are repressed or closed down.

Second, Russians and Ukrainians are 'one people' with a single language, culture, and common history (Zolotukhin 2018, 67–85). Russian information warfare and western histories of 'Russia' portray Ukraine as a place without its own history and identity. Ukrainians are a 'brotherly nation' who are 'part of the Russian people,' and reunification, Putin (2017) told the Valdai Club, will inevitably take place. 'One people inhabits Ukraine and the Russian Federation, for the time being, divided (by the border),' Russian Security Council Secretary Nikolai Petrushev (2016) has said.

Third, the Ukrainian language does not exist and what is spoken in Ukraine are dialects of Russian. Although the USSR promoted Russification, it nevertheless recognised the existence of the Ukrainian language. The Russian information agency Rex published an article claiming that the 'Ukrainian language is a weapon in the hybrid war' because the Ukrainian language is 'artificial.' The Ukrainian language is a form of hybrid, 'brain programming' political technology (Yermolenko 2019).

Fourth, the Ukrainian nation is a conspiracy directed against Russia. This idea was first promoted by Russian *nationalists (imperialists)* in the late-nineteenth century when the Tsarist Russian and Austrian-Hungarian empires competed over control of western Ukraine. This myth is closely tied to that of an artificial Ukrainian state as a puppet of the West seeking to divide the 'All-Russian People.'

Tsarist authorities and Russian political parties claimed that the Ukrainian people do not exist and are a mere fiction dreamt up by Austrians and other foreign powers to divide the 'All-Russian People' (Weeks, 1996). Incredibly, Putin (2020b) has revived this late-nineteenth century Tsarist nationalist (imperialist) view of Austrians creating a fictitious Ukrainian nation: 'The Ukrainian factor was specifically played out on the eve of World War I by the Austrian special service. Why? This is well-known – to divide and rule (the Russian people).'

White *émigrés* perpetuated this Russian chauvinistic myth, which has been rehabilitated in Putin's Russia. White *émigrés* Prince Alexandre Wolkonsky (1920), Pierre Bregy, and Prince Serge Obolensky (1940) would feel at home in Putin's Russia. One hundred White *émigré* aristocrats living in western Europe signed an open letter of support for Russia during the 2014 crisis (Laruelle 2020b, 353–354; Belton 2020, 259–260, 272–273, 324–329, 385, 427–429).

These nineteenth century and pre-World War II views of Ukraine and Ukrainians were espoused by Russian nationalists (imperialists) and fascists, and were incorporated into the discourse of Russian leaders. Four years prior to Putin talking about an Austrian conspiracy lying behind a separate Ukrainian nation, the leader of the Russian Imperial Movement, Stanislav Vorobyev (2020), made the same statement. Vorobyev (2020) *and* Putin (2015a, 2015b) view 'Russians' as the most divided people in the world and believe that Ukrainians are illegally occupying 'Russian' lands.

Girkin, also a member of the Russian Imperial Movement, believes that the 'real separatists' are 'the ones in Kyiv, because they want to split Ukraine off from Moscow' (Bidder 2015). Girkin's brand of 'imperial nationalism' defines 'Russians' as encompassing three eastern Slavs and all Russian speakers (Plokhy 2017, 342). Vorobyev (2020) has stressed that Ukrainians 'are not an ethnos' but a 'socio-political group of separatists' who, after the USSR disintegrated, 'obtained Russian historic lands of the Russian people (as in 4.2. Map): *Malorossiya* (Little Russia), *Slobozhanshchyna* (Kharkiv region), *Hetmanshchyna* (central Ukraine), 'New Russia,' and Crimea, and as a result of this crime they have obtained lands that never belonged to them.' As in Western histories of 'Russia,' Ukrainians are again squatters on primordial 'Russian lands.'

Contemporary Russian leaders have revived the Tsarist Russian nationalist (imperialist) concept of the three branches of the 'All-Russian People' with Ukrainians as 'Little Russians.' Ukrainians breaking away from *triyedinyy russkij narod* are the separatists – not Russian proxies in the Donbas. A

Russian mercenary fighting for Russian proxies was asked if he supported independence for the Donbas, to which he replied, 'Independence from whom?' He had travelled to the Donbas to 'protect the Russian people' (understood as the *triyedinyy russkij narod*) and stand up for 'this brotherly people' (Goryanov and Ivshina 2015).

Putin and the Russian Imperial Movement agree that Ukrainians do not exist. Similar to Suslov (2020), Vorobyev (2020) has said, 'Ukrainians are some socio-political group who do not have any ethnos. They are just a socio-political group that appeared at the end of the nineteenth century by means of manipulation of the occupying Austro-Hungarian administration, which occupied Galicia.' There is no difference between the nationalist (imperialist) attitudes of President Putin towards Ukraine and Ukrainians and those of Vorobyev's fascist Russian Imperial Movement. This explains why national Bolsheviks, anti-Semites, and Russian chauvinists support Putin on Ukraine (Dugin 2014; Glazyev 2019; Surkov 2020).

Fifth, Russia's civilisation is unique and in competition with the West, whose 'fifth column' in Eurasia and the Russian World is the 'puppet' state of Ukraine led by Galician nationalists who came to power in the Euromaidan (Laruelle 2016c). Russia is not fighting Ukrainians who belong to the 'All-Russian People' living in 'New Russia' and 'Ukraine,' and who are being prevented from being part of the Russian World. Ukraine is always portrayed as a country without real sovereignty, which only exists because it is propped up by the West. Similar to Soviet propaganda and ideological campaigns, Ukrainian 'nationalists' are depicted as the West's puppets and since 2014 have been doing the West's bidding by dividing the 'All-Russian People.' Russian information warfare describes Poroshenko and President Volodymyr Zelenskyy as 'puppets' of Ukrainian nationalists and the West. [8]

Similarly derogatory descriptions are made by Cohen (2019, 145), who describes US Vice President Joe Biden as Ukraine's 'pro-consul overseeing the increasingly colonized Kyiv.' President Poroshenko was not a Ukrainian leader, but 'a compliant representative of domestic and foreign political forces,' who 'resembles a pro-consul of a faraway great power' running a 'failed state' (Cohen 2019, 36).

Cohen (2019) and Glazyev (2019), both with a history of support for left-wing politics, agree about Ukraine as a Western puppet state. Glazyev (2019) writes: 'By itself, the election of a new president of Ukraine does not change the situation,' because it is 'obvious that in the top three candidates who won

---

[8] https://euvsdisinfo.eu/report/zelenskyys-ruling-is-complete-failure-nazis-feel-well-ukraine-remains-anti-russia/

the majority of votes in the first round of the presidential "election," there was not a single candidate who did not swear allegiance to the American occupation authorities.'

Sixth, Russian media and information warfare routinely dehumanise Ukraine and Ukrainians by belittling the idea that they can exist without external support, whether that support is Russian or western.[9] One example of this idea is found in the mocking and ridiculing of Ukraine on Russian television as possessing a navy during the November 2018 Russian-Ukrainian naval confrontation in the Azov Sea.

Seventh, spreading disillusionment in Ukraine's reforms and European integration is an outgrowth of previous themes. Ukraine and Ukrainians, because of their artificiality, are unable to introduce reforms and fight corruption, and therefore the goal of joining the European Union will end in failure. Ukraine is plagued by corruption and ruled by oligarchs. To hammer this point home, a final point is made that nobody is waiting for Ukraine in Brussels and that eventually Kyiv will understand this and return to Russia's bosom.[10]

One important reason for propagating this theme is that the potential threat of the success of Ukrainian reforms and their destabilising influence on Putin's authoritarian system. Ukraine is a hub for anti-Putin opposition activities and exiled journalists.

Eighth, drawing on Soviet ideological campaigns against 'Nazi collaborators' in the Ukrainian diaspora, Ukraine is depicted as a country ruled by (Galician) 'Nazis' and 'fascists'[11] – even after Zelenskyy, who is of Jewish-Ukrainian descent, was elected Ukrainian president. Soviet propaganda and ideological campaigns attacked dissidents and the nationalist opposition as 'bourgeois nationalists,' who were in cahoots with Nazis in the Ukrainian diaspora and in the pay of western and Israeli secret services. Today, a 'Ukrainian nationalist' in Moscow's eyes is anybody who supported the Euromaidan and Ukraine's future outside the Russian World.

With President Zelenskyy continuing his predecessor's support for the goal of Ukraine joining the EU and NATO, Russia has also begun criticising him as a 'nationalist.' Director of the Foreign Intelligence Service (SVR) and Chairman

---

[9] https://euvsdisinfo.eu/dehumanizing-disinformation-as-a-weapon-of-the-information-war/?highlight=Ukraine%20has%20a%20special%20place%20within%20the%20disinformation%20%28un%29reality
[10] https://euvsdisinfo.eu/ukraine-under-information-fire/?highlight=EU%20ukraine
[11] https://euvsdisinfo.eu/ukraine-will-turn-into-a-banana-republic-ukrainian-elections-on-russian-tv/?highlight=ukraine%20land%20of%20fascists

of the Russian Historical Society, Sergei Naryshkin (2020), commenting on the statements of the Ukrainian president during his visit to Poland said, 'It is clear that Mr. Zelenskyy is more and more immersed in the ideas of Ukrainian nationalism.' With Glazyev's (2019) background in the national-Bolshevik *Rodina* party, it is unsurprising that he reacted to Zelenskyy's election with an anti-Semitic diatribe (on anti-Zionism and anti-Semitism, see Kuzio 2017c, 118–140).

A common theme in Russian information warfare and diplomacy is the claim that, with 'nationalists' and 'Nazis' ruling Ukraine, there is an existentialist threat to Russian speakers. Putin (2019) refuses to countenance the return of Ukrainian control over the Russian-Ukrainian joint border because of the alleged threat of a new 'Srebrenica-style' genocide of Russian speakers similar to that perpetrated by Serbian forces against Muslim Bosnians in July 1995.

With Russian nationalists (imperialists), convinced that 'New Russia' is inhabited by 'Russians,' they are unable to fathom the very concept of Russian-speaking Ukrainian patriotism. Mocking Russia's obsession with searching for 'fascists' in Ukraine, Jewish-Ukrainian oligarch Ihor Kolomoyskyy began wearing tee-shirts emblazoned with *Zhydo-Banderivets* (Jew-Banderite), a sarcastic reference to his status as an alleged Jewish supporter of Ukrainian nationalist leader Bandera.

Ninth, Soviet anti-Zionism, a camouflaged form of anti-Semitism, has been revived in Russian information warfare against Ukraine and by Russian proxies in the DNR and LNR. Glazyev (2019) linked Zelenskyy's election to the 'general inclination of the Trump administration towards the extreme right-wing forces in Israel.' Glazyev does not attempt to hide his anti-Semitism, bizarrely claiming that the Trump administration will 'set new tasks for the renewed Kyiv regime. I do not exclude, for example, the possibility of a massive relocation to the lands of Southeast Ukraine "cleansed" from the Russian population of the inhabitants of the Promised Land who were tired of permanent war in the Middle East, just as Christians fleeing from Islamised Europe.' This anti-Semitic claim was made by one of Putin's senior advisers on Ukraine, who together with Medvedchuk was a joint architect of Russian strategy that pushed Ukraine to crisis in 2013–2014.

Ukraine's oligarchs, such as Jewish-Ukrainian Kolomoyskyy, who took a decisive stance against Russia as governor of Dnipropetrovsk in 2014, are pillorised as being in bed with Ukrainian nationalists. Ukraine is being colonised by the EU, US, and the West as part of a liberal, elite conspiracy that promotes globalisation to destroy the sovereignty of nation-states.

Globalisation, with George Soros as a favourite target, is synonymous with a world-wide Jewish conspiracy.

The tenth theme has its origins in the USSR, which covered up crimes it had committed against its own people and those undertaken by its security forces and assassins abroad. The 1933 *Holodomor*, for example, was denied by the USSR until 1990 (Applebaum 2017). Those who wrote about the *Holodomor* in the Ukrainian diaspora and well-known historians, such as Robert Conquest, were castigated as anti-Soviet 'Cold War warriors' (see Tottle 1987). Tarik Amar (2019; see Kuzio 2019b) continues this genre in devoting 20 of his 24-page review of Applebaum (2017) not to the *Holodomor*, the subject of her book, but to the evils of 'Ukrainian nationalism' (see Kuzio 2019b).

The rehabilitation of Stalin is accompanied by the denial of Stalinist crimes against Poles, such as the Molotov-Ribbentrop Pact and 1940 Katyn massacres, the *Holodomor*, and the 1939 occupation of the three Baltic states. Sputnik International, an important weapon of Russian disinformation abroad, published the '*Holodomor* Hoax: Anatomy of a Lie Invented by the West's Propaganda Machine' (Blinova 2015) nearly three decades after the same arguments were used by Canadian communist Douglas Tottle (1987). In 2015, books by Polish Jewish scholar and lawyer Raphael Lemkin, who developed the concept of genocide after World War II and wrote about and testified on the *Holodomor*, were included in Russia's Federal List of Extremist Materials. In August 2020, on the eve of Ukraine's Independence Day, the monument to a little starving girl called the 'Bitter Memory of Childhood' outside Kyiv's National Museum of *Holodomor* Genocide was vandalised in what the General Director of the museum, Olesya Stasyuk, described as an 'inadmissible offense against the memory of an entire nation.'[12]

Russian information warfare continues in the Soviet tradition of covering up crimes committed by the Kremlin. Blame for the shooting down of the civilian airliner MH17 is shifted away from Russia and the existence of Russian security forces in eastern Ukraine. Distraction of blame over the shooting down of MH17 has gone through 200 disinformation stories,[13] which have been regurgitated in pseudo-academic writing (Pijl 2018).

Russia has always denied the existence of Russian forces in eastern Ukraine

---

[12] https://holodomormuseum.org.ua/news-museji/vandaly-namahalysia-zruinuvaty-skulpturu-pro-holodomor/
[13] https://euvsdisinfo.eu/pro-kremlin-disinformation-desperation-mh17-and-wwii/?highlight=mh17

and, when these forces have been caught, has blamed soldiers 'getting lost' or 'being on holiday.' Nearly two-thirds of Ukrainians (65%) believe that Russian troops are in Ukraine, whereas only 27% of Russians believe this. Additionally, 72% of Ukrainians (but only 25% of Russians) believe that their two countries are at war (Poshuky Shlyakhiv Vidnovlennya Suverenitetu Ukrayiny Nad Okupovanym Donbasom: Stan Hromadskoyii Dumky Naperedodni Prezydentskykh Vyboriv 2019; Shpiker 2016).

Conclusion

This chapter has provided evidence and analysis of Russian nationalism (imperialism) and chauvinism towards Ukraine and Ukrainians. Nevertheless, nationalism (imperialism) in Putin's Russia continues to be downplayed, marginalised, or described as temporary by Western scholars. Between the 2004 Orange Revolution and Putin's re-election in 2012, Russian nationalism (imperialism) rehabilitated Tsarist Russian and White *émigré* views of Ukraine and Ukrainians into official discourse, military aggression, and information warfare. In 2007, the two branches of the Russian Orthodox Church were re-united, and the Russian World Foundation was created. Between 2008–2012, Putin evolved into viewing himself as the 'gatherer of Russian lands,' which include Ukraine. The most extreme example of this evolution was Putin (2020b) incorporating into official discourse the late-nineteenth century Tsarist Russian conspiracy of Austrians creating a fake Ukrainian people that had been earlier rehabilitated by Russian fascists (Vorobyev 2020).

In the same manner as western orientalism had earlier imagined in a negative manner peoples fighting for their national self-determination in their colonies, *Putinversteher* scholars have copied Kremlin templates about the evils of 'Ukrainian nationalism.' Ukraine, which has one of the lowest levels of electoral support for extreme right parties in Europe, is allegedly over-run by Nazis. At the same time, western scholars can find little or no evidence of nationalism in Russia, where it dominates domestic politics, underpins a cult of the murderous tyrant Stalin, and fuels territorial conquest and military aggression against Georgia and Ukraine. In reality, nationalism in Ukraine has become more civic since 2014.

This chapter has analysed how academic orientalism permeates the writings of western political scientists on the 2014 crisis, Russian-Ukrainian War, and Russian and Ukrainian nationalism. The next chapter takes my application of academic orientalism further by applying it to claims of a 'civil war' taking place in Ukraine to show that this is a false narrative that is not supported by what took place or by Ukrainians. The roots of the 2014 crisis go as far back as 1991 (D'Anieri 2019) and concern Russian intervention in Ukraine in the decade prior to the annexation of Crimea and hybrid warfare in Donbas. The next chapter provides evidence of a Russian-Ukrainian War taking place. The false narrative of a 'civil war' dovetails with Ukraine being portrayed as a country with acute regional divisions between Russian and Ukrainian speakers, which was captured by Galician-based 'Ukrainian nationalists' during the Euromaidan.

5

Russian Military Aggression or 'Civil War'?

There has always been Russian invasion, annexation, and military and other forms of aggression in what Oscar Jonsson and Robert Seely (2015) describe as 'full spectrum conflict.' There has never been a 'civil war' in Ukraine. Misplaced use of the term 'civil war' to describe the Russian-Ukrainian War is correlated with three factors. First, denial or downplaying of Russian military and other forms of involvement against Ukraine. Second, claims that Russian speakers are oppressed and threatened by Ukrainianisation with an additional claim that eastern Ukraine has a 'shared civilization' with Russia (Cohen 2019, 17). Third, highly exaggerated claims of regional divisions in Ukraine that point to the country as an 'artificial' construct.

This chapter is divided into four sections. The first section discusses terminology on civil wars and provides evidence from Ukrainian opinion polls that Ukrainians see what is taking place as a war with Russia, not a 'civil war.' The second section analyses how the Russian-Ukrainian War should be understood as taking place between Ukrainians, who hold a civic identity and patriotic attachment to Ukraine, and a small number of Ukrainians in regions such as the Donbas and their external Russian backers, whose primary allegiance is to the Russian World and the former USSR. An example of civic nationalism is Dnipropetrovsk in 2014–2015 when the region was led by two Jewish-Ukrainians (regional Governor Kolomoyskyy and Deputy Governor Hennadiy Korban) and an ethnic Russian (Deputy Governor and, since 2015, Mayor of the city of Dnipro Borys Filatov), who prevented Russian hybrid warfare from expanding west of Donetsk.The third section analyses the period, usually ignored by scholars, prior to 2014 when Russia provided training and support for separatists and violence during the Euromaidan Revolution, and the crucial period between 2012–2013 when Putin implemented policies as the 'gatherer of Russian lands.' The fourth section provides a detailed analysis of 'full spectrum conflict' that includes Russian intelligence activities, Russian nationalist (imperialist) mercenaries, Putin's rhetoric providing signaling to Russian nationalists (imperialists), information warfare and cyber-attacks, Russian discourse on limited sovereignty, and Russian military invasion of Ukraine.

Theory, Terminology, and Why Ukrainians Do Not See a 'Civil War'

Terminology is problematic in discussions about whether a 'civil war' is taking place in Ukraine. Tymofil Brik (2019) took Jesse Driscoll (2019) to task for ignoring the local context, neglecting census results and Ukrainian opinion polls and research (a typical problem found in academic orientalism), and being influenced by his experience working in Central Asia and the Caucasus, 'which is not often applicable to Russian-Ukrainian relations, neither current nor historical.' The Donbas War is not an ethnic conflict, unlike conflicts in Georgia and Azerbaijan, as Russian speakers are fighting in both Ukrainian security forces *and* Russian proxy forces.

A civil war is defined by Patrick M. Reagan (2000) and Nicholas Sambanis (2002, 218) as a war between organised groups within the same state leading to high intensity conflict and casualties of over 1,000 people, a definition which applies to the Donbas. James Fearon (2007) defines a civil war as a violent conflict within a country fought by organised groups that aim to take power at the centre or in a region, or to change government policies. A civil war challenges the sovereignty of an internationally recognised state, takes place within the boundaries of a recognised state, and involves rebels that are able to mount organised, armed opposition.

Sambanis (2002) analyses how grievances have transformed into mass violence. A violent rebellion would be likely if the state unleashed repression against minorities who hold political grievances. Ted Gurr (2000) has stressed the salience of ethno-cultural identities and their capacity to mobilise, the importance of levels of grievance, and the availability of opposition political activities. Scholars have also debated the causes of civil wars as either 'greed' or 'grievance,' which can arise from contestation over identity, religious, and ethnic factors. The World Bank's Collier-Hoeffler model investigates the availability of finances, opportunity costs of rebellion, military advantage and terrain, ethnic and regional grievances of minorities dominated by majorities, the size of population, and the period of time since the last conflict (Wong 2006).

Sambanis (2002) argues that realism and neo-realism are unable to explain the outbreak, duration, and termination of civil wars because both sets of theories assume that the state is a unitary actor and cannot therefore explain why ethnic, religious, and class divisions emerge and threaten a state's sovereignty. Neo-liberal theories, Sambanis (2002, 225) believes, are better equipped to explain the outbreak of civil wars and the role of non-state actors in fomenting them.

Constructivists believe that mobilisation of protestors is the work of elites (defined as 'ethnic entrepreneurs') who fashion beliefs, preferences, and identities in ways that socially construct and reinforce existing cleavages (Fearon and Laitin 2002). In the Ukrainian case, this argument would point to Manafort's racist 'Southern Strategy' being used by the Party of Regions in the decade prior to 2014. An argument against defining the Donbas conflict as a 'civil war' is therefore the long-term work of Russian and Donbas 'ethnic entrepreneurs' during the decade prior to the 2014 crisis (Na terrritorii Donetskoy oblasty deystvovaly voyennye lagerya DNR s polnym vooruzheniyem s 2009 goda 2014). A constructivist approach has particular resonance in the Donbas, where oligarchs and the Party of Regions political machine dominated Ukraine's only Russian-style managed democracy.

An important discussion of 'civil war' in Ukraine has been made by Sambanis, Stergios Skaperdas, and William Wohlforth (2017), who discuss how an external sponsor, in this case Russia, 'can use different combinations of the different instruments at its disposal to induce rebellion and civil war.' Russia's intervention 'activated' cleavages and increased polarisation, 'making it harder for the state to suppress the rebellion' (Sambanis, Skaperdas and Wohlforth 2017, 13). As polarisation increased, inflamed by Russia's information warfare and politicians' rhetoric and outright disinformation, violence escalated. Without Russia's intervention, anti-Maidan protestors in the Donbas would not have transformed into armed insurgents (Wilson 2015).

What is often ignored in discussions about whether what is taking place in the Donbas should be described as a 'civil war' is Ukrainian public opinion. Ploeg (2017, 177) dislikes the fact that only 13.6% of Ukrainians believe that there is a 'civil war' in their country and blames this on 'anti-Russian' media. Petro (2016, 198; 2018, 326) refuses to accept Ukrainian polling data, believing that they understate pro-Russian feelings, exaggerate anti-Russian attitudes, and downplay regional divisions.

Polls conducted in 2015 and 2018 found that 16.3% and 13.4%, respectively, of Ukrainians believed that a 'civil war' was taking place in Ukraine (Perspektyvy Ukrayinsko-Rosiyskykh Vidnosyn 2015; Viyna na Donbasi: Realii i Perspektyvy Vrehulyuvannya 2019). In a 2018 poll, the Donbas conflict was viewed as a 'civil war' by a low of 5.1% in western Ukraine and a high of 26.5% in eastern Ukraine. The number of those who believed in a 'civil war' in the east (26.5%) was lower than the 34.2% in eastern Ukraine, who viewed the conflict as a Russian-Ukrainian War (Viyna na Donbasi: Realii i Perspektyvy Vrehulyuvannya, 2019).

Furthermore, 72% of Ukrainians believe that there is a Russian-Ukrainian War, ranging from a high of 91% in the west to 47% in eastern and 62% in southern Ukraine. In Ukrainian-controlled Donbas, views are evenly split between 39%, who believe a Russian-Ukrainian War taking place, and 40% who do not (Poshuky Shlyakhiv Vidnovlennya Suverenitetu Ukrayiny Nad Okupovanym Donbasom: Stan Hromadskoyii Dumky Naperedodni Prezydentskykh Vyboriv 2019). Respectively, 76% and 47% of residents of Ukrainian-controlled Donetsk and Luhansk believe that Russia is a party to the conflict, with 12% and 31% respectively disagreeing (Public Opinion in Donbas a Year After Presidential Elections 2020).

Civic Ukrainian versus Russian World Loyalties

Arguments in favour of a 'civil war' fuelled by competing regional and national identities are only made possible by ignoring Russia's long-standing chauvinistic attitudes towards Ukrainians, the many aspects of Russia's 'full spectrum conflict,' and the intervention in Ukraine from February 2014 (Kudelia and Zyl, 2019, 807). Regional versus national identities provide a weak explanation for why protestors transformed into armed insurgents in the Donbas, but not in the other six *oblasts* of southeastern Ukraine. Transforming minority support for separatism in Donetsk (27.5%) and Luhansk (30.3%) was only possible because Russia provided far more resources in its 'full spectrum conflict' to these two regions. The Donbas had deprecated and denigrated Ukrainian majorities, while aggressive pro-Russian minorities were accustomed to undertaking violence against their opponents.

Some scholars emphasise the local roots of the crisis in the Donbas (Matveeva 2018; Kudelia 2017; Kudelia and Zyl 2019; Himka 2015). Tor Bukkvoll (2019, 299) attempts to have it both ways, confusingly describing the conflict as an 'insurgency' until August 2014 'even though Russian political agents and special forces most probably played an important role in its instigation.' A regional versus national identities framework of the 'civil war' is at odds with the claim of an 'absence of an ideology' among pro-Russian forces in the Donbas (Kudelia and Zyl 2019, 815). This can only be undertaken by ignoring Putin's belief of himself as the 'gatherer of Russian lands' implemented through Medvedchuk and Glazyev's strategy (O komplekse mer po vovlecheniyu Ukrainy v evraziiskii integratsionyi protsess 2013) and Ukraine's participation in the Russian World (Zygar 2016, 258).

Matveeva (2018, 2) is one of a small number of scholars who describes the conflict as one between civilisations, emphasising allegiance to the Russian World as 'politicized identity.' Scholars writing about identity in the Euromaidan have also talked about 'civilisation choices' (Lena Surzhko-Harned and Ekateryna Turkina 2018, 108) In contrast, 'Ethnicity is a poor marker in Ukraine, and loyalty and identity are weakly correlated with it' (Matveeva 2018, 25). From 2006, Putin began to talk of Russia as the centre of a Eurasian civilisation with superior values and distinct to the EU, which he portrayed as a harmful actor (Foxall 2019). This took place a year before the creation of the Russian World, three years before the launch of the EU's Eastern Partnership, and four years before the creation of the CIS Customs Union. Attachment to civilisation identity (civic Ukrainian or Russian World), rather than language, is a better marker of loyalty in the Donbas War as there are Russian speakers fighting on both sides.

Nevertheless, Matveeva's (2018) discussion of civilisation is confusing, as she wrongly defines it in civic terms as corresponding to *Rossiyskie* citizens of the Russian Federation. Tolz (2008a, 2008b) and other western scholars have long noted that civic identity is weak in the Russian Federation. The 1996 Russian-Belarusian union, a precursor to the Russian World, was a 'challenge to the civic model of Russian nationality' (Plokhy 2017, 319).

The Russian World is, in fact, a claim to the allegedly common *Russkij* ethno-cultural, religious, and historical identity of the three eastern Slavs. Russia is a 'state-civilisation,' and Putin is gathering 'Russian' lands that he believes are part of the Russian World. Taking their cue, leaders of the 'Russian spring' spoke of an 'artificially divided Russian people' (Matveeva 2018, 221). In both cases, they were saying that Ukraine is a 'Russian land' and that Ukrainians are a branch of the 'All-Russian People.' The Russian Orthodox Church concept of 'Holy Rus' supports the rehabilitation of Tsarist Russian nationality policy of a 'All-Russian People' with three branches. The Russian World and Russian identity are defined in ethno-cultural, not in civic terms (Plokhy 2017, 327–328, 331).

Kudelia (2017) believes that a clash over identities was fuelled by the influence of Ukrainian nationalism in the Euromaidan, which allowed Russian authorities to paint it as a 'nationalist putsch.' A more insightful way is presented by Matveeva (2018) who discusses a 'civilisational' divide between Ukrainians in the Donbas, who were oriented to the Russian World, and Ukrainians whose civic allegiance was to Ukraine (Kuzio 2018, 540).

This civilisation divide is perhaps what Dominique Arel (2018, 188) refers to when he writes of the 'rebellion of Russians' (that is, those living in the Donbas who thought of themselves as part of the 'All-Russian People'). Arel

(2018) alludes to an understanding of 'Russian' (i.e. All-Russian People') identity as encompassing the three eastern Slavs. This also shows that those in the Donbas who viewed themselves as members of the 'All-Russian People' agreed with Russian leaders that Russians and Ukrainians are 'one people' (D'Anieri 2019, 162–163). Ukrainians in the Donbas who thought of themselves as 'Russians' were most likely the same as those who claimed to hold a Soviet identity. Russian and Soviet were *de facto* the same in the USSR.

The 2001 census recorded 17% of Ukraine's population as Russians, but only 5% of these were exclusively Russian with the remainder exhibiting a mixed Ukrainian-Russian identity (The Views and Opinions of South-Eastern Regions Residents of Ukraine). During the 2014 crisis, sitting on the fence was no longer possible, and many Ukrainians who had held a mixed identity adopted a civic Ukrainian identity to show their patriotism. The proportion of the Ukrainian population declaring themselves to be ethnic Ukrainians increased to 92%. Currently, only 6% of Ukrainians declare themselves to be ethnically Russian, down from 22% in the 1989 Soviet census and 17% in the 2001 Ukrainian census (Osnovni Zasady ta Shlyakhy Formuvannya Spilnoyi Identychnosti Hromadyan Ukrayiny 2017, 5).

Between two opinion polls conducted in April and December 2014, mixed Russian-Ukrainian identities in southeastern Ukraine collapsed (O'Loughlin and Toal 2020, 318). Six years on, mixed identities have declined even further. In Dnipropetrovsk, those with mixed identities halved from 8.2 to 4.5%. In Zaporizhzhya and Odesa, mixed identities collapsed from 8.2 and 15.1% to 2 and 2.3%, respectively. Mixed identities were never strong in Kherson and Mykolayiv, where they collapsed to a statistically insignificant 0.6 and 1.6%, respectively. Kharkiv registered the lowest decline, from 12.4 to 7.7%. This is what Kharkiv scholar Zhurzhenko (2015) called the 'end of ambiguity' in eastern Ukraine. Ukraine no longer has a pro-Russian 'east.'

Russian Intervention in the Decade Prior to the 2014 Crisis

Training and Support for Separatism in Ukraine

In November 2004, Russia supported a separatist congress in Severodonetsk in Luhansk *oblast*, organised by Yanukovych in protest to the Orange Revolution denying him his fraudulent election victory. In February 2014, a similar congress of the Ukrainian Front in Kharkiv was planned after Yanukovych fled from Kyiv, but failed to go ahead after regional leaders from southeastern Ukraine and the president failed to turn up.

Yanukovych's plans in 2004 and 2014 drew on a long tradition of creating pro-Russian fronts. So-called 'Internationalist Movements' were established by the Soviet secret services in the late 1980s in Ukraine, Moldova, and the three Baltic States to oppose their independence. The Donetsk Republic Party, which is one of two parties ruling the DNR, is a successor to the Inter-Movement of the Donbas founded in 1989 by Andrei Purgin, Dmitri Kornilov, and Sergei Baryshnikov. Its allies were the Movement for the Rebirth of the Donbas and Civic Congress, which changed its name to the Party of Slavic Unity (Kuzio 2017c, 88–89).

The Donetsk Republic Party was launched in 2005, not coincidentally a year after the 2004 Orange Revolution with support from Russian intelligence (Na terrritorii Donetskoy oblasty deystvovaly voyennye lagerya DNR s polnym vooruzheniyem s 2009 goda 2014). The Donetsk Republic Party and similar extremist groups were provided with paramilitary training in summer camps organised by Dugin (see Shekhovtsov 2016, 2017, 2018, 253; Likhachev 2016). The Donetsk Republic Party was banned by the Ukrainian authorities in 2007, but continued to operate 'underground' with the connivance of the Party of Regions, which monopolised power in the Donbas.

Baryshnikov, Dean of Donetsk University in the DNR, and other leaders of the Donetsk Republic Party have always been extreme Russian chauvinists and Ukrainophobes. Baryshnikov believes that 'Ukraine should not exist' because it is an 'artificial state.' He admits, 'I have always been against Ukraine, politically and ideologically,' showing the long ideological continuity between the Soviet Inter-Movement and the Donetsk Republic Party (Na terrritorii Donetskoy oblasty deystvovaly voyennye lagerya DNR s polnym vooruzheniyem s 2009 goda 2014).

Baryshnikov unequivocally states that Ukrainians 'are Russians who refuse to admit their Russia-ness;' in other words, he supports the Tsarist Russian nationality policy of three branches of the 'All-Russian People,' which was rehabilitated by Putin. Baryshnikov supports the destruction of Ukrainian national identity 'by war and repression,' because it 'can be compared to a difficult disease, like cancer' (Judah 2015, XVI, 11, 150, 152–153).

In spring 2014, Russia's information warfare and Russian neo-Nazis on the ground in Donetsk helped to swell the number of members of the hitherto marginal Donetsk Republic Party (Melnyk 2020). Toal (2017, 252) writes that many Donbas and Crimean Russian proxies were 'genuine neo-Nazis.' The Donetsk Republic Party (Na terrritorii Donetskoy oblasty deystvovaly voyennye lagerya DNR s polnym vooruzheniyem s 2009 goda 2014) is one of two ruling parties in the DNR after winning 68.3% of the vote in its fake 2014 'election.'

Russian Penetration of Ukraine's Security Forces

Sakwa (2017a) and Matveeva (2018) seek to downplay Yanukovych as a friend of Russia and, in doing so, minimise Russia's intervention in Ukrainian affairs prior to 2014. Sakwa (2017a, 159, 153) writes, 'Yanukovych had never been a particular friend of Russia' and 'relations with Moscow during his presidency remained strained.' This chapter provides evidence that this is not true. Russia penetrated Ukrainian security forces during Yanukovych's presidency extensively (see Kuzio 2012; Belton 2020, 387). Jonnson and Seely (2015) place Russia's 'full spectrum conflict' in the long-term context of Russian subversion that, over a number of years, strove to weaken its opponents' security forces and increase its ties with Russia, for example through pro-Russian political forces, Russian-language media, think tanks, and NGOs (Gonchar, Horbach, and Pinchuk 2020, 41–51). The work of Russian intelligence services and the strategic use of corruption are two of the most widely used Russian tools in its 'full spectrum conflict.' Russia's biggest export has always been corruption – not energy.

Security Service of Ukraine and military officers undertook espionage for Russia in the critical early stages of the conflict in 2014. The extent of Russia's penetration is evident to the present day, with senior military and Security Service of Ukraine officers detained and charged with treason (Gonchar, Horbach and Pinchuk 2020, 3–22).[1] When Poroshenko said in March 2015 that 80% of Security Service of Ukraine officers defected in spring 2014 in Crimea, his claim was met with disbelief, but he was not exaggerating. The extent of Russia's success in fomenting treason in Ukraine's security forces in Crimea in spring 2014 can be seen in Table 5.1.

5.1. Table of Defections from Ukrainian Security Forces in Crimea, Spring 2014.
Source: Gonchar, Horbach, and Pinchuk 2020, 13.

Total Number of Security Forces in Crimea	Of those, the number who returned to Ukraine	Defectors as a percentage of the total number of Ukrainian security forces in Crimea
13,468 military (4,637 officers and 8,831 sergeants and soldiers)	3,991 (1, 649 officers, 2,342 sergeants and soldiers)	70%
1,235 Security Service of Ukraine officers	217	86.4%
2,489 Ministry of Interior Internal Troops	1,398	44%

---

[1] https://www.pravda.com.ua/news/2020/04/14/7247830/

Violence and Nationalism during the Euromaidan

Claiming that a dominating influence of 'Ukrainian nationalism' in the Euromaidan is correlated with defining what is taking place in the Donbas as a 'civil war,' Keith Darden and Lucan Way (2014) exaggerate the influence of nationalism on the Euromaidan and portray 'nationalists' as ethnically based and originating from western Ukraine. Olga Onuch and Gwendolyn Sasse (2018, 28) provide a detailed counter-analysis, stressing the diversity of the protestors among whom they estimate nationalists accounted for only 5%, rising to 10–20% during the violence. The majority of protestors were 'ordinary citizens' with no previous history of political activity (Onuch 2014). Calling into 'question the salience and stability of ethno-linguistic and regional identities,' they argue that 'a conceptualization of Ukrainian politics as being driven by ethno-linguistic or regional demands is too simplistic' (Onuch and Sasse 2018, 30–31).

Exaggerating the influence of 'Ukrainian nationalism' is closely correlated with exaggerating regional divisions in Ukraine, repeating claims and stereotypes that are usually the exclusive prerogative of those who believe in an 'artificial Ukraine' and 'two Ukraines' (Sakwa 2015; Hahn 2018, Petro 2015). Kolsto (2016, 708) describes southeastern Ukraine as exhibiting 'a more Russian character than the rest of Ukraine,' which if true would have led to the success of Russia's 'New Russia' project in 2014 (see Kuzio 2019a).

Ukrainian nationalists stereotypically painted as 'western Ukrainian' are often from eastern Ukraine. Nationalist *Pravyy Sektor* (Right Sector) Party leaders Dmytro Yarosh and Andriy Tarasenko are from Dnipropetrovsk, initial support for and leaders of the Azov battalion came from Kharkiv, Minister of Interior Arsen Avakov is a Russian-speaking Armenian from Kharkiv, and oligarch Kolomoyskyy is a Russian-speaking Jewish-Ukrainian from Dnipropetrovsk (as was his deputy Korban), while his other deputy (Filatov) was an ethnic Russian. The highest number of military veterans of the Donbas conflict are found in Dnipropetrovsk, Kharkiv, and Poltava (Kolumbet 2020), and the highest number of casualties of Ukrainian security forces are from Dnipropetrovsk (see 6.2 map).

President Yanukovych's use of violence against protestors was lobbied for by Putin during his one-on-one meetings with the Ukrainian president and by Putin's senior advisers Surkov and Glazyev. Violence during the Euromaidan 'radicalised the protestors' (Friesendorf 2019, 112). The *Berkut* forces that undertook human rights abuses and killed protestors were brought to Kyiv from Crimea, the Donbas, and elsewhere in eastern Ukraine in the belief that Kyiv-based *Berkut* would be unreliable. When these *Berkut* officers returned home, they were greeted as heroes and, in many cases, deserted to Russian forces in Crimea or joined Russian proxy forces in Donbas. The *Berkut* was disbanded by the Euromaidan revolutionaries after they took power (Crimea welcomes riot cops after murdering Euromaidan protestors 2014).

High levels of participation of eastern Ukrainians in volunteer battalions in 2014 (Aliyev 2019, 2020) grew out of the Euromaidan. In eastern Ukraine, football 'ultras' (members of football fan clubs) and civil society activists created self-defence groups to protect local Maidans against Party of Regions and pro-Russian vigilantes. The most active of these self-defence groups were found in Kharkiv, Dnipropetrovsk, Zaporizhzhya, Odesa, and to a lesser extent Donetsk (Fisun 2014).

2012–2013: 'Gathering Russian Lands' versus Post-Modern EU

Some western scholars ignore Russia's pressure on Yanukovych prior to the 2014 crisis and instead focus their entire criticism on the EU in 2014. The EU undertook a 'reckless provocation' in compelling Yanukovych 'in a divided country to choose between Russia and the West' (Cohen 2019, 17). Enlarging NATO to 'Russia's borders' and the EU pushing its Association Agreement split Ukraine, because the east has a 'shared civilization' with Russia (Cohen 2019, 17). For a historian, it is surprising that Cohen (2019) believes that civilisations and identities are set in stone and never change. Western (or Russian) 'political aggression' allegedly undermined 'centuries of intimate relations between large segments of Ukrainian society and Russia, including family ties' (Cohen 2019, 83).

D'Anieri (2019) provides a more balanced critique of EU and Russian policies towards Ukraine in the run up to the 2014 crisis, pointing out that 'Ukraine's policy of picking which component of an agreement to adhere to would no longer be accepted' (D'Anieri 2019, 192). D'Anieri (2019, 264) writes that Putin 'put immense pressure' on Yanukovych to not sign the Association Agreement (see also Sambanis, Skaperdas and Wohlforth 2017).

Impartial scholars would apportion blame on both the EU *and* Russia, both of which pressured Yanukovych to make a decision in their favour. The EU could not understand the depth of Russia's hostility to Ukraine joining the Association Agreement because they did not believe it was aimed against Russia. The EU did not understand that Russia made no distinction between membership and Eastern Partnership offers of integration. 'Putin saw the Association Agreement as threatening the permanent loss of Ukraine, which it had, since 1991, seen as artificial and temporary' (D'Anieri 2019, 251).

The Ukraine crisis was ultimately a clash between a post-modern, twenty-first century EU and Russia, whose thinking had stagnated to the nineteenth century, or at the very least prior to World War II. This was evident in the rehabilitation of Tsarist Russian White *émigré* ideologies and thinking of Russia and its neighbours. Polish Foreign Minister Radek Sikorski rejected Russia's 'nineteenth-century mode of operating towards neighbours' (D'Anieri 2019, 203). D'Anieri (2019, 276) believes that 'Russia seeks an order based on the dominance of great powers that was widely accepted in the era prior to World War I.'

Medvedchuk has been Putin's representative in Ukraine since at least 2004, the year Putin and Svetlana Medvedev, wife of former Russian Prime Minister Medvedev, became godparents to his daughter Darina. Writing about Medvedchuk, Neil Buckley, and Roman Olearchyk (2017) say, 'Many suspect him of being Mr Putin's agent.' Zygar (2016, 123) believes that Medvedchuk has long been the 'main source of information about what was happening in Ukraine.' Medvedchuk is the only person Putin has fully trusted in Ukraine, and he is 'effectively Putin's special representative in Ukraine' (Zygar 2016, 167).

With accusations from his Soviet past of being a KGB informer, Medvedchuk 'shared some of the "Ukrainophobia" of Moscow officialdom' (Zygar 2016, 84). In the USSR, Medvedchuk had been a Soviet-appointed attorney for Ukrainian dissidents Yuriy Litvin and Vasyl Stus between 1979–1980. Although he was their 'defence attorney' he supported the court's convictions, and Lytvyn and Stus died in the Siberian gulag in 1984 and 1985, respectively (Tytykalo 2020).

Medvedchuk and Glazyev implemented Putin's goal of 'gathering Russian lands' by bringing Ukraine into the Russian World and CIS Customs Union (from 2015, the Eurasian Economic Union). In spring 2012, at the same time as Putin was re-elected, Medvedchuk launched the Ukrainian Choice political party, which resembled more a 'front for the Kremlin than independent organization' (Hosaka 2018, 341). Russia and its representatives in Ukraine promoted Eurasian integration for its alleged benefits of Ukrainian access to markets and cheaper gas deals (Molchanov 2016). According to them, Ukraine could only maintain its identity at the centre of Eurasia rather than on the edge of Europe; Ukraine's growing trade with the EU since 2014 shows this to be untrue.

Russia's active measures against Ukraine were launched in early 2013, which targeted ideological, political, economic, and information factors (Hosaka 2018). In summer 2013, Medvedchuk and Glazyev devised a strategy that included a trade war and a range of other policies to pressure President Yanukovych to turn away from the EU Association Agreement and join the CIS Customs Union (O komplekse mer po vovlecheniyu Ukrainy v evraziiskii integratsionyi protsess 2013). This strategy may have been what Belarusian President Lukashenka was referring to when he said that he had seen Russian plans in May 2013 to invade Crimea and 'New Russia' (Leshchenko 2014, 215).

Putin did not fully trust Yanukovych and threatened to back Medvedchuk in the 2015 elections if he did not withdraw from the EU Association Agreement (Hosaka 2018; Melnyk 2020, 18). Putin and Medvedchuk's allies worked with the Russian nationalist wing of the Party of Regions led by Igor Markov, Oleg Tsarev, and Vadym Kolesnichenko. All three supported Russia's interventions and military invasion in 2014. Kolesnichenko was a co-author of the divisive 2012 language law and was one of the organisers of the failed Ukrainian Front in Kharkiv (Kulick 2019, 359).

The Medvedchuk-Glazyev strategy was fully implemented. One part of the strategy was 'Operation Armageddon,' launched on 26 June 2013, just three weeks after Prime Minister Nikolai Azarov agreed to bring Ukraine into the CIS Customs Union as an 'observer.' One of 'Operation Armageddon's' most important periods of activity was from 1 December 2013, when the Euromaidan took off, to 28 February 2014, a day after Russia launched its invasion of Crimea. 'Operation Armageddon' was complimented by 'Operation Infektion,' launched in February 2014 and continued to the present day (Nimmo, Francois, Eib, Ronzaud, Ferreira, Hernon, and Kostelancik 2020). 'Operation Armageddon' was a 'Russian state-sponsored cyber espionage campaign' designed to give Russia military advantage in any future conflict with Ukraine and, to this end, it targeted Ukrainian government, military, and law enforcement to obtain an insight into Ukrainian intentions and plans (Operation Armageddon 2015).

In summer 2013, Ukraine was subjected to a trade boycott and demands for payment of its debts to Gazprom, actions that were combined with a 'massive diplomatic offensive against Ukraine' (Svoboda 2019, 1694). Putin and Yanukovych held numerous one-on-one meetings prior to and during the Euromaidan, which 'underlined the importance of the issue for Russia and the seriousness of the situation' (Svoboda 2019, 1695). In the year before the outbreak of military conflict, Russia 'combined diplomacy, propaganda, economic pressure, and even the threat of military action' (Svoboda 2019, 1700; see also Haukkala 2015).

Included in the Medvedchuk-Glazyev strategy was an invitation to Putin and

Kirill to speak at the July 2013 Kyiv conference to promote 'Orthodox-Slavic values' and Ukraine's civilisation choice in favour of the Russian World (D'Anieri 2019, 193; Kishkovsky 2013; Zygar 2016, 258). As Patriarch of the Russian Orthodox Church, Kirill had strongly identified with the Russian World since becoming Patriarch in 2009 and supported the rehabilitation of the Tsarist Russian nationality policy of three eastern Slavic branches of the 'All-Russian People.' Kirill agreed with Putin that Russians and Ukrainians were 'one people' (Plokhy 2017, 331). As 'Holy Rus,' the three eastern Slavs were the core of the Russian Orthodox Church with the Russian World a contemporary reincarnation of 'Kievan Russia' (Kyiv Rus).

Putin and Kirill used the celebrations of the anniversary of the 1,025th anniversary of the Christianisation of Kyiv Rus to rebuild a contemporary eastern Slavic Union in the Russian World. Eastern Slavic and Russian World values were claimed to be superior to European liberal values, a message that Russia has increasingly promoted as it has reached out to and supported populist nationalist and neo-fascist groups in Europe hostile to the EU (see Shekhovtsov 2018).

Putin told Medvedchuk's conference: 'The baptism of Rus was a great event that defined Russia's and Ukraine's spiritual and cultural development for the centuries to come. We must remember this brotherhood and preserve our ancestor's land' (D'Anieri 2019, 193–194). In a clear reference to himself as the 'gatherer of Russian lands,' Putin described 'Russians' as the most divided people in the world (Laruelle 2015; Teper 2016).

'Full Spectrum Conflict' and the 2014 Crisis

Downplaying Russia's Military Invasion

Scholars who use the term 'civil war' ignore 10 important factors that took place in the decade prior to and during spring 2014 (see Belton 2020, 384, 387–389, 419–427):

1. Russian interference in the 2004 presidential elections;
2. Russian support for and training of separatists and extremist Russian nationalists;
3. Russian backing for an alliance between the Party of Regions and Crimean Russian nationalists-separatists;
4. Evolution of Russian views away from the Soviet concept of close but different Russians and Ukrainians towards Tsarist Russian *and* White émigré denial of Ukraine and Ukrainians (Belton 2020, 422–424);
5. President Medvedev's (2009) open letter laying out demands which President Yanukovych fulfilled;

6. Russian infiltration and control over Ukrainian security forces during Yanukovych's presidency and how this led to defections, treason and leakage of intelligence in the 2014 crisis;
7. Implementation of Putin's 'gathering of Russian lands' after his re-election in 2012–2013, including pressure on Yanukovych to drop Ukraine's integration into the EU;
8. Russia offering exile to Yanukovych and other Party of Regions leaders who had stolen upwards of $100 billion from Ukraine[2] and committed treason (Roth 2019);
9. How Russia's annexation of Crimea, 'Russian spring' and 'New Russia' project impacted upon Ukrainian policy decisions to combat Russian proxies in the Donbas; and
10. Focusing on only Russian military boots on the ground while ignoring the many components of Russian 'full spectrum conflict' (Jonsson and Seely 2015) which are chronicled in Table 5.2.

Denial, obfuscation, minimising, or ignoring evidence of Russia's 'full spectrum conflict' is used to give credence to the claim that a 'civil war' is taking place in Ukraine. Matveeva (2018, 112) writes that Putin 'was elusive, zigzagging, and non-committal.' In support of her claim that separatists were not Russian proxies, Matveeva (2018, 217) writes that 'military supplies switched on and off,' ignoring many other aspects of Russian involvement and Russia's intervention prior to the Euromaidan and immediately after Yanukovych fled from Kyiv.

It cannot be true, as Sakwa (2017a) writes, that Russia sought to extricate itself from the Donbas at the same time as it built up a huge army and military arsenal controlled by GRU (Russian military intelligence) officers and 5,000 Russian occupation troops based in the DNR and LNR. Cohen's (2019) denial of Russia's military invasion in Ukraine is in keeping with his denial of Russian hacking of the 2016 US elections, chemical weapons attack against Russian defector Sergei Skripal in Britain, and every other nefarious action of which Russia is accused of undertaking. Just some of the Russians who have been poisoned include Navalnyi, Anna Politkovskaya, Vladimir Kara Murza (twice), Yuri Schchekochikin, Emilian Gebrev in Bulgaria, Alexander Litvinenko, Alexander Perepilichny, and Skripal in the UK.

Hahn (2018, 268) downplays Russian forces in spring 2014 as 'negligible' and 'non-existent,' and minimises Russia military intervention. In writing that 'it is fundamentally a civil war,' Hahn (2018, 270) views the conflict taking place between 'western Ukrainian nationalists' and 'good,' pro-Russian eastern

---

[2] https://www.reuters.com/article/us-ukraine-crisis-yanukovich/toppled-mafia-president-cost-ukraine-up-to-100-billion-prosecutor-says-idUSBREA3T0K820140430

Ukrainian Russian speakers. Western Ukrainian 'fascists' came to power in a *coup d'état* during the Euromaidan and made Russian speakers a 'stigmatised minority' (Hahn, 2018, 45), closed Russian language media, and demonised President Putin. Putin's policies are described as 'reactive and defensive' and as a 'countermove to mitigate the loss incurred in and potential threat from Kiev' (Hahn 2018, 21). This is a novel way to describe the annexation of a neighbour's territory. Putin had 'solid arguments' for 'Russian intervention in the crisis and especially in Crimea' (Hahn 2018, 237).

Serhiy Kudelia (2017, 226) applies 'civil war' to the entire period until summer 2014, when Russia invaded Ukraine. Kudelia (2017, 228) blames only Ukraine for launching 'the military stage,' a view he shares with Sakwa (2015), Matveeva (2016, 2018), and Cohen (2019). Similarly, Matveeva (2018, 272) writes, 'Before the crisis, Moscow's role in Ukraine was not particularly active,' and 'Moscow did not support any independent activism of a pro-Russian nature in Ukraine.' Hiroaki Kuromiya (2019, 252, 257), the leading historian of the Donbas, believes that 'violence was encouraged and supported by Moscow' because, on their own, 'the local separatists were simply not determined enough to engage in war.'

5.2. Russian 'Full Spectrum Conflict,' February–April 2014
Source: Compiled by author.

Date	Event
22 February	Yanukovych fled from Kyiv.
23 February	Large Russian military exercises by 150, 000 troops (38% of Russian ground forces) are held on the Ukrainian-Russian border.
27 February	Russia invades Crimea.
28 February	State Duma Chairman Sergei Naryshkin threatens that Russia would intervene to 'defend' Russians and Russian speakers in a telephone call with acting Ukrainian head of state Oleksandr Turchynov during an emergency meeting of Ukraine's National Security and Defence Council (RNBO).
1 March	Putin is given the green light by the Federation Council to militarily intervene in Ukraine until 'normalisation of the socio-political situation takes place' to 'protect the interests of Russian citizens and compatriots.' On the same day, from exile in Russia, Yanukovych calls for Russian troops to intervene in Ukraine. Pro-Russian rallies are launched in 11 *oblast* centres in southeastern Ukraine (Harding 2014).
1–4 March	Donetsk Republic Party's 'People's Militia of Donbas' stormed the *oblast* council building in Donetsk and replaced the Ukrainian with a Russian flag. Pavel Gubarev is proclaimed 'People's Governor.'
9, 13–14 March	Violence was unleashed against pro-Ukrainian rallies in Donetsk and Luhansk and an attack was launched on the Ukrainian nationalist HQ in Kharkiv which led to the deaths of two Russian nationalists.

7–9 April	Pro-Russian forces occupy state administration buildings in Donetsk, Luhansk and Kharkiv. The DNR is proclaimed. In Kharkiv, Russian citizens and pro-Russian activists are forcibly removed by Ministry of Interior 'Jaguar' *spetsnaz* who made 64 arrests.
12 April	GRU officer Igor ('Strelkov') Girkin and 50 Russian *spetsnaz* intervened into mainland Ukraine from Crimea and travel to Donetsk to lead pro-Russian forces.
16 April	Ukraine launches the Anti-Terrorist Operation (ATO).
17 April	Putin first talks of southeastern Ukraine as 'New Russia' openly questioning Ukraine's territorial integrity.
27 April	Luhansk People's Republic (LNR) is proclaimed.
12 May	DNR and LNR hold referenda and declare independence from Ukraine.

Russian Intelligence

Russian intelligence actively financed, trained, and cooperated with anti-Maidan activists in the decade before and during the Euromaidan (see The Battle for Ukraine 2014). In 2009, Russian diplomats in Odesa and Crimea were expelled for supporting separatists. Russian volunteers who were trained in Russian camps joined the conflict. There is a mass of evidence, collected by the Security Service of Ukraine, that Russian intelligence officers undertook training and coordination with, and provided leadership to separatist forces throughout 2014.

Intercepted telephone conversations of FSB intelligence officer Colonel Igor Egorov ('Elbrus') (2020), who was first deputy commander of the 'New Russia' army, provide evidence that he coordinated the so-called DNR Ministry of Defence (Bellingcat 2020a). Egorov (2020) is a senior officer from the FSB elite *spetsnaz* unit, which is a successor to the KGB's V Department's elite *Vympel spetsnaz* unit. Bellingcat's (2020b, 2000c) research and captured documents released by the Security Service of Ukraine show the close ties between Surkov, Yevgeny Prigozhin, Wagner Group mercenaries, the Moscow headquarters of GRU, and FSB and Russian intelligence on the ground in Ukraine, who coordinated and supplied military equipment to Russian proxies in the Donbas in 2014.

The 12 April 2014 intervention of mainland Ukraine by GRU officer Girkin and 50 Russian *spetsnaz* soldiers is evidence of Russian military boots on the ground at the beginning of the conflict. A day after his intervention in mainland Ukraine, the Security Service of Ukraine published intercepted telephone calls between Girkin (2014) and his handlers in Moscow, including to and from his Russian telephone number. His invasion was a 'key escalatory move' (Sambanis, Skaperdas and Wohlforth 2017, 32). As Girkin had participated in

Russia's annexation of Crimea and intervened in mainland Ukraine from Russian-occupied Crimea, he undoubtedly 'coordinated his actions with Moscow, above all with Glazyev' (Zygar 2016, 285). Girkin 'acted in accordance with a directive from Moscow' (Kuromiya 2019, 257; Sokolov, 2019). Girkin admitted that he had coordinated his action with Crimean Prime Minister Aksyonov. Girkin's *spetsnaz* soldiers were augmented the following month by Chechen mercenaries loyal to President Ramzan Kadyrov, who fought in the Donbas between May–July 2014 (Vatchagaev 2015).

Mercenaries in the Service of Russian Nationalism (Imperialism)

'Political tourists' were bussed into Kharkiv and other Ukrainian cities from Russia or into Odesa from the Russian-occupied Trans-Dniestr region of Moldova to act as fake Ukrainian protestors (Shandra and Seely 2019). It is not coincidental that rallies simultaneously began on 1 March 2014 in 11 southeastern Ukrainian cities on the same day that Putin received authorisation from the Federation Council to intervene militarily in Ukraine. Kudelia's (2014) argument that the violent seizure of official buildings 'happened sporadically and in a decentralized manner' is simply naïve and unbelievable. It is improbable that rallies would have broken out coincidentally on the same day in 11 locations when only 11.7% of the population in southeastern Ukraine supported the seizure of buildings and a very high 76.8% opposed this action. In Donetsk and Luhansk, where there was the highest support in the eight *oblasts* of southeastern Ukraine, only 18.1 and 24.4% of people, respectively, supported the seizure of buildings, while a much higher 53.2 and 58.3% opposed such action (The Views and Opinions of South-Eastern Regions Residents of Ukraine).

Yevhen Zakharov, head of the Kharkiv Human Rights Protection Group, believes that 'these pan-Ukrainian rallies were carefully co-ordinated' (Harding 2014). Pro-Russian activists admitted that, before they stormed the State Administration in Kharkiv, they 'met with Russian intelligence agents who were working in the east' and who were from 'the Russian military and intelligence agencies' (Jones 2014). In Kharkiv, '20 to 40 buses' from the nearby Russian city of Belgorod arrived in the centre' (Harding 2014). Kharkiv journalist Andriy Borodavka estimated that 'around 200' Russian citizens had been bused from Russia to Kharkiv. 'They delivered hardcore Kremlin activists, he said, some dressed in military-style fatigues. They waved Russian flags and cried: 'Russia, Russia' (Harding 2014). 'Together with local thugs, the "tourists" stormed the main administrative building, at the opposite end of the square, and evicted the Ukrainian nationalists who had been occupying it, brutally beating several of them,' Luke Harding (2014) reported from Kharkiv. A clash outside the Kharkiv headquarters of the Ukrainian nationalist organisation Patriots of Ukraine led to two attackers from the pro-Russian *Oplot* (Bulwark)[3] being shot and killed (Harding 2014).

Oplot grouped together athletic members of a Kharkiv sports club who had acted as Ministry of Interior vigilantes during the Euromaidan and were most likely involved in some of the killings of protestors.[4] The *Oplot* members interviewed by the PBS (Public Broadcasting Service) for its documentary on Kharkiv had admitted to being financed and trained by Russian intelligence to attack Euromaidan supporters (Jones 2014). After the failure of the Kharkiv People Republic, *Oplot* members fled to the DNR and joined Russian proxy forces. At the same time, as part of a Russian-sponsored terrorist campaign throughout Ukraine, *Oplot* were behind terrorist attacks in Kharkiv; one such attack in February 2015 killed four people (see Kuzio 2015b, 2015c).

Moscow student blogger Arkady Khudyakov replaced the Ukrainian flag on the roof of the Kharkiv State Administration building with a Russian flag. He posted video and photos of his exploits on the social network site LiveJournal' (Harding 2014). It cannot be a coincidence that a Russian flag was also raised by Russian citizen Mikhail Chuprikov on Donetsk city hall on the same day as in Kharkiv (Roth 2014). Rallies, beatings, and seizures of state buildings were 'secretly organized, financially backed, and ideologically underpinned by the Russian leadership' (Gomza and Zajaczkowski 2019).

The Glazyev tapes 'vividly illustrate Moscow's covert support for the still unarmed anti-government protests in Ukraine several weeks before the actual war started' (Umland 2016). Russia intervened to organise, support, and enlarge pro-Russian rallies 'immediately after the victory of the Maidan revolution in early 2014' (Umland 2016). Russia 'actively fanned the flames of pre-existing ethnic, cultural and political tensions in the region' (Umland 2016).

Russian 'political tourists' and neo-Nazis, with the assistance of Russian intelligence, tipped peaceful anti-Kyiv protests into violence and then armed insurgencies. Russia's 'full spectrum conflict' (Jonsson and Seely 2015) had the effect of 'emboldening insurgents in eastern Ukraine to ramp up demands and take armed actions' (Sambanis, Skaperdas and Wohlforth 2017, 30). The escalation of protests into a full-blown war would have been unlikely without 'increased expectations of intervention' (Sambanis, Skaperdas and Wohlforth 2017, 30). Expectations of Russian military invasion in 'New Russia' following

---

[3] On *Oplot* see https://news.24tv.ua/ru/oplot_chto_jeto_harkov_chto_stoit_znat_ob_organizacii_oplot_n1224554

[4] https://news.24tv.ua/ru/ford-motor-company-pochemu-soznatelno-prodavali-novosti-v-mire_n1435549

that in Crimea influenced both sides to persevere throughout 2014 (Sambanis, Skaperdas and Wohlforth 2017, 31). The arrival of Russian neo-Nazis in the Donbas led to violent attacks against pro-Ukrainian protestors, confirming that external intervention was a central factor in the transition from peaceful protests to violent conflict. On 5 March 2014, Russian neo-Nazi extremists violently attacked pro-Ukrainian protestors in Donetsk on the same day that *Rossija-1* TV channel aired inflammatory reports of US mercenaries arriving in the Donbas with *Pravyy Sektor* Ukrainian nationalists to ethnically cleanse Russians and Russian speakers (Hajduk and Stepniewski 2016, 45).

It would be truly incredulous to believe that Russian intelligence was not involved in coordinating pro-Russian 'uprisings' in southeastern Ukraine, or that they were not behind Chuprikov in Donetsk and Khudyakov in Kharkiv. 'I don't believe that in one day across the entire east and south of Ukraine, the same protest breaks out,' former head of the politics division in Donetsk city council Viktor Nikolaenko said (Ioffe 2014). 'Then all of a sudden, an armed resistance rises. I've been in politics too long to believe in such a coincidence. The synchronization is obvious,' Nikolaenko added (Ioffe 2014). That most of the violent protestors were actually Russian 'tourists' proved to be comical in Kharkiv, where they took control of the Opera House mistakenly believing the building to be the city hall.

Putin, Suslov, Medvedchuk, and Glazyev aimed to transform these protests into pro-Russian uprisings, which would take control of *oblast* and city councils and state administrations. These councils would vote to refuse to recognise the Euromaidan revolutionary government in Kyiv as Ukraine's legitimate authorities (on Kharkiv see Harding 2014), which would be followed by the establishment of 'people's republics.' These so-called 'people's republics' would invite Russian forces to intervene to 'protect' ethnic Russians and Russian speakers from 'Ukrainian nationalists.'

Russia's strategy was to have the fig leaf of 'Ukrainians' supporting these goals, and then 'Moscow would support them' (Zygar 2016, 284) in 'a convincing picture of genuine local and even internal support for Russian ideas in Ukraine' (Shandra and Seely 2019, 22). In reality, these actions were 'micromanaged by Kremlin officials' (Shandra and Seely 2019, 38). The low number of participants in pro-Russian rallies in 'New Russia' and weak support for pro-Russian goals found in opinion polls point to the artificiality of these pro-Russian 'uprisings' and why they failed (Kuzio 2019a).

These different aspects of Russia's 'full spectrum conflict' (Jonsson and Seely 2015) are ignored by many scholars writing about 2014 in Ukraine (Cohen 2019). Kudelia (2017, 214) incredulously writes, 'Without question Russia exploited these events, but it did not define them.' This is not true; different aspects of Russian 'full spectrum conflict' (Jonsson and Seely 2015) had the goal of 'converting a marginal movement into a mass phenomenon' (Wilson 2015, 645). Leaks of Surkov's emails (Shandra and Seely 2019), Glazyev's telephone conversations (Umland 2016), and a February 2014 Russian strategy document (Russian 'road map' for annexing eastern Ukraine) provide abundant evidence of Russian intervention during the Euromaidan and in spring 2014.

Putin's Signalling and Nationalist (Imperialist) Coalitions

Erin K. Jenne (2007) believes that external lobbying and external patrons are key factors in determining the mobilisation of minorities because they signal an intention to intervene, which radicalises demands towards the central government. Actual or expected intervention shapes bargaining calculations (Sambanis, Skaperdas and Wohlforth 2017, 27). Pro-Russian forces and Russian nationalists understood Putin's signalling as Russia's intention to either annex 'New Russia' in the same way as it had Crimea or to detach the region and create a semi-independent state aligned with Russia in the Eurasian Economic Union.

In February–April 2014, the presence of Russian nationalists (imperialists), activities of Russian intelligence operatives, and intervention into mainland Ukraine by Girkin's Russian *spetsnaz* (chronicled in Table 5.2) at the same time as Russia annexed Crimea heightened fears among Ukrainian policymakers that Russia was seeking to dismember Ukraine. This is clearly evident in the minutes of the emergency meeting of Ukraine's National Security and Defence Council (RNBO) held on 28 February 2014 (National Security and Defence Council 2016). Melnyk (2020, 18) believes that the annexation of Crimea and destabilisation of southeastern Ukraine should be treated together.

Foreign powers have intervened in the majority of civil wars and, the longer the civil war continues, the more likely it is that there will be outside intervention. Sambanis (2002, 235) writes that 'expected intervention has a robustly positive and highly significant association with civil war.' Foreign powers should be reasonably confident of success; the projected time horizon of the intervention is short and domestic opposition is minimal. These three factors were only partly present in Ukraine in 2014 (Sambanis 2002).

In February 2014, Putin took a gamble when Russian forces invaded Crimea, but they met no resistance; large-scale infiltration of Ukrainian security forces by Russian intelligence led them to calculate that Ukrainian resistance would be minimal. Russia's invasion of Crimea 'radically transformed expectations of intervention in other Ukrainian regions, notably Donbas' (Sambanis, Skaperdas and Wohlforth 2017, 27). In Kyiv and the Donbas, Russia's occupation of Crimea was viewed as a blueprint by pro-Russian groups, which would be followed by Russia further detaching territories from southeastern Ukraine (Osipan 2015, 138).

It is highly improbable that Russia spontaneously launched a military operation on 27 February 2014, only five days after Yanukovych fled from Kyiv. D'Anieri (2019, 230) writes, 'At a minimum, Russia had made plans for the military seizure of Crimea well in advance.' Plans for Crimea were prepared as a contingency during earlier crises in Russian-Ukrainian relations in 2004, between 2008–2009, and after Putin's 2012 re-election. Sanshiro Hosaka (2018, 363) rules out a last-minute improvisation and views Russia's invasion of Crimea as a 'well-considered and proactive move' to maintain Ukraine within Russia's orbit.

Russia's invasion and annexation of Crimea strongly influenced perceptions of Russian policies towards mainland Ukraine among Ukrainian policymakers. The lack of Ukrainian resistance in Crimea 'incentivized the Kremlin to press for continuing gains' (Bowen 2019, 334). Russia's annexation of Crimea led to a belief that 'the Kremlin would unleash in the Donbas a similar operation to that in Crimea' which, in turn, influenced the decisions and expectations of Kyiv and pro-Russian forces (Gilley 2019, 323).[5] Hosaka (2018, 324–325) believes that Crimea's annexation was part of Russia's 'strategic goal' of 'keeping Ukraine in Russia's orbit.'

Soviet and Russian nationalist (imperialist) nostalgia 'was already present in the 'red brown' (communist-fascist) coalition of 1993' (D'Anieri 2019, 256), which came to the fore in the 'Russian spring' (see Melnyk 2020, 22). In spring 2014, Putin's rhetoric signalled support for the goals of the 'brown' (fascist), 'white' (monarchist and Orthodox fundamentalist), and 'red' (Communist) Russian nationalist (imperialist) coalition (Laruelle 2016a). The ranks of Putin's senior advisers on Ukraine (Surkov 2019, Glazyev 2020) and influential Russians (Dugin 2014) are dominated by Russian nationalists (imperialists) and anti-Semites (see Likhachev 2016; Laruelle 2016a; Shekhovtsov 2017). Putin's rhetoric emboldened Russian nationalists (imperialists) to believe that Russian authorities were no longer abiding by treaties they had signed with Ukraine, and they therefore viewed Ukraine as a target for dismemberment or re-configuration into a loose confederation aligned with Russia in the Eurasian Economic Union (Melnyk 2020, 28–29).

---

[5] Igor Girkin interviewed by *Nezavisimoye Voyennoye Obozreniye*, 23 August 2019. http://nvo.ng.ru/

Russian Information Warfare

Most western scholars ignore Putin's obsession with Ukraine and Ukrainophobia, which permeates Russia's information warfare and was analysed in chapter 4. Matveeva (2018) devotes little space to Russia's massive information war against Ukraine, which played a central role in the 2014 crisis; while not denying the power of the Russian media at the same time Matveeva (2018) barely mentions it. It is untrue that Russia had 'few soft power instruments at its disposal' prior to and in 2014 (Matveeva 2018, 273).

Russian information warfare and disinformation were central components of its 'full spectrum conflict' towards Ukraine. Talking of Kharkiv, Borodavka admitted, 'Yes, the FSB plays a role in supporting pro-Russian groups. But the most important vector is the Russian media' (Harding 2014) in mobilising violent conflict and political instability. The Russian media 'have effectively been on a war footing since the spring of 2014' (Fedor 2015, 1). Hysteria, hatred, aggression, and xenophobia have 'reached alarmingly high levels,' and political murders and violence have 'become unremarkable' (Fedor 2015, 1, 5). Russia's information warfare was that of the 'language of hate' from its inception (Bonch-Osmolovskaya 2015, 182), creating a climate favourable to local support for military and political operations in Crimea and Donbas (Hajduk and Stepniewski 2016, 46–47). Protestors were radicalised by Russian propaganda and information warfare and Russian hybrid warfare transformed protestors into an armed insurgency (Wilson 2015).

An information campaign of this nature and intensity would be viewed by every country it would be directed against as an act of aggression by a foreign power. NATO's understanding of the growing importance of Russian cyber warfare, information warfare, and disinformation led to the opening of a NATO Strategic Communications Centre of Excellence in Riga, a Cooperative Cyber Defence Centre of Excellence in Tallinn, and a Communications and Information Agency in The Hague. To counter Russian disinformation, the EU created the East StratCom Task Force (which publishes the excellent weekly *Disinformation Review*), and the US government established a Global Engagement Centre.[6]

Russia as a Great Power and Ukraine's 'Limited Sovereignty'

Sakwa (2017a, 106, 131) claims that Russia is not a 'genuine revisionist power' because it aims to 'ensure the universal and consistent application of

---

[6] https://www.stratcomcoe.org/; https://ccdcoe.org/; https://www.ncia.nato.int/; https://euvsdisinfo.eu/; https://www.state.gov/bureaus-offices/under-secretary-for-public-diplomacy-and-public-affairs/global-engagement-center/

existing norms.' Russia has pushed back since February 2007, when Putin gave a speech to the Munich Security Conference, after which 'the stage was set for confrontation' and Russia was not 'seeking to destroy the sovereignty of its neighbors' (Sakwa 2017, 27, 35). One can only read this with incredulity following Russia's 2008 recognition of the independence of the Georgian regions of Abkhazia and South Ossetia and annexation of Crimea. Ukrainian opinion polls show that nearly three-quarters (71%) of Ukrainians believe that Russia is seeking to destroy Ukrainian sovereignty (Perspektyvy Ukrayinsko-Rosiyskykh Vidnosyn 2015, 61).

Sakwa (2017a, 263) denies that Russia never sought 'a return to spheres of influence,' which is untrue because Russia believes it can be a great power only by controlling and the West recognising its exclusive sphere of influence in Eurasia. Russia has always sought US and international recognition of Eurasia as its exclusive sphere of influence. Mikhail Suslov (2018, 4) writes that 'the idea of a sphere of influence' is hardwired into the 'Russian World' imagery. The Russian World demands an exclusive Russian sphere of influence over the three eastern Slavs based on 'common' culture, values, language, and religion. The 'Russian' presence abroad is where Russia's sphere of influence extends, especially in Ukraine and Belarus, which are viewed as branches of the 'Russian nation.' 'The Russian World is where Russians are' (Suslov 2018) and, if Ukrainians and Russians are 'one people,' then Ukraine is an inalienable part of the Russian World.

Similarly, Laruelle (2015, 96) believes that there is no nationalism in Russian foreign policy and that Putin 'does not advance a nationalist agenda.' At the same time, Laruelle (2015) confusingly writes that nationalism (in this book, it is defined as imperialism) *does* shape Russian foreign policy on identity questions, such as 'Russians' as a divided nation, and in other areas. A rehabilitation of Tsarist Russian and White *émigré* views of Ukraine and Ukrainians is evidence of a nationalistic (imperialistic) Russian foreign policy. Beyond western political scientists working on Russia, there are few government policymakers, think tank experts, or journalists who would believe that Russian foreign policy is not nationalist.

W. Wayne Merry (2016) views Putin's war against Ukraine as a clash of sovereignties because Russia is at odds with the UN and international law in not viewing Ukraine and most former Soviet states as 'sovereign' entities. Claiming the status of first among equals for itself and seeking a nationalist (imperialist) primacy of its own interests, Russia is in 'pursuit of suzerainty,' whereby a great power exercises control over its neighbours' external relations while giving internal autonomy to a satrap, such as Lukashenka. The Lukyanov Doctrine, now confined to the territory of the former USSR, is a 'conceptual successor' to the Brezhnev Doctrine, which the USSR used to justify invasions of eastern European communist states (Gretskiy 2020, 21). Since 1991, Russia has pursued a Lukyanov Doctrine by undermining the territorial integrity of former Soviet republics, aggravating their security threats, promoting separatism, using economic blackmail, and training and equipping non-state actors (such as the Donetsk Republic Party) for military purposes (Gretskiy 2020, 7).

The Lukyanov Doctrine provided the ideological underpinnings for Russia's belief in spring 2014 that it had a right to intervene in what it viewed as a disintegrating and chaotic Ukrainian state, which it had always believed was 'failed,' 'artificial,' and 'Russian.' After Yanukovych fled from Kyiv, 'The general feeling (in Moscow) was that Ukraine had ceased to exist as a state' (Zygar 2016, 283). This factor should be understood within the broader context of Russia viewing Ukraine as an artificial state together with Russia's view of its Eurasian neighbours possessing limited sovereignty.

Editor of *Russia in Global Affairs*, Fyodr Lukyanov, does not deny that Russia intervened in spring 2014, saying, 'It would be strange if it weren't there' (Ioffe 2014). Russian had two goals. The first goal was to show to the international community that Ukraine could not control all of its territory, and the second goal was to prevent the emergence of an 'anti-Russian' Ukraine (Ioffe 2014).

Military Invasion

Jonsson and Seely (2015) define 'full spectrum conflict' as combining military, informational, economic, energy, and political components. Russian aggression towards Ukraine included 'a mixture of strategic 21st century tactics, *maskirovka* [Russian military deception], and hybrid warfare' (Bodie 2017, 306). Military (kinetic violence) and non-military components came under one command. Aiming to avoid a large-scale war, 'full spectrum conflict' fell back on the use of the Russian military if its proxy forces were on the verge of defeat, as in August 2014 when Russia invaded Ukraine.

Military forms of hybrid warfare only work when there is popular support among the local population, which clearly did not exist in six of the eight *oblasts* of southeastern Ukraine; even in the Donbas, the population was divided. A full-scale Russian invasion would have 'destroyed the fiction that Russia was not involved' (D'Anieri 2019, 245) and would have had two strategic consequences. The first consequence would have been that the Russian public would have found out they are at war with Ukraine. Until now, Russians, with limited access to independent sources of information, have believed the myth of Russia's non-involvement in the 'civil war' in Ukraine. It is highly improbable that Russian information warfare could spin Russian forces as openly fighting a war against Ukrainians. The second consequence is that a Russian invasion would have led to a full-blown crisis with the West, NATO placed on high alert, and the introduction of a far more severe sanctions regime, similar to that pursued against Iran.

In a detailed study of Russian control over the parts of Donbas it has occupied, Donald N. Jensen (2017) brushes this aside as an outcome resulting from 'civil war' or 'popular uprising,' and believes that the conflict was manufactured by Russia to prevent Ukraine's integration into the West. Jensen (2017) documents how Donbas proxies were controlled by Russia from its inception with all major military decisions made in Moscow. Evidence of Russia's invasion is available from an array of official sources, think tanks, and academic studies, including within Ukraine. Ukrainian views of a Russian-Ukrainian War, as opposed to a 'civil war,' are echoed by international organisations, European and North American journalists, and governments (Harding 2016, 304–305). On a weekly basis, the US Mission to the OSCE refutes Russia's claims of a 'civil war' taking place in Ukraine: 'We all know the truth – the brutal war in Donbas is fomented and perpetuated by Russia' (Ongoing Violations of International Law and Defiance of OSCE Principles and Commitments by the Russian Federation in Ukraine 2018). US Ambassador Kurt Volker, former Special Representative for Ukraine Negotiations, has said, 'Russia consistently blocks expansion of OSCE border mission and its forces prevent SMM from reliably monitoring the border as it sends troops, arms, and supplies into Ukraine; all while claiming it's an "internal" conflict and spouting disingenuous arguments about Minsk agreements.'[7]

Russia supplies training, leadership, fuel, ammunition, military technology, and intelligence, and there is a presence of Russian military, intelligence, mercenaries who fought in frozen conflicts in Eurasia, members of organised crime, and nationalist extremists. Control is exercised through Kremlin 'curators,' such as Suslov in 2014–2020. Military 'advisers' and Russian intelligence coordinate their policies through the Centre for the Management of Reconstruction. The Inter-Ministerial Commission for the Provision of Humanitarian Aid for the Affected Areas in the Southeast of the Regions of Donetsk and Luhansk acts as Russia's shadow government.

Andrew S. Bowen (2019, 325) believes that a Russian strategy only became clear in late 2014. Nevertheless, large military exercises on the border, and training and coordination of non-state actors were used by Russia from the inception of the crisis, and 'Russia's supporting hand was evident from the

---

[7] https://twitter.com/specrepukraine/status/1028739476074450945?s=12

beginning' (Bowen 2019, 325). From the beginning of the crisis, 'Russian troops, intelligence officers, and political advisers were alleged to be either supporting or directly controlling the separatists' (Bowen 2019, 331). From May 2014, there is little doubt, as noted by the UNHCHR during the period between 2 April-6 May 2014, that '[t]hose found to be arming and inciting armed groups and transforming them into paramilitary forces must be held accountable under national and international law' (Report on the human rights situation in Ukraine 2014).

From May 2014, Russia has provided surface-to-air missiles, which were used to shoot down five Ukrainian helicopters, 2 fighter jets, an AN-30 surveillance plane, and Ilyushin IL-76 over the course of two months. Russian artillery fired a huge number of shells into Ukraine over July and August 2014. Because of a high number of casualties among Russian proxies and Russian forces from Ukrainian air power, Russia sought to change the military balance on the battlefield by suppling the sophisticated surface-to-air BUK missile system that shot down MH17.

Conclusion

Five factors explain Russia's actions in 2014. The first factor emerged in the decade prior to the 2014 crisis with the rehabilitation of Tsarist Russian and White émigré nationalist (imperialist) views of Ukraine and Ukrainians, and Putin's view of himself as the 'gatherer of Russian lands.' The second and third factors are inter-connected. Putin's personal anger at being humiliated for a second time by a western-backed Ukrainian revolution undermined his 'gathering of Russian lands' that would have turned Ukraine away from the EU and toward the Russian World and Eurasian Economic Union. The fourth factor is Russia's long-standing territorial claims against Crimea going back to the early 1990s. The final factor is the Lukyanov Doctrine's view of Ukraine as possessing limited sovereignty, which is a product of both the Soviet-era Brezhnev Doctrine and the first point; namely, Ukraine being perceived as an artificial state.

Russia's 'full spectrum conflict' began following the Orange Revolution and continued through to 2013. Between 2012–2013, Russia launched a massive trade, intelligence, cyber, and informational operation to pressure Ukrainian leaders to drop EU integration. In the decade prior and in 2014, pro-Russian extremists were given paramilitary training, and Russian intelligence infiltrated Ukrainian security forces, especially in Crimea. With a high level of infiltration, it is unsurprising that Russian intelligence was active on the ground in Ukraine between 2013–2014 during the Euromaidan and after Yanukovych fled Kyiv. Russian *spetsnaz* soldiers intervened in mainland Ukraine from occupied Crimea and, with the assistance of Russian nationalists (imperialists) and political tourists trained in Russia and bussed into Ukraine, transformed protestors into armed insurgents. Pro-Russian Chechen proxies were sent by Kadyrov. Russian information warfare was placed on a war footing. Military equipment was supplied throughout 2014, from June of that year, artillery attacks were taking place from Russia into Ukraine, and Russia invaded Ukraine on Ukrainian Independence Day (24 August). Taken together, these different aspects of Russian 'full spectrum conflict' constituted Russian intervention from the first day of the 2014 crisis. Western scholars should place greater trust in the Ukrainian public, which has never seen evidence of a 'civil war' in Ukraine.

The impact of the full range of Russian 'full spectrum conflict' was the opposite to that which Putin sought, and three areas of which are analysed in the concluding chapter. Putin's policies towards Ukraine undermined a pro-Russian 'east' and the Soviet concept of Russian-Ukrainian 'brotherly' peoples, thereby increasing Ukrainian civic national integration and severely curtailing Russian soft power in Ukraine. Putin's inability to comprehend his mistakes in these three areas and his longevity in power for another sixteen years make the chances for peace low.

6

Conclusion: Impact of War and Prospects for Peace

Since 1991, there has been an in-built tension in Russian-Ukrainian relations, because 'the more Ukraine asserted its sovereignty, the more Russia questioned it, and vice versa' (D'Anieri 2019, 63). The 2014 crisis cannot be understood without 'looking at its long-term sources' because to do so would be to tackle them 'out of context and therefore to misinterpret them' (D'Anieri 2019, 253). The sources of the 2014 crisis lie in Russia's inability to recognise Ukraine and Ukrainians, which hark back to the early 1990s. The 2014 Russian-Ukrainian crisis is not fundamentally different from the many disagreements the two sides have had since December 1991 (D'Anieri 2019, 265–266).

This chapter is divided into two sections. The first section analyses the impact of Russian annexation and military aggression on the disintegration of Ukraine's 'east,' which comprised eight southeastern Ukrainian *oblasts* prior to 2014; the replacing of the Soviet concept of Russians and Ukrainians as close, but different 'brothers' with the Tsarist Russian and White *émigré* denial of Ukraine and Ukrainians, which particularly impacted upon Russian-speaking eastern Ukrainians; and the collapse in Russian soft power in Ukraine. The second section discusses the prospects for a peaceful settlement of the Russian-Ukrainian War. Former President Poroshenko was never the obstacle to peace, and President Zelenskyy will not become the harbinger of peace because the roots of the Russian-Ukrainian War do not lie in the choice of Ukrainian president, but rather in Russian nationalist (imperialist) attitudes towards Ukraine and Ukrainians, which will remain as long as Putin is *de facto* president for life.

Impact of the War

Pro-Russian Ukrainian 'East' is No More

Russian-speaking southeastern Ukrainians have undertaken the majority of the fighting against Russian and Russian proxy forces, and they account for the highest rate of casualties of Ukrainian security forces.[1] Over two million IDPs and refugees are Russian speakers from the Donbas. Russia is not fighting 'western Ukrainian nationalists,' but is primarily killing, wounding, and harming Russian-speaking Ukrainians. Eastern Ukraine has the highest proportion of military veterans and the highest rate of casualties among Ukrainian security forces (see 6.2 map).

6.1. Photographs in Kyiv and Dnipropetrovsk *Oblast* of Ukrainian Security Forces Killed in the Russian-Ukrainian War.
Source: Author's photographs.

Note: Top photograph: long wall alongside Kyiv's Mykhayivskyy Zolotoverkhnyy Monastyr (St. Michael's Golden-Domed Monastery) with photographs of Ukrainian security forces killed in the Russian-Ukrainian war; bottom left photograph: one section of the large military cemetery in the city of Dnipro of Ukrainian security forces killed in the Russian-Ukrainian war; bottom right photograph: one of the many glass obelisks in the Alley Heroyiv (Alley of Heroes) in the centre of the city of Dnipro dedicated to the Nebesna Sotnya (Heavenly Hundred) killed during the Euromaidan Revolution and Ukrainian security forces killed in the Russian-Ukrainian war.

---

[1]   http://memorybook.org.ua/indexfile/statbirth.htm

Russian information warfare and *Putinversteher* scholars (Sakwa 2015, 2017; Cohen 2019) depict volunteer battalions as dominated by extreme right ideologies and western Ukrainians; in fact, they were largely filled by Russian speakers and national minorities (Aliyev 2020). Huseyn Aliyev (202) writes that ethnic nationalism was 'one of the least probable causes of wartime mobilization.' Azov and *Pravyy Sektor* battalions, the two battalions demonised for their 'nationalist' ideologies most often, included Georgians, Jews, Russians, Tatars, and Armenians.

6.2. Map of Ukrainian Security Forces Killed in the Russian-Ukrainian War by *Oblast*
Source: http://memorybook.org.ua/indexfile/statbirth.htm. Used with permission.

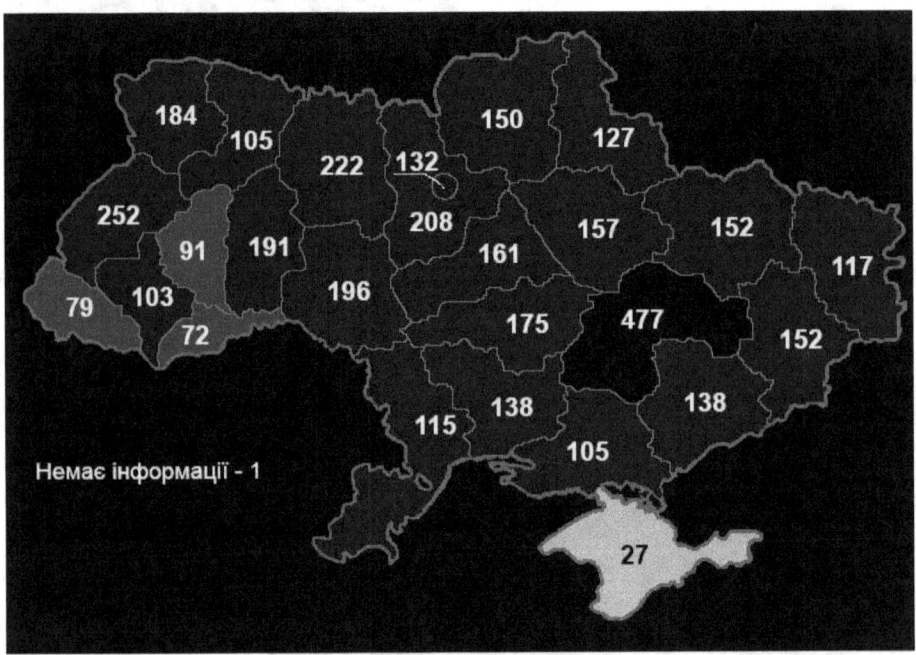

Note: Total of 4,270 known casualties as of 1 March 2020. Note, the highest number of 477 casualties is in Dnipropetrovsk oblast.

Six years of Russian military aggression have changed Ukraine, Ukrainian views of Russia, and Ukrainian-Russian relations. Russia's annexation of Crimea and on-going military aggression in eastern Ukraine have two long-lasting consequences for scholarly research on Ukraine. The first consequence is the disappearance of a pro-Russian 'east,' and the second is the collapse in Russian soft power. Since 2013, Russian policies have been counter-productive and have deepened Ukraine's break with Russia.

Tatyana Zhurzhenko (2015, 52) writes that 2014 represented a 'new rupture in contemporary history, a point of crystallization for identities, discourses, and narratives for decades to come.' Ukraine's fault line is no longer east versus west, but Ukraine versus the Donbas. Medical volunteer Natalya Zubchenko, based in the city of Dnipro, said, 'We don't think of ourselves as east or west. We're central' (Sindelar 2015). The fracturing of Ukraine's 'east' and its reduction to two Donbas *oblasts* represent ground-breaking changes in Ukrainian identity and the country's regional configuration (Zhurzhenko 2015; Kuzyk 2018; Kulyk 2016, 2018, 2019).

The collapse in pro-Russian sentiments and growth in Ukrainian patriotism in Dnipropetrovsk created a 'domino effect,' which spread to neighbouring regions because of the *oblast*'s industrial power and size. Opinion polls show that there is now a belt of four *oblasts* – Dnipropetrovsk, Zaporizhzhya, Kherson, and Mykolayiv – within the former eight pro-Russian *oblasts* of southeastern Ukraine that no longer hold pro-Russian views or pro-Russian foreign policy orientations. Changes in Kharkiv and Odesa were not as dramatic, but even there, pro-Russian sentiment has declined. Ukrainian identity is also growing in Ukrainian-controlled Donbas (Sasse and Lackner 2018; Haran, Yakovlyev and Zolkina 2018).

Russian speakers in Ukraine are loyal to a multi-ethnic country where the Russian and Ukrainian languages are both spoken *and* disloyal to the Russian World. This is reflected in three-quarters of Ukrainians describing the conflict as a Russian-Ukrainian War (Poshuky Shlyakhiv Vidnovlennya Suverenitetu Ukrayiny Nad Okupovanym Donbasom: Stan Hromadskoyii Dumky Naperedodni Prezydentskykh Vyboriv 2019). Russia's invasion led Russian-speaking Ukrainian patriots to view DNR and LNR leaders as Russian puppets; that is, Russian proxies (Aliyev 2019).

Until 2014, centrist Ukrainian and Russian speakers were not anti-Russian and adhered to the Soviet concept of Ukrainians and Russians being closely related, but different 'brothers.' They would never accept the Tsarist Russian and White *émigré* view of Ukrainians as one of three branches of the 'All-Russian People' and the non-existence of a Ukrainian state.

Putinversteher scholars believe that peace can be achieved in the Donbas by Ukraine embracing its 'bicultural' Ukrainian-Russian identity (Petro 2015, 33). Hahn (2018, 176) agrees with Russian leaders that left- and right-bank Ukrainians and Russians are a 'single nation,' 'having common historical roots and common fates, a common religion, a common faith, and a very similar culture, languages, traditions and mentality.' The failure of Putin's 'New Russia' project shows that Ukraine never had a 'bi-cultural' identity, and adopting Petro's (2015) proposals would have been impossible prior to 2014 and, after six years of war and bloodshed, his proposal is illusory.

Low levels of Ukrainian allegiance to the Russian World were already evident before the 2014 crisis (Wawrzonek 2014) and in 2014. A majority of Ukrainians in southeastern Ukraine did not believe that they were part of the Russian World. Of Ukraine's eight southeastern *oblasts*, the Russian World was thoroughly unpopular in Dnipropetrovsk, Zaporizhzhya, Kherson, and Mykolayiv, had only slightly higher support in Kharkiv and Odesa, and had the highest support in the Donbas. Overall, only 27.4% in southeastern Ukraine felt that they belonged to the Russian World (O'Loughlin, Toal and Kolosov 2016, 760). Russian military aggression 'killed any appeal' for the Russian World in Ukraine (Plokhy 2017, 345).

In spring 2014, Russia's strategy to organise pro-Russian rallies that would capture official buildings, declare non-recognition of the Euromaidan government's authority, and establish 'people's republics,' which would seek protection through Russian military invasion, had low levels of support throughout southeastern Ukraine (The Views and Opinions of South-Eastern Regions Residents of Ukraine 2014). If Russia had invaded eastern Ukraine to 'protect' Russian speakers, only 7% in southeastern Ukraine would have greeted these Russian troops (The Views and Opinions of South-Eastern Regions Residents of Ukraine 2014).

Russians and Ukrainian are No Longer 'Brothers

The 1863 thesis of *tryedynstva russkoho naroda* was revived in a refashioned form after 1934, when Ukrainians and Russians were presented as different, but at the same time close 'brotherly peoples' whose fate was forever bound together. During Putin's presidency, Russian discourse and policies towards Ukraine stagnated from this Soviet 'brotherly peoples' concept to the Tsarist Russian and White *émigré* concept of *tryedynstva russkoho naroda*, which considers Ukraine an artificial state, Ukrainians and Russians as 'one people,' and Ukraine as including 'Russian lands' that were wrongly allocated by the Soviet regime. Such views have always had very limited support in Ukraine outside of Crimea and the Donbas.

It is also important to remember that sharp breaks in 1991 and 2014 followed changes that had taken place earlier. In 1991, the disintegration of the USSR and Ukrainian independence came after six years of civil strife, nationalist mobilisation, splits in the Soviet Communist Party of Ukraine, and opposition success in Soviet Ukrainian and local elections. The 2014 crisis similarly came after a quarter of a century of nation-building in an independent

Ukrainian state, and the growing importance of national identity and memory politics following the Orange Revolution. Ukrainian nation-building progressed rapidly after 1991 and 2014, but this development had been set in motion by earlier periods of slower changes in identity.

The official Soviet historiography of Kyiv Rus as the joint inheritance of three eastern Slavs remained influential until the Orange Revolution. In a 2006 opinion poll asking which statement they supported, 43.9% of Ukrainians agreed that Ukrainian history was an integral part of eastern Slavic history, while 24.5% believed that Ukraine had exclusive title to Kyiv Rus (Rehionalni Osoblyvosti Ideyno-Politychnykh Orientatsiy Hromadyan Ukrayiny v Konteksti Vyborchoyi Kampanii 2006, 5). A decade later, this had changed, and 59% of Ukrainians believed that Kyiv Rus and other historical developments were exclusively Ukrainian, with 32% continuing to believe that Ukrainian history is part of eastern Slavic history (Konsolidatsiya Ukrayinskoho Suspilstva: Vyklyky, Mozhlyvosti, Shlyakhy 2016). Two years later, another poll found that 70% of Ukrainians believed that Ukraine is the exclusive successor to Kyiv Rus (rising from 54% in 2008), with 9% disagreeing (Dynamics of the Patriotic Moods of Ukrainians 2018). Within twelve years, the number of Ukrainians who claimed exclusive title to Kyiv Rus history had nearly tripled from 24.5% to 70%.

Five years after Russia launched its military aggression against Ukraine, only voters for the pro-Russian Opposition Platform-for Life (88%) believed that Ukraine is part of eastern Slavic history. Most of these voters live in the shrunken 'east' of Ukrainian-controlled Donbas. Most voters for the Fatherland Party (*Batkivshchina*, 62%), Zelenskyy's Servant of the People Party (*Sluhu Narodu,* 61%), Voice Party (*Holos*, 54%), and Poroshenko's European Solidarity Party (*Yevropeyska Solidarnist*, 54%) do not believe that Ukrainian history is part of eastern Slavic history (Ukrayina Pislya Vyboriv: Suspilni Ochikuvannya, Politychni Priorytety, Perspektyvy Rozvytku 2019). Could we deduce from this that Zelenskyy's voters are more 'nationalistic' than those who support Poroshenko?

The Soviet 'brotherly peoples' concept gave eastern Ukrainians and Russian speakers a Ukrainian identity and a close relationship to Russia. Russian-Ukrainian 'brotherly' relations were undermined by the rehabilitation of Tsarist Russian and White *émigré* views of Ukrainians, and by Russia's annexation of Crimea and invasion of Ukraine. This was reflected in the outrage present in Anastastiya Dmytruk's poem at the beginning of this book, which says that Russians will no longer be the brothers of 'Ukrainians.'

Vasyl Kremen and Vasyl Tkachenko (1998, 18), two political consultants in President Kuchma's team, stressed that unity in Kyiv Rus 'does not mean "eternal unity" of the three eastern Slavic peoples.' Plokhy (2017, 346) concludes, 'The imperial construct of a big Russian nation is gone, and no restoration project can bring it back to life, no matter how much blood and treasure may be expended in the effort to revive a conservative utopia.' By 2018, 66% of Ukrainians believed they had been brothers with Russians, but this was no longer the case, while another 16% believed that Russians and Ukrainians had *never* been brothers (Mishchenko 2018). This means that a high 82% of Ukrainians no longer view Russians as their 'brothers' (Kulchytskyy and Mishchenko 2018, 192).

The first nuclear bomb against Russian-Ukrainian 'brotherly' relations detonated around Crimea. Plokhy (2017, 345) writes: 'The Russian World was now associated not just with Pushkin and the Russian language but with a land grab that had cost thousands of dead and wounded and disrupted millions of lives.' Putin's (2020c) claim that Russia's annexation of Crimea was not the reason why relations with Ukraine were poor is untrue, because Crimea was one of the central components of the Soviet nationalities policy of Russian-Ukrainian 'brotherhood.' In 1954, the peninsula was transferred from the Russian SFSR to Soviet Ukraine on the symbolically important 300th anniversary of the reunion of Ukraine and Muscovy in the 1654 Treaty of Pereyaslav.

The second nuclear bomb detonated in response to Russia's invasion of Ukraine. Putin chose Ukrainian Independence Day to invade Ukraine in 2014. Russian speakers who joined Ukrainian volunteer battalions viewed Russian-controlled Donbas as run by 'gangsters' that misrepresented Ukraine (Aliyev 2019). They were especially resentful at Russia's invasion in August 2014, which for them crossed a 'red line' and turned the conflict into a Russian-Ukrainian War.

Putin offered 'guarantees' for the withdrawal of Ukrainian forces, who were surrounded by an invading Russian force. Putin lied and, near the Donetsk *oblast* town of Ilovaysk, Russian forces killed 366 Ukrainian soldiers, wounded 429, and took 300 prisoners. The General Prosecutor's Office of Ukraine described Putin's *maskirovka* as a war crime and sent the case to the Office of the Prosecutor of the International Criminal Court.[2] An additional war crime was 'Russian servicemen and the irregular illegal armed formations under their control' who murdered and wounded Ukrainian soldiers.[3] Ilovaysk buried Ukrainian-Russian 'brotherhood.'

---

[2] https://www.ukrinform.net/rubric-defense/3085849-ukraine-sends-evidence-of-russias-war-crimes-near-ilovaisk-to-icc.html
[3] https://www.gp.gov.ua/ua/news?_m=publications&_c=view&_t=rec&id=279120

15% of Ukrainian voters are veterans of the Donbas War or are family members of veterans. By the end of Putin's term in office in 2036, a far higher proportion of Ukrainian voters will be veterans of the Donbas War. Veterans are very active in civil society and party politics.[4] Streets and roads have been renamed throughout Ukraine in honour of Ukrainian soldiers who have died fighting in the Donbas. New sections of cemeteries for casualties of Ukrainian security forces who died fighting in the Russian-Ukrainian War are now commonly found alongside graves of Soviet soldiers who fought in the Great Patriotic War and in Afghanistan, and Ukrainian nationalists who fought for the Western Ukrainian People's Republic (ZUNR) and Ukrainian Insurgent Army (UPA). As of December 2019, 523 plots of Ukrainian soldiers killed in the Russian-Ukrainian can be found throughout Ukraine, containing a total 1,636 graves.[5]

Military casualties and veterans of the war increase support for radical post-Euromaidan memory politics, breaking with Soviet and Russian interpretations of Ukrainian history and Ukraine's divorce from Russia (Identychnist Hromadyan Ukrayiny v Novykh Umovakh: Stan, Tendentsii, Rehionalni Osoblyvosti 2016). In 2016, 69% of veterans, compared to 46% of Ukrainians overall, condemned the Soviet regime and backed the prohibition of communist symbols. Meanwhile, 58% of Donbas War veterans supported one of four de-communisation laws (Law No. 314-VIII) providing legal status and honouring those they consider to be their predecessors in the fight for Ukrainian independence (Identychnist Hromadyan Ukrayiny v Novykh Umovakh: Stan, Tendentsii, Rehionalni Osoblyvosti 2016). Veterans and soldiers of the Russian-Ukrainian War are largely in the 20–45 age group, which also makes them more radical proponents of Ukrainian identity and negative towards Russia. More Ukrainians under the age of 59 support (than oppose) one of the de-communisation laws banning communist and Nazi symbols and denouncing the USSR and Nazi Germany as totalitarian states. Only the 60–69 and above 70 age groups had higher numbers of opponents than supporters of de-communisation (Shostyy rik dekomunizatsii: stavlennya naselennya do zaborony symboliv totalitarnoho mynuloho 2020).

Russia's invasion had its greatest impact upon eastern Ukrainians, such as Russian-speaking Anatoliy Korniyenko, whom I interviewed in the city of Dnipro in 2019 and 2020. His 22-year-old son Yevhen had been killed in the Russian-Ukrainian War on 12 August 2014, and Anatoliy Koniyenko volunteered for combat duty at the age of 58 (the last time he had served was

---

[4] See photos and video footage of 20,000 veterans marching in Kyiv on Independence Day on 24 August 2020 at https://www.pravda.com.ua/news/2020/08/24/7263980/

[5] https://uinp.gov.ua/pres-centr/novyny/de-pohovani-geroyi-suchasnoyi-rosiysko-ukrayinskoyi-viyny-infografika

in the Soviet army in the 1970s). He served four years on the Ukrainian-Russian front line. I asked him why he had enlisted, to which he replied, 'I wanted revenge.' There are very many Korniyenko's in Ukraine, particularly in the east and south, who have lost loved ones to Russian military aggression or who have friends who have lost family members in the war.

6.3. Yevhen and Anatoliy Korniyenko, First Museum of the ATO in Dnipro and Donbas War Zone.
Source: Author's photographs.

Note: On the left is a memorial to Yevhen Korniyenko (5 March 1992–12 August 2014) in the Pershyy Muzey ATO Dnipro (First Museum of the ATO in Dnipro).[6] On the right is his father, Anatoliy Koniyenko, when he was in the Donbas war zone.

Another example of the re-thinking of Ukrainian attitudes brought about by the war can be found in Canadian-Ukrainian Andrew Fesiak. His father was one of a few who managed to escape a massacre perpetrated by Polish nationalists against his family and the majority of the inhabitants of a Ukrainian village in June 1945 on the current Polish-Ukrainian border.[7] The irony is that Polish nationalists then did not view Ukraine as a real nation, similar to contemporary Russian nationalists. The leader of the Polish nationalist group, Józef Zadzierski ('Wołyniak'), who committed the massacre, and many other crimes against the Ukrainian minority is considered a hero in Poland today.[8]

---

[6] https://www.facebook.com/UkrainesFirstATOMuseum and http://www.museum.dp.ua/tag/%d0%b0%d1%82%d0%be

[7] http://euromaidanpress.com/2019/01/03/my-family-in-the-polish-ukrainian-borderlands-killing-zone/ and https://www.nasze-slowo.pl/moya-simya-ta-smertelna-zona-polsko-ukra%D1%97nskogo-prikordonnya/

[8] Dionizy Garbacz, Wołyniak, legenda prawdziwa (Warsaw: Polish Institute of National Remembrance, 2015). https://ipn.poczytaj.pl/ksiazka/wolyniak-legenda-prawdziwa-cd-dionizy-garbacz,72549

Andrew Fesiak's mother was one of the 150,000 Ukrainians who were ethnically cleansed in the spring 1947 *Akcja Wisła* (Operation Vistula) by the Polish communist authorities from southeastern Poland to the former German territories that had been included in post-war Poland.

Fesiak has lived in Kyiv for two decades and has a Ukrainian family. He comes from a town in Canada's province of Ontario, where he attended the St. John the Baptist Ukrainian Orthodox Church. He went to Ukrainian school with children from the Ukrainian nationalist community, but had little in common with them ideologically or religiously (the nationalist community tended to be Greek-Catholic). When I met Fesiak for the first time in Toronto in 2001, he held mild pro-Soviet and pro-Russian views, which is no longer the case. Fesiak explained his gradual evolution prior to 2014 and his rapid change since then:

> Various things that Russia did since Ukraine's independence slowly changed my mind. First and foremost was their disrespect for everything Ukrainian. Russian efforts to constantly denigrate Ukraine, Ukrainians, and the language and culture was increasingly evident under Putin. I previously believed it would be in Ukraine's interests to have a close economic relationship with Russia and other former Soviet countries as the world was forming into economic unions and the EU was not offering Ukraine membership. But Russia's economic war against Ukraine proved they could not be trusted even in this area. When Yanukovych was in power, a language law was adopted that upgraded Russian to a *de facto* second state language, to the detriment of the Ukrainian language. Russian economic warfare against Ukraine continued, regardless of the fact that Yanukovych was pro-Russian. This annoyed me so much that when I went on a business trip to Moscow in 2012, I purposefully spoke Ukrainian instead of Russian.

> The point of no return was Russia's annexation and invasion in 2014. This was a real stab in the back that no generation of Ukrainians would ever forget. The fact they could do this in the twenty-first century in Europe just blew my mind. Russia's military aggression forced me to re-examine every episode of Ukrainian history and its relations with Russia. Prior to Russia's invasion, when looking at history, I may have said sure, 'that' particular negative historical event happened, but it was a long time ago and times have changed.

After Russia's annexation and invasion, I see that what Russia did in 2014, was a continuation of their 'normal' state of affairs, which they have been doing for centuries. I was also shocked and dismayed by another big stab in the back from the Russian people themselves, with 85% of them supporting the Kremlin's treacherous act of stealing Crimea from Ukraine. This is just as bad, if not worse, than the actual invasion and annexation, in terms of Ukrainians being betrayed by their so-called 'brothers.' It's one thing for a government to commit a crime, it's another thing when their citizens massively support that crime, especially against a country and people that they consider to be their 'brothers.'

Collapse in Russian Soft Power

The disintegration of Ukraine's pro-Russian 'east' is part of an overall implosion of Russian soft power influence in Ukraine (Zarembo 2017, 47). In September 2014, Ukraine ended the broadcasting of Russian television channels (Ukrainian State Film Agency 2014) and, from 2016, began curtailing imports of banned Russian books and films (Ukrainian Parliament 2016a; Ukrainian State Film Agency 2016). From 2017, Ukraine banned the entry of Russians deemed a threat to Ukrainian national security. Russian social media and some online sources, such as the Russian Internet search engine *Yandex*, the Russian equivalent of Facebook *VKontakte*, *Odnoklassniki*, and email domain .ru (Poroshenko 2017), were closed down because they were part of Russia's information warfare against Ukraine. President Zelenskyy (2020) extended these bans.

In southeastern Ukraine, only 4% watch Russian television. A mere 1% of Ukrainians younger than the age of 29 watch Russian television, and only 7% of young Ukrainians visit Russian websites (Zarembo 2017, 21). Facebook is now far more popular than *VKontakte* and, by 2020, 60% of Ukrainians used Facebook and only 7% used *VKontakte* (Sotsialno-politychna sytuatsiya v Ukrayini 2020). Western search engines such as Google Chrome are used far more often than *Yandex*, and Gmail has wiped out use of .ru.

Loss of Russian soft power and geopolitical influence is evident in religious affairs. All Ukrainian presidents (except Yanukovych) and every Ukrainian parliament supported autocephaly (independence) for Ukrainian Orthodoxy from the Russian Orthodox Church (Yushchenko 2008; Poroshenko 2018; Ukrainian Parliament 2016c; Ukrainian Parliament 2018). A 2018 opinion poll showed that Ukrainians supported religious independence from Moscow, with 52% believing that the pro-autocephalous Ukrainian Orthodox Church-Kyiv

Patriarch was the historical successor to the Orthodox Church in Kyiv Rus. Only 12% believed that the Russian Orthodox Church to be the historical successor (Dynamics of the Patriotic Moods of Ukrainians 2018).

The Kyiv Metropolitan had been under the canonical jurisdiction of the Constantinople Patriarch until 1686, when Muscovy, sensing the weakness of Constantinople under Turkish occupation, illegally transferred the Ukrainian Church under the Moscow Patriarch. Until the seventeenth century, Belarus came under the Kyiv Metropolitan.

In October 2018, Constantinople Patriarch Bartholomew I declared the 1686 transfer to have been 'uncanonical' and returned Ukrainian Orthodox believers under Constantinople's jurisdiction. In response, the Russian Orthodox Church broke off communications with the Constantinople Patriarch, and Putin called an emergency session of Russia's Security Council. A March 2020 summit to condemn Ukrainian autocephaly showed the isolation of the Russian Orthodox Church when only three (Russia, Serbia, Jerusalem) of fourteen Orthodox Churches attended.

In January 2019, Bartholomew I issued a *Tomos* granting autocephaly to the Orthodox Church of Ukraine; following a merger between the Ukrainian Orthodox Church-Kyiv Patriarch, the Ukrainian Autocephalous Orthodox Church, and defectors from the Russian Orthodox Church in Ukraine. With 40% (12,000) of the total number of 30,000 Russian Orthodox Church parishes found in Ukraine, Ukraine's autocephaly has dramatically reduced the influence of the Russian Orthodox Church inside Ukraine and in the broader Orthodox world. Russia is no longer the biggest Orthodox Church with the Romanian and Russian Orthodox Churches now approximately similar in size with 16,000 parishes each.

Russian soft power in Ukraine's economy, trade, and energy has collapsed. Ukraine's trade is individually higher with China (17.74%) and Germany (12.33%) than it is with Russia (10.94%), and trade with Poland (8.31%) is growing.[9] Trade with the EU, which is now the biggest destination for Ukrainian exports, has grown from 26% to 47% since 2013. Ukraine is the third largest exporter of grain to the EU after the US and Brazil. In 2013, 29% of Ukrainian fruit and vegetables were exported to Russia which, by 2019, had collapsed to only 3.5%; the highest proportion is now exported to the EU (67%), the Middle East (14%), and Belarus (7%). Nicolai N. Petro (2016) and Mikhail Molchanov (2016, 2018) were wrong to believe that Ukraine would not survive economically without Russia.

---

9   https://open4business.com.ua/main-trade-partners-of-ukraine-in-from-total-volume-import-from-other-countries-to-ukraine-in-jan-may/

For many Ukrainians, especially the younger generation, the negotiation of a visa-free regime with the EU, along with Ryan Air, Wizz Air, and other low-cost airlines, makes travel to the EU affordable. Since 2017, a quarter of Ukrainians have travelled visa-free to the EU. The highest numbers flying to the EU are from Kharkiv, Odesa, Lviv, and Kyiv *oblasts* (Getmanchuk and Litra 2019). Flights to Greece, the Czech Republic, and Germany have increased by 46%, 38%, and 31% respectively. Passenger traffic from Kyiv's Borispil airport has more than doubled from 6 to 14 million, with similar high growth rates from Lviv, Zaporizhzhya, and Kharkiv airports.

Nearly as many Ukrainians travel into Russia (3.9 million) as travel to Hungary (3.4 million). Approximately 700,000 Ukrainians flew to Poland in 2019, up from 204,000 in 2017, facilitated by Ukrainians ability to fly to eight Polish cities from Kyiv's two airports. Approximately 463,000 Ukrainians work permanently in Poland (representing three-quarters of foreign workers) together with one million Ukrainians who work temporarily and travel back and forth for trade. Approximately 25,000 Ukrainians study in Poland.

Odesa, Kharkiv, Dnipropetrovsk, Lviv, and Sumy *oblasts* have high levels of participation in educational and cultural exchanges with the EU (Getmanchuk and Litra 2019). In comparison, in Russia and Belarus, which do not have visa-free regimes with the EU, only 12,000 Russians and 38,000 Belarusians work in Poland. Ukraine receives the largest remittances from abroad of any country in Europe, which amounted to $15.8 billion, or 10% of GDP, in 2019.

Since the introduction of a visa-free regime between Ukraine and the EU in 2017, a growing number of Ukrainians from its southeastern *oblasts* have travelled to Poland (Olearchyk 2019). The southern Ukrainian *oblast* of Mykolayiv has the highest indicator of European integration of any Ukrainian region (Getmanchuk and Litra 2019). The highest rates of European investment, and the largest number of projects funded by the European Investment Bank and European Bank for Reconstruction and Development are found in the southeastern Luhansk, Sumy, Donetsk, Kharkiv, Dnipropetrovsk, Zaporizhzhya, Mykolayiv, and Kherson *oblasts* (Getmanchuk and Litra 2019).

Russian political influence through corrupt networks has declined since Autumn 2015, when Ukraine ended imports of Russian gas (Ukraine's Fight Against Corruption: The Economic 2018). Since 2015, oligarchs have no longer been able to make huge profits from opaque gas intermediaries, using some of these funds to finance pro-Russian political forces, such as the Party of Regions. Gas tycoon Dmytro Firtash is fighting extradition to the US on charges of corruption and to Spain over collusion with Russian organised crime. With the loss of corrupt rents from the gas trade, Ukraine's pro-

Russian Opposition Platform-For Life is completely reliant on Russian funding through Medvedchuk, Putin's representative in Ukraine. With the disappearance of Ukraine's 'east,' this reduces its attractiveness to voters even further.

Russia's attempt to bypass Ukraine with Nord Stream II were thwarted by US sanctions, forcing Putin to agree to a five-year transit agreement for gas through Ukraine beginning in January 2020. Ukraine's energy needs are met by importing gas from central Europe and, since 2019, US liquefied natural gas and oil transported through Poland. Ironically, Putin's military aggression has been a decisive factor in making Ukraine energy independent of Russia.

Prospects for Peace

In an environment where the rule of law is non-existent and is always flouted at home and abroad, it is unsurprising that treaties and agreements signed by Ukraine with Russia were worthless pieces of paper during the 2014 crisis. This has increased Ukrainian distrust in Putin's promises. D'Anieri (2019, 258) writes that the 1997 Russian-Ukrainian treaty 'brought little in the way of friendship,' opposed as it was by many Russian elites and the treaty 'had little impact on Ukrainian-Russian relations.' Russia had 'deep and fundamental' disagreements over Ukraine and always insisted that Moscow 'considered a voice in Ukraine as essential' (D'Anieri 2019, 258–259).

Democracy and geopolitics first merged in the Orange Revolution and, since then, 'Ukraine's conflict with Russia and the West's conflict with Russia were tightly bound together' (D'Anieri 2019, 137). The Orange Revolution 'changed everything' because 'the two conflicts have become one' (D'Anieri 2019, 137). Ukraine's democratisation signifies the enlargement of western influence into what Russia views as its exclusive sphere of influence. Ukraine's European integration was unacceptable to Russia in 2014, and this remains true today.

Russian and Russian Proxy Forces in Crimea and the Donbas[10]

Crimea	Russian-Controlled Donbas	Russian forces on the Russian-Ukrainian Border
32,500 Russian armed forces. Of these, 11,500 military servicemen form the 22nd Army Corps	35,000 security forces comprised of Ukrainians and Russian nationalist mercenaries in the 1st (DNR) Corps and 2nd (LNR) Corps	
	5,000 GRU, FSB, Russian military officers, advisers, logistical support and trainers	Military supplies and fuel are delivered through the section of the Russian-Ukrainian border which is exclusively controlled by Russia since 2014
200 armoured personnel carriers 31 tanks	914 armoured personnel carriers 481 tanks	Up to 2,600 armoured personnel carriers and 1,100 tanks
100 artillery systems	720 artillery systems	Up to 1,100 artillery systems
100 helicopters		330 combat aircraft and 230 helicopters

Ukraine would have to agree to many Russian demands to achieve peace, which would be tantamount to capitulation for many Ukrainians. These demands include relinquishing sovereignty over Crimea and changing its constitution to provide 'special status' to the DNR and LNR. Russia demands that the 35,000-strong security forces of the DNR and LNR be re-organised into a local militia, which would amount to the legalisation of Russian-controlled forces. Ukraine demands the de-militarisation and withdrawal of all foreign forces, but it is impossible for a withdrawal to take place as long as Russia sticks to the fiction that it has no security forces in the Donbas. Russia has also rejected returning control over the border to Ukraine until Ukraine meets all of its demands.

Russia seeks a neutral Ukraine that relinquishes its goal of joining NATO and

---

[10] Sources: https://empr.media/news/occupied-crimea/the-military-strength-of-the-russian-troops-in-crimea-becomes-known/ and https://www.ukrinform.net/rubric-defense/3056432-1100-russian-tanks-330-warplanes-along-border-with-ukraine.html#:~:text=Ukrainian%20and%20American%20experts%2C%20as,large%2Dscale%20offensive%20against%20Ukraine.

the EU, two objectives that are enshrined in Ukraine's constitution since February 2019. Changing the constitution requires a majority two-thirds vote by parliament, which would be impossible and is opposed by large majorities of Ukrainians, who now support membership in both organisations. Support for NATO membership has skyrocketed since 2014 and a high majority would support membership in a referendum. Approximately 69% of Ukrainians would participate in a referendum on NATO membership, of whom 70% would vote in favour, up from 66% in 2017 (Pidsumky 2018; *Hromadska Dumka* 2018). In Ukrainian-controlled Donbas, 31% of people support NATO membership, despite miniscule support prior to 2014 (Observations of Public Attitudes in Donbas 2020).

One of Zelenskyy's election promises was to bring peace to the Donbas, and he remained naively confident in pushing the peace process forward during his first year in office (see Kuzio 2020b). President Zelenskyy's inability to move the peace process forward confirms that neither President Poroshenko nor 'Ukrainian nationalists' were the obstacles. Zelenskyy's decision to withdraw from three contact points on the front line was unpopular. With Russian and Russian proxy forces continuing to engage Ukrainian forces on a daily basis, the withdrawals failed to achieve a significant reduction in hostilities.

Zelenskyy also oversaw two prisoner exchanges, which earned him good will as a populist exercise, but also criticism. Of those transferred to Russia, six prisoners were *Berkut* riot police guilty of killing protestors during the Euromaidan. Another was Volodymyr Tsemakh, who had been kidnapped by Security Service of Ukraine special forces in a daring raid and was wanted by the Hague-based Joint Investigations Team due to his involvement in the downing of MH17.

Despite his good will and willingness to compromise, Zelenskyy was unable to achieve any major success in the peace process for reasons which are the same as those under Poroshenko. An inability to push the peace process forward points to deeper issues; after all, Zelenskyy is a centrist, Russian-speaking politician from eastern Ukraine who (unlike his predecessor) would have been willing to make difficult compromises. Typically, in Russian policies towards Ukraine, Putin does not attempt to engage with Zelenskyy or adopt compromises, in this case towards the goal of achieving peace. Russian demands towards Kyiv are not modified and Zelenskyy is simply expected to abide by them.

In April 2019, the month Zelenskyy was elected, Putin slapped him twice in the face. Russia began issuing passports to residents of Russian-controlled

Donbas, forecasting that, by the end of 2020, one million residents of the DNR and LNR would possess them. The residents of Russian-controlled Donbas returned their gratitude and voted for constitutional amendments in the July 2020 Russian referendum. In the same month, Russia introduced sanctions on 140 goods (on top of the 200 goods sanctioned by Russia earlier in December 2018), including coal, crude oil, and oil products, which could no longer be exported to Ukraine.

Conclusion

Stereotypes of a divided Ukraine on the verge of disintegration, and Ukrainians and Russians as very close people were wrong prior to 2014 and are outdated in the face of the tectonic changes that have occurred since then (see Kuzyk 2019). While Ukraine has been removed from the Russian Orthodox Church's canonical territory, Ukraine remains 'Russian territory' for western historians of 'Russia,' who did not change their approach following the emergence of independent Russia and Ukraine. This makes this author sceptical that they will take into account the impact of the Russian-Ukrainian War and Ukrainian Orthodox autocephaly on the writing of 'Russian' history.

Putin's rehabilitation of Tsarist Russian and White *émigré* views, which deny the existence of a Ukrainian people and portray Ukraine as an 'artificial' and failed state, annexation of Crimea, and invasion and war with Ukraine have fundamentally changed the Ukrainian-Russian relationship. A pro-Russian 'east' has disappeared, Ukrainians no longer view Russians as their 'brothers,' and Russian soft power in Ukraine has disintegrated. Ukrainian opinion polls show dramatic changes in identity, views of Ukrainian history and relations with Russia.

D'Anieri (2019) believes that the West's goals of seeking to keep Russia satisfied and Ukraine independent are mutually incompatible. NATO is not Russia's only problem; a democratising Ukraine integrating into Europe within the EU's Eastern Partnership is also unacceptable to Russia. Putin does not distinguish between integration (on offer in the Eastern Partnership) and membership (which is not). Integration into Europe means that Putin cannot fulfil his destiny of 'gathering Russian lands' because Ukraine would not be part of the Russian World. Russian leaders believe that 'Russian lands,' wrongly included in Ukraine, are being prevented from joining the Russian World by Galician Ukrainian nationalists. Russian leaders have continued to believe this fallacy after Zelenskyy's election.

With Russian nationalism (imperialism) driving Putin's policies towards Ukraine, it is difficult to see how peace in the Donbas can be achieved. With

Putin in power for another 16 years, the policies he has pursued, however counter-productive they have been to Russian goals, will continue towards Ukraine.

References

Ad hoc Report on the situation of national minorities in Ukraine adopted on 1 April 2014. (2014). Advisory Committee on the Framework Convention for the Protection of National Minorities, Council of Europe, 2 April. https://rm.coe.int/CoERMPublicCommonSearchServices/DisplayDCTMContent?documentId=09000016800c5d6f

Alexseev, M. and Hale, E.H. (2016). 'Rallying round the leader more than the flag: Changes in Russian national public opinion 2013-2014' in: P. Kolsto and H. Blakkisrud eds., *The New Russian Nationalism. Imperialism, Ethnicity, and Authoritarianism.* Edinburgh: Edinburgh University Press, 192-220.

Aliyev, H. (2019). 'The Logic of Ethnic Responsibility and Pro-Government Mobilization in East Ukrainian Conflict,' *Comparative Political Studies*, 52 (8): 1200-1231.

Aliyev, H. (2020). 'When neighbourhood goes to war. Exploring the effect of belonging on violent mobilization in Ukraine,' *Eurasian Geography and Economics*, 2020. https://doi.org/10.1080/15387216.2020.1756366

Amar, T. C. (2019). 'Politics, Starvation, and Memory: A Critique of Red Famine,' *Kritika: Explorations in Russian and Eurasian History*, 20 (1): 145-169.

Applebaum, A. (2017). *Red Famine. Stalin's War on Ukraine.* London: Allen Lane.

Arel, D. (2018). 'How Ukraine has become more Ukrainian,' *Post-Soviet Affairs*, 34 (2-3): 186-189.

AR Krym: Lyudy, Problemy, Perspektyvy. (2008). Razumkov Centre for Economic and Political Studies, *Natsionalna Bezpeka i Oborona*, 8. http://razumkov.org.ua/uploads/journal/ukr/NSD104_2008_ukr.pdf

Ascher, A. (2002). *Russia: a short history.* Oxford: Oneworld.

Bacon, E. (2015). 'Putin's Crimean Speech, 18 March 2014: Russia's Changing Public Political Narrative,' *Journal of Soviet and Post-Soviet Politics and Society*, 1(1): 13-36.

Barth F. ed., (1969). *Ethnic Groups and Boundaries. The Social Organization of Cultural Difference.* Long Grove, IL: Wavelength Press.

Belafatti, F. (2014). 'Orientalism reanimated: colonial thinking in Western analysis's comments on Ukraine,' *Euromaidan Press*, 27 October. http://euromaidanpress.com/2014/10/27/western-commentators-should-rid-themselves-of-old-prejudices-dating-back-from-the-age-of-colonialism-before-commenting-on-eastern-european-affairs/

Bellingcat. (2020a). 'Identifying FSB's Elusive "Elbrus": From MH17 to Assassinations in Europe.' *Bellingcat*, 24 April. https://www.bellingcat.com/news/uk-and-europe/2020/04/24/identifying-fsbs-elusive-elbrus-from-mh17-to-assassinations-in-europe/

Bellingcat. (2020b). '"K" for Kurator or Catch Me If You Can,' 9 July. https://www.bellingcat.com/news/uk-and-europe/2020/07/09/k-for-kurator-or-catch-me-if-you-can/ and https://www.bellingcat.com/app/uploads/2020/07/transcript.pdf

Bellingcat. (2020c). 'Putin Chef's Kisses of Death: Russia's Shadow Army's State-Run Structure Exposed,' 14 August. https://www.bellingcat.com/news/uk-and-europe/2020/08/14/pmc-structure-exposed/

Belton, C. (2020). *Putin's People. How the KGB Took Back Russia and Then Turned on the West*. London: William Collins.

Bidder, B. (2015). 'The Man Who Started the War in Ukraine.' *Der Spiegel International*, 18 March. https://www.spiegel.de/international/europe/the-ukraine-war-from-perspective-of-russian-nationalists-a-1023801.html

Billington, J.H. (1970). *The Icon and the Axe. An Interpretative History of Russian Culture*. New York: Vintage Books.

Blakkisrud, H. (2016). 'Blurring the boundary between civic and ethnic: The Kremlin's new approach to national identity under Putin's third term' in: P. Kolsto and H. Blakkisrud eds., *The New Russian Nationalism. Imperialism, Ethnicity, and Authoritarianism*. Edinburgh: Edinburgh University Press, 249-274.

Blinova, E. (2015). 'Holodomor Hoax: The Anatomy of a Lie Invented by West's Propaganda Machine,' *Sputnik News*, 19 October. https://sputniknews.com/politics/201510191028730561-holodomor-hoax-invented-hitler-west/

Bodie, J. (2017). 'Modern Imperialism in Crimea and Donbas,' *Loyola of Los Angeles International and Comparative Law Review*, 40 (267): 267-308.

Bolton, J. (2020). *The Room Where It Happened: A White House Memoir*. New York: Simon and Schuster.

Bonch-Osmolovskaya T., (2015). 'Combatting the Russian State Propaganda Machine: Strategy of Information Resistance,' *Journal of Soviet and Post-Soviet Politics and Society*, 1 (1): 175-218.

Bowen A.S. (2019). 'Coercive diplomacy and the Donbas: Explaining Russian strategy in Eastern Ukraine,' *Journal of Strategic Studies*, 42 (3-4): 312-343.

Brandenberger, D. L. and Dubrovsky, A. M. (1998). 'The People Need a Tsar': The Emergence of National Bolshevism as Stalinist Ideology, 1931-1941.' *Europe-Asia Studies*, 50(5): 873-892.

P. Bregy, P. and Obolensky, S. (1940). *The Ukraine – a Russian Land.* London: Selwyn and Blount.

Brik, T. (2019). '"Civil War" and Other Clichés. Why is it Important to Study Terminology, Context, and Data?' *Vox Ukraine*, 20 February. https://voxukraine.org/en/civil-war-and-other-cliches-why-is-it-important-to-study-terminology-context-and-data/

Brown, A., Kaiser M., and Smith, G. S. eds., *The Cambridge Encyclopaedia of Russia and the Former Soviet Union.* Cambridge and New York: Cambridge University Press.

Brudny, Y.M. (1998). *Reinventing Russia. Russian Nationalism and the Soviet State, 1953-1991.* Cambridge, MA: Harvard University Press.

Bulmer, M. and Solomos, J. (1998). 'Re-thinking Ethnic and Racial Studies,' *Ethnic and Racial Studies*, 21 (5): 829-837.

Bureiko, N. and Moga, T.L. (2019). 'The Ukrainian–Russian Linguistic Dyad and its Impact on National Identity in Ukraine,' *Europe-Asia Studies*, 71 (1): 137-155.

Buckley, N. and Olearchyk, R. (2017). 'Putin's friend emerges from shadows in Ukraine,' *Financial Times*, 24 April.

Bukkvoll, T. (2016). 'Why Putin went to war: ideology, interests, and decision-making in the Russian use of force in Crimea and Donbas,' *Contemporary Politics*, 22 (3): 267-282.

Bukkvol, T. (2019). 'Fighting on behalf of the state – the issue of pro-government militia autonomy in the Donbas war,' *Post-Soviet Affairs*, 35 (4): 293-307.

Canada's indigenous people are still overlooked. (2017). *The Economist*, 29 July. https://www.economist.com/news/americas/

Carey, H. F. and Raciborski, R. (2004). 'Postcolonialism: A valid Paradigm for the Former Sovietized States and Yugoslavia?' *East European Politics and Societies*, 18 (2): 191-235.

Chaisty, P. and Whitefield, S. (2015). 'Putin's Nationalism Problem' in: A. Pikulicka-Wilczewska and R. Sakwa eds., *Ukraine and Russia: People, Politics, Propaganda and Perspectives.* Bristol: E-International Relations, 165-172.

Channon, J. and Hudson, R. (1995). *Penguin Historical Atlas of Russia*. London: Penguin Books.

Charap, S. and Colton, T. J. (2017). *Everyone Loses. The Ukraine Crisis and Ruinous Contest for Post-Soviet Eurasia*. London: International Institute for Strategic Studies.

Chernenko, A.M. (1994). *Ukrayinska Natsionalna Ideya*. DDU: Dnipropetrovsk.

Chornokondratenko, M. and Williams, M. (2018). 'Ukrainians relive bloodshed of Kiev's Maidan in virtual reality,' *Reuters*, 17 September. https://www.reuters.com/article/us-ukraine-crisis-vr-idUSKCN1LX148

Chraibi, C. (2020). 'Kremlin planned to destabilize Ukraine in the early 1990s by smearing "all forms of nationalism," KGB file reveals,' *Euromaidan Press*, 23 July. http://euromaidanpress.com/2020/07/23/kgb-file-reveals-how-the-kremlin-planned-to-destabilize-ukraine-in-the-early-1990s/

Clarke, R. (2018). '2014: Ultra-Right Threats, Working Class Revolt and Russian Policy Responses' in: B. Kagarlitsky, R. Desai, and A. Freeman eds., *Russia, Ukraine and Contemporary Imperialism*. London: Routledge, 46-67.

Clem, R. S. (2014). 'Dynamics of the Ukrainian state-territory nexus,' *Eurasian Geography and Economics*, 55 (3): 219-235.

Clover, C. (2016). *Black Wind, White Snow. The Rise of Russia's New Nationalism*. New Haven, Conn.: Yale University Press.

Coalson, R. (2014). 'Is Putin 'Rebuilding Russia' According to Solzhenitsyn's Design?' *RFERL*, 1 September. http://www.rferl.org/content/russia-putin-solzhenitsyn-1990-essay/26561244.html

Cohen, A. (1996). *Russian Imperialism. Developments and Crisis*. Westport, CA: Praeger.

Cohen, S. F. (2019). *War with Russia?: From Putin & Ukraine to Trump and Russiagate*. New York: Skyhorse Publishing.

Connor, W. (1972). 'Nation-Building or Nation-Destroying?' *World Politics*, 24 (3): 319-355.

Cordier, B. De. (2017). 'A Look at the "Resistance Identity" of the Donbas Insurgency,' *Russian Analytical Digest*, 198, 14 February. https://css.ethz.ch/content/dam/ethz/special-interest/gess/cis/center-for-securities-studies/pdfs/RAD198.pdf

Coynash, H. (2014). 'Putin's Neo-Nazi Helpers,' *Kharkiv Human Rights Protection Group*, 10 March. http://khpg.org/index.php?id=1394442656

Coynash, H. (2017). 'Cross and Icons seized, Archbishop assaulted in barbaric new attack on Ukrainian Cathedral in Russian-occupied Crimea,' *Kharkiv Human Rights Protection Group*, 1 September. http://khpg.org/en/index.php?id=1504187187

Coynash, H. and Charron, A. (2019). 'Russian-occupied Crimea and the state of exception: repression, persecution, and human rights violations,' *Eurasian Geography and Economics*, 60 (1): 28-53.

Coynash, H. (2020a). 'Crimea is our land. We did not give it to Russia, nor did we sell it" Powerful final court address by Crimean Tatar human rights defender,' *Kharkiv Human Rights Protection Group*, 25 June. http://khpg.org/en/index.php?id=1593356319

Coynash, H. (2020b). 'Russia admits its constitutional changes are aimed at making return of Crimea to Ukraine "impossible",' *Kharkiv Human Rights Protection Group*, 26 June. http://khpg.org/en/index.php?id=1593031626

Crimea: Five Years. (2019). Levada Centre, 11 April. https://www.levada.ru/en/2019/04/11/crimea-five-years/

Crimea welcomes riot cops after murdering Euromaidan protestors. (2014). https://www.youtube.com/watch?v=efii3FK9W7A

D'Anieri, P.D., Kravchuk, R., and Kuzio, T. (1999). *Politics and Society in Ukraine*. Boulder, CO: Westview.

D'Anieri, P. (2018). 'Gerrymandering Ukraine? Electoral Consequences of Occupation,' *East European Politics and Societies*, 33 (1): 89-108.

D'Anieri, P. (2019). *Ukraine and Russia. From Civilized Divorce to Uncivil War*. Cambridge: Cambridge University Press.

Darden, K. and Way, L. (2014). 'Who are the Protestors in Ukraine?' *The Washington Post*, 12 February. https://www.washingtonpost.com/news/monkey-cage/wp/2014/02/12/who-are-the-protesters-in-ukraine/

Davies, N. (1996). *Europe. A History*. Oxford: Oxford University Press.

Dawisha, K. (2014). *Putin's Kleptocracy: Who Owns Russia?* New York, Simon & Schuster.

Defenders Day of Ukraine (2020). Rating Sociological Group, 14 October. http://ratinggroup.ua/en/research/ukraine/fbb3f3c52d452cdd1646d4a62b69dba5.html

Delcour, L. and Wolczuk, K. (2015). 'Spoiler or facilitator of Democratization? Russia's role in Georgia and Ukraine,' *Democratization*, 22 (3): 459-478.

Despite Concerns About Governance, Ukrainians Want to Remain One Country. (2014). Pew Research Centre, 8 May. https://www.pewresearch.org/global/2014/05/08/despite-concerns-about-governance-ukrainians-want-to-remain-one-country/

Dmytryshyn, B. (1973). *Medieval Russia. A Source Book, 900-1700*. New York: Praeger.

Dolgov A. (2014). 'Navalny Wouldn't Return Crimea, Considers Immigration Bigger Issue Than Ukraine,' *Moscow Times*, 16 October. https://www.themoscowtimes.com/2014/10/16/navalny-wouldnt-return-crimea-considers-immigration-bigger-issue-than-ukraine-a40477

Driscoll, J. (2019). 'Ukraine's Civil War: Would Accepting This Terminology Help Resolve the Conflict?' *Ponars Policy Memos*, 572, February. http://www.ponarseurasia.org/memo/ukraines-civil-war-would-accepting-terminology-help-resolve-conflict

Dugin, A. (2014). 'Putin's Advisor Dugin says Ukrainians must be 'killed, killed, killed,'' 12 June. https://www.youtube.com/watch?v=MQ-uqmnwKF8

Dynamics of the Patriotic Moods of Ukrainians. (2018). Rating Sociological Group, 21 August. http://ratinggroup.ua/en/research/ukraine/dinamika_patrioticheskih_nastroeniy_ukraincev_avgust_2018.html

Dwyer, P. and Nettlebeck, A. (2018). 'Savage Wars of Peace': Violence, Colonialism and Empire in the Modern World' in: P. Dwyer and A. Nettlebeck eds., *Violence, Colonialism, and Empire in the Modern World*. New York and London: Palgrave and Macmillan, 1-24.

Egorov, I. (2020). 'SBU maye audio pro te, yak verbuvalnyk Shaytanova keruvav boyovykamy na Donbasi,' *Ukrayinska Pravda*, 9 July. https://www.pravda.com.ua/news/2020/07/9/7258728/

Emerson, R. (1967). *From Empire to Nation*. Cambridge, MA: Harvard University Press.

European Parliament. (2016). 'Motion for a Resolution on the Crimean Tatars,' 10 May. https://www.europarl.europa.eu/doceo/document/B-8-2016-0588_EN.html?redirect

Fearon, J. (2007). 'Iraq's Civil War.' *Foreign Affairs*, 86 (2): 2-15. https://www.foreignaffairs.com/articles/iraq/2007-03-01/iraqs-civil-war

Fearon, J. and Laitin, D. (2000). 'Violence and social construction of ethnic identity,' *International Organization*, 54 (4): 845-877.

Fedor, J. 2015. 'Introduction: Russia Media and the War in Ukraine,' *Journal of Soviet and Post-Soviet Politics and Society*, 1 (1): 1-12.

Feklyunina, V. (2016). 'Soft power and identity: Russia, Ukraine and the 'Russian world(s),' *European Journal of International Relations*, 22(4): 773-796.

Fisun, O. (2014). 'Ukrainian Nationalism, Soccer Clubs, and the Euromaidan,' *Ponars Policy Memos*, 324, July. https://www.ponarseurasia.org/memo/ukrainian-nationalism-soccer-clubs-and-euromaidan-0

Fitzpatrick, C.A. (2014). 'Russia This Week.' *The Interpreter*, 11 April. https://www.interpretermag.com/russia-this-week-communist-wins-mayoral-elections-in-novosibirsk/

Florinsky, M. (1953). *Russia. A History. Two volumes*. New York: Macmillan.

Follow-up of the situation in the Autonomous Republic of Crimea (Ukraine). (2019). United Nations Educational, Scientific and Cultural Organisation, 13 September. https://unesdoc.unesco.org/ark:/48223/pf0000370522/PDF/370522eng.pdf.multi

Forsberg, T. and Sirke, T. (2019). 'Russian Discourse on Borders and Territorial Questions – Crimea as a Watershed?' *Russian Politics*, 4 (2): 211-241.

Fournier, A. (2010). 'Mapping Identities: Russian Resistance to Linguistic Ukrainisation in Central and Eastern Ukraine,' *Europe-Asia Studies*, 54 (3): 415-433.

Foxall, A. (2019). 'From Evropa to Gayropa: A Critical Geopolitics of the European Union as Seen from Russia,' *Geopolitics*, 24 (1): 174–193.

Franklin, S. and Shepard, J. (1996). *The Emergence of Rus 750-1200*. London and New York: Longman.

Freeze, G.L. (2002). *Russia: a history*. Oxford, NY: Oxford University Press.

Freedman, L. (2019). *Ukraine and the Art of Strategy*. Oxford: Oxford University Press.

Friesendorf, C. (2019). 'Police Reform in Ukraine as Institutional Bricolage.' *Problems of Post-Communism*, 66 (2): 109-121.

Frye, T. (2017). 'Russian Studies is Thriving, not Dying.' *The National Interest*, 3 October. https://nationalinterest.org/feature/russian-studies-thriving-not-dying-22547

Galeotti, M. (2016). *Hybrid War or Gibridnaya Voina? Getting Russia's Non-Linear Military Challenge Right.* Morrisville, NC: Lulu Press.

Gessen, M. (2017). *The Future is History: How Totalitarianism Reclaimed Russia.* New York: Riverhead Books.

Getmanchuk, A. and Litra, L. eds., (2019). *The European Map of Ukraine. Rating of European Integration of Regions.* Kyiv: New Europe Centre. https://rpr.org.ua/wp-content/uploads/2019/11/Euromap-eng-web.pdf

Gilbert, M. (1993). *Dent Atlas of Russian History.* London: Routledge.

Gilley, C. (2019). 'Review of Anna Matveeva,' *Europe-Asia Studies*, 71(2): 321-323.

Girkin, I. (2014). 'SBU: Peremovyny chleniv dyversiynoyi hrupy svidchat pro shyrokomasshtabnu viyskovu ahresiyu RF proty Ukrayiny,' 14 April. https://www.youtube.com/watch?v=xVDx-TqeWj4&feature=emb_logo

Giuliano, E. (2018). 'Who supported separatism in Donbas? Ethnicity and popular opinion at the start of the Ukraine crisis,' *Post-Soviet Affairs*, 34 (2-3): 158-178.

Glazyev, S. (2019) 'Okkupatsiya,' *Glazev.ru*, 7 May. https://glazev.ru/articles/153-geopolitika/67422-okkupatsija

Goble, P. (2015). 'Putin conducting 'hybrid genocide' against Crimean Tatars, Muzhdabayev says,' *Euromaidan Press*, 7 April. http://euromaidanpress.com/2015/04/07/putin-conducting-hybrid-genocide-against-crimean-tatars-muzhdabayev-says/

Gomza, I. (2019). 'Quenching Fire with Gasoline. Why Flawed Terminology Will Not Help to Resolve the Ukraine Crisis,' *Ponars Policy Memos*, 576, February. http://www.ponarseurasia.org/memo/quenching-fire-gasoline-flawed-terminology-will-not-help-resolve-ukraine-crisis

Gomza, I. and Zajaczkowski, J. (2019). 'Black Sun Rising: Political Opportunity Structure Perceptions and Institutionalization of the Azov Movement in Post-Euromaidan Ukraine,' *Nationalities Papers*, 47 (5): 774-800.

Gonchar, M., Horbach, V. and Pinchuk, A. (2020). *Russian Octopus in Action. Case "Ukraine."* Kyiv: Centre for Global Studies (Strategy XXI), Institute for Euro-Atlantic Cooperation. https://geostrategy.org.ua/en/analysis/research/rosiyskiy-sprut-u-diyi-keys-ukrayina

Goryanov, A. and Ivshina, O. (2015). 'Boyets "spetsnaza DNR": pomosh Rossii byla reshayushchey,' *BBC Russian Service*, 31 March. https://www.bbc.com/russian/international/2015/03/150325_donetsk_rebel_interview

Gregory, P. R. (2014). 'Putin's "Human Rights Council" Accidentally Posts Real Crimean Election Results.' *Forbes*, 5 May. https://www.forbes.com/sites/paulroderickgregory/2014/05/05/putins-human-rights-council-accidentally-posts-real-crimean-election-results-only-15-voted-for-annexation/#34f49be4f172

Gretskiy, I. (2020). 'Lukyanov Doctrine: Conceptual Origins of Russia's Hybrid Foreign Policy – The Case of Ukraine,' *Saint Louis University Law Journal*, 64 (1): 1-22.

Gurr, T. (2000). *Peoples Versus States: Minorities at Risk in the New Century*. Washington DC: US Institute of Peace.

Hahn, G. M., (2018). *Ukraine Over the Edge. Russia, the West and the new 'Cold War.'* Jefferson, NC: McFarland and Company.

Hajduk, J. and Stepniewski, T. (2016). 'Russia's Hybrid War with Ukraine: Determinants, Instruments, Accomplishments and Challenges,' *Studia Europejskie*, 2: 37-52.

Hale, H. E. (2016). 'How nationalism and machine politics mix in Russia,' in: P. Kolstø and H. Blakkisrud eds., *The New Russian Nationalism. Imperialism, Ethnicity and Authoritarianism*. Edinburgh: Edinburgh University Press, 221-248.

Haran, O., Yakovlyev M., and Zolkina, M. (2018). 'Identity, war, and peace: public attitudes in the Ukraine-controlled Donbas,' *Eurasian Geography and Economics*, 60 (6): 684-708.

Harding, L. (2014). 'Ukraine nationalist attacks on Russia supporters – fact or Kremlin fairytale?' *The Guardian*, 20 March. https://www.theguardian.com/world/2014/mar/20/ukraine-nationalist-attacks-russia-supporters-kremlin-deaths

Harding, L. (2016). *A Very Expensive Poison. The Definitive Story of the Murder of Litvinenko and Russia's War with the West.* London: Guardian Books.

Harris, E. (2020). 'What is the Role of Nationalism and Ethnicity in the Russia–Ukraine Crisis?' *Europe-Asia Studies*, 72 (4): 1-21.

Haukkala, H. (2015). 'From Cooperative to Contested Europe? The Conflict in Ukraine as a Culmination of a Long-Term Crisis in EU-Russian Relations,' *Journal of Contemporary European Studies*, 23 (1): 25-40.

Hickman, M. J. (1998). 'Reconstructing, deconstruct, 'race': British political discourses about the Irish in Britain,' *Ethnic and Racial Studies*, 21 (2): 288-307.

Himka, J-P. (2015). 'The History behind the Regional Conflict in Ukraine,' *Kritika*, 16 (1): 129-136.

Horbulin, V. (2017). *The World Hybrid War: Ukrainian Forefront.* Kyiv: National Institute of Strategic Studies.

Horvath, R. (2015). 'The Euromaidan and the crisis of Russian nationalism,' *Nationalities Papers*, 43 (6): 819-839.

Hosaka, S. (2018). 'The Kremlin's Active Measures Failed in 2013: That's Why Russia Remembered its Last Resort – Crimea,' *Demokratizatsiya: The Journal of Post-Soviet Democratization*, 26 (3): 321-364.

Hosking, G. (1997). *Russia. People & Empire, 1552-1917.* London: Harper-Collins.

Hosking, G. (1998). 'Can Russia become a Nation-state?' *Nations and Nationalism*, 4 (4): 449-462.

Horvath, R. (2011). 'Apologist of Putinism? Solzhenitsyn, the Oligarchs, and the Specter of Orange Revolution,' *The Russian Review*, 70 (1): 300-318.

Howard, M. (1995). 'Ethnic Conflict and International Security,' *Nations and Nationalism*, 1 (3): 285-295.

Hrushevsky, M.A (1970). *History of Ukraine*. N.P.: Archon Books. Reprint of a 1941 edition published by Yale University Press.

Hunter, M. (2018). 'Crowdsourced War: The Political and Military Implications of Ukraine's Volunteer Battalions 2014-2015,' *Journal of Military and Strategic Studies*, 18 (3): 78-124.

Hutchings, S. and Tolz, V. (2015). *Nation, Ethnicity and Race on Russian Television. Mediating Post-Soviet Difference.* London: Routledge.

In Crimea serious human rights violations and attacks on minorities and journalists require urgent action. (2014), Council of Europe, 27 October. https://www.coe.int/en/web/commissioner/-/in-crimea-serious-human-rights-violations-and-attacks-on-minorities-and-journalists-require-urgent-action

Identychnist Hromadyan Ukrayiny v Novykh Umovakh: Stan, Tendentsii, Rehionalni Osoblyvosti (2016). Razumkov Centre for Economic and Political Studies, *Natsionalna Bezpeka i Oborona*, 3–4. http://razumkov.org.ua/uploads/journal/ukr/NSD161-162_2016_ukr.pdf

In some countries in Central and Eastern Europe, roughly one-in-five adults or more say they would not accept Jews as fellow citizens. (2018). Pew Research Centre, 27 March. https://www.pewresearch.org/fact-tank/2018/03/28/most-poles-accept-jews-as-fellow-citizens-and-neighbors-but-a-minority-do-not/ft_18-03-26_polandholocaustlaws_map/

Ioffe, J. (2014). 'Will Russia Invade Ukraine?' *The New Republic*, 9 April. https://newrepublic.com/article/117314/will-russia-invade-ukraine

Janmaat, J.G. (2000). *Nation-Building in Post-Soviet Ukraine. Educational Policy and the Response of the Russian speaking Population*. Amsterdam: Netherlands Geographical Studies.

Jatras, J. G. (2011). '*Svoboda*: 'A Kind of 'Freedom' Ukraine Doesn't Need.' *American Institute in Ukraine*, 12 March.

Jenne, E.K. (2007). *Ethnic Bargaining: The Paradox of Minority Empowerment*. Ithaca, NY: Cornell University Press.

Jensen, D. N. (2017). Moscow in the Donbas: Command, Control, Crime and the Minsk Peace Process, *NDC Research Report*, 1. March. Rome: NATO Defence College. http://www.ndc.nato.int/news/news.php?icode=1029

Jones, J. (2014). 'The Battle for Ukraine,' *PBS Frontline*, 27 May. https://www.pbs.org/wgbh/frontline/film/battle-for-ukraine/ and https://www.pbs.org/wgbh/frontline/film/battle-for-ukraine/transcript/

Jonsson, O. and Seely, R. (2015). 'Russian Full-Spectrum Conflict: An Appraisal After Ukraine,' *Journal of Slavic Military Studies*, 28 (1): pp.1-22.

Joo, H-m., (2008). 'The Soviet origin of Russian chauvinism: Voices from below,' *Communist and Post-Communist Studies*, 41 (2): 217-242.

Judah, T. (2014). 'Ukraine: Two Poets in the War,' *New York Review of Books*, 28 November. https://www.nybooks.com/daily/2015/04/06/ukraine-two-poets/

Judah, T. (2015). *In Wartime. Stories from Ukraine.* New York: Tim Duggan Books.

Kaihko, I. (2018). 'A nation-in-the-making, in arms: control of force, strategy and the Ukrainian volunteer battalions,' *Defence Studies*, 18 (2): 147-166.

Kaul, E. C. (2020). 'From Orange to Red: Why the Security Service of Ukraine Changed the Approach to Handling Protests from 2004 to 2014,' *East European Politics and Societies and Culture.* https://doi.org/10.1177/0888325420926607.

Kalakura, Y. (2004). *Ukrayinska Istoriohrafiya.* Kyiv: Heneza.

Katchanovski, I. (2016). 'The Maidan Massacre in Ukraine: A Summary of Analysis, Evidence, and Findings' in: J.L. Black and M. Johns eds., *The Return of the Cold War: Ukraine, the West and Russia.* Abingdon: Routledge, 220-224.

Kedourie, E. (1979). *Nationalism*, London: Hutchinson.

Keenan, E. L. (1994). 'On Certain Mythical Beliefs and Russian Behaviors' in: S. Frederick ed, *The Legacy of History in Russia and the New States of Eurasia.* Armonk, NY and London: M.E. Sharpe, 19-40.

Kennedy, P.M. (1973). 'The decline in nationalistic history in the West: 1900—1970,' *Journal of Contemporary History*, 8 (11): 77-100.

Kent, N. (2016). *Crimea. A History.* London: Hurst & Co.

Kishkovsky, S. (2013). 'Putin in Ukraine to Celebrate a Christian Anniversary,' *New York Times*, 27 July. https://www.nytimes.com/2013/07/28/world/europe/putin-in-ukraine-to-celebrate-a-christian-anniversary.html

Kochan, L. (1974). *The Making of Modern Russia.* Harmondsworth: Penguin Books.

Kohut, Z. E. (1994). 'History as a Battleground: Russian-Ukrainian Relations and Historical Consciousness in Contemporary Ukraine' in: S. F. Starr ed., *The Legacy of History in Russia and the New States of Eurasia.* Armonk, NY and London: M.E. Sharpe, 123-146.

Kolsto, P. (2000). *Political Construction Sites. Nation-Building in Russia and the Post-Soviet States* (Boulder, CO: Westview.

Kolsto, P. (2014). 'Russian nationalists flirt with democracy,' *Journal of Democracy*, 25 (3): 120-134.

Kolsto, P. (2016a). 'Crimea vs. Donbas: How Putin Won Russian Nationalist Support—and Lost It Again,' *Slavic Review*, 75 (3): 702-725.

Kolsto, P. (2016b). 'Introduction: Russian nationalism is back – but precisely what does it mean?' in: P. Kolsto and H. Blakkisrud eds., *The New Russian Nationalism. Imperialism, Ethnicity, and Authoritarianism*. Edinburgh: Edinburgh University Press, 1-17.

Kolsto, P. and Blakkisrud H. eds., (2016c). *The New Russian Nationalism. Imperialism, Ethnicity, and Authoritarianism*. Edinburgh: Edinburgh University Press.

Kolsto, P. (2019). 'Is imperialist nationalism an oxymoron?' *Nations and Nationalism*, 25 (1), 2019, 18–44.

Kolumbet, A. (2020). Interview, *New Eastern Europe*, 7 April. https://neweasterneurope.eu/2020/04/07/donbas-veterans-establish-their-place-in-ukrainian-society/

Konsolidatsiya Ukrayinskoho Suspilstva: Vyklyky, Mozhlyvosti, Shlyakhy. (2016). Razumkov Centre for Economic and Political Studies, *Natsionalna Bezpeka i Oborona*, 7-8. http://razumkov.org.ua/uploads/journal/ukr/NSD165-166_2016_ukr.pdf

Kotsur, V. P. and Kotsur, A. O. (1999). *Istoriohrafiya Istorii Ukrayiny*. Chernivtsi: Zoloti Lytavry.

Krastev, I. (2005). 'Russia's post-orange empire,' *Open Democracy*, 19 October. https://www.opendemocracy.net/en/postorange_2947jsp/

Kravchenko, V. (2016). 'Review of Richard Sakwa, Frontline Ukraine. Crisis in the Borderlands.' *East/West: Journal of Ukrainian Studies*, 3 (1): 155-163. https://www.ewjus.com/index.php/ewjus/article/view/173/68

Kremen, V. and Tkachenko, V. (1998). *Ukrayina: Shlyakh do sebe: problemy suspilnoyi transformatsii*. Kyiv: Druk.

Kuchma, L. (1996). *Mykhailo Hrushevsky*. Kyiv: Ukrayina.

Kudelia, S. (2014). 'Domestic Sources of the Donbas Insurgency,' *Ponars Policy Memos* 351, September. http://www.ponarseurasia.org/memo/domestic-sources-donbas-insurgency

Kudelia, S. (2017). 'The Donbas Rift.' *Russian Social Science Review*, 58 (1): 212-234.

Kudelia, S. and Zyl, J. van. (2019). 'In My Name: The Impact of Regional Identity on Civilian Attitudes in the Armed Conflict in Donbas,' *Nationalities Papers*, 47 (5): 801-821.

Kulick, O. (2019). 'Dnipropetrovsk Oligarchs: Lynchpins of Sovereignty or Sources of Instability?' *The Soviet and Post-Soviet Review*, 46 (3): 352-386.

Kulyk, V. (2014). 'Ukrainian Nationalism Since the Outbreak of Euromaidan,' *Ab Imperio*, 3: 94-122.

Kulyk, V. (2016). 'National Identity in Ukraine: Impact of Euromaidan and War,' *Europe-Asia Studies*, 68 (4): 588-608.

Kulyk, V. (2018). 'Shedding Russianness, Recasting Ukrainianness: The Post Euromaidan Dynamics of Ethnonational Identifications in Ukraine,' *Post-Soviet Affairs*, 34 (2–3): 119-138.

Kulyk, V. (2019). 'Memory and Language: Different Dynamics in the Two Aspects of Identity Politics in Post-Euromaidan Ukraine,' *Nationalities Papers*, 47 (6): 1030-1047.

Kuromiya, H. (2019). 'The War in the Donbas in Historical Perspective,' *The Soviet and Post-Soviet Review,* 46 (3): 245-262.

Kuzio, T. (1998). *Ukraine. State and Nation-Building*. London: Routledge.

Kuzio, T. (2001a). 'Transition in Post-Communist States: Triple or Quadruple?' *Politics*, 21 (3): 169-178.

Kuzio, T. (2001b). 'Post-Soviet Ukrainian Historiography in Ukraine,' *Internationale Schulbuchforschung/International Textbook Research*, 23 (1): 27-42.

Kuzio, T. (2002). 'The Myth of the Civic State: A Critical Survey of Hans Kohn's Framework for Understanding Nationalism,' *Ethnic and Racial Studies*, 25 (1): 20-39.

Kuzio, T. (2005). 'Nation-State Building and the Re-Writing of History in Ukraine: The Legacy of Kyiv Rus,' *Nationalities Papers*, 33 (1): 30-58.

Kuzio, T. (2007). 'Russians and Russophones in the Former USSR and Serbs in Yugoslavia: A Comparative Study of Passivity and Mobilisation' in: T. Kuzio, *Theoretical and Comparative Perspectives on Nationalism: New Directions in Cross-Cultural and Post-Communist Studies. Soviet and Post-Soviet Politics and Society series 71,* Hannover: Ibidem-Verlag, 177-216.

Kuzio, T. (2010). 'State-led violence in Ukraine's 2004 elections and orange revolution,' *Communist and Post-Communist Studies*, 43 (4): 383-395.

Kuzio, T. (2012). 'Russianization of Ukrainian National Security Policy under Viktor Yanukovych,' *Journal of Slavic Military Studies*. 25 (4): 558-581.

Kuzio, T. (2015a). 'The Rise and Fall of the Party of Regions Political Machine,' *Problems of Post-Communism*. 62 (3):174-186.

Kuzio, T. (2015b). 'Ukraine Reignites. Why Russia Should be Added to the State Sponsors of Terrorism List,' *Foreign Affairs*, 25 January. https://www.foreignaffairs.com/articles/russian-federation/2015-01-25/ukraine-reignites

Kuzio, T. (2015c). 'Is Russia a State Sponsor of Terrorism?' *New Eastern Europe*, 22 January. https://neweasterneurope.eu/2015/01/22/russia-state-sponsor-terrorism/

Kuzio, T. (2017a). 'Ukraine between a Constrained EU and Assertive Russia,' *Journal of Common Market Studies*. 55 (1): 103-120.

Kuzio, T. (2017b). 'Stalinism and Russian and Ukrainian National Identities,' *Communist and Post-Communist Studies*, 50 (4): 289-302.

Kuzio, T. (2017c). *Putin's War Against Ukraine. Revolution, Nationalism, and Crime*, Toronto, Chair of Ukrainian Studies.

Kuzio, T. (2017d). 'Why are Russian Opposition Leaders Democrats at Home and Imperialists Abroad?' *Atlantic Council of the US*, 22 May. https://www.atlanticcouncil.org/blogs/ukrainealert/why-are-russian-opposition-leaders-democrats-at-home-and-imperialists-abroad/

Kuzio, T. (2019a). 'Russian Stereotypes and Myths of Ukraine and Ukrainians and Why Novorossiya Failed,' *Communist and Post-Communist Studies*, 52 (4): 297-309.

Kuzio, T. (2019b). 'Ideological Zealots Fighting a Non-Existent Ukrainian Nationalist Enemy: A Reply to Tarik Amar's Review of Red Famine,' *Kyiv Mohyla Humanities Journal*, 6: 209-216. http://kmhj.ukma.edu.ua/article/view/189122/188548

Kuzio, T. (2020a). 'Empire Loyalism and Nationalism in Ukraine and Ireland. Comparing the Sources of Conflict in the Donbas and Ulster,' *Communist and Post-Communist Studies*, 53 (3): 88-106.

Kuzio, T. (2020b). 'Time for Zelenskyy to turn from populism to pragmatism,' *Atlantic Council of the US*, 12 October. https://www.atlanticcouncil.org/blogs/ukrainealert/russo-ukrainian-war-time-for-zelenskyy-to-turn-from-populism-to-pragmatism/

Kuzyk, P. (2019). 'Ukraine's national integration before and after 2014. Shifting 'East–West' polarization line and strengthening political community,' *Eurasian Geography and Economics*, 60 (6): 709-735.

Kymlicka, W. (1996). *Multicultural Citizenship*. Oxford: Oxford University Press.

Kymlicka, W. (1997). *The Rights of Minority Cultures*. Oxford: Oxford University Press.

Lagan, B. (2018). 'Australia Day marked by biggest protests,' *The Times*, 26 January. https://www.thetimes.co.uk/article/record-crowds-turn-out-to-protest-against-australia-day-qlxprck6k21724386-governments-intentions-are-good-righting-historic-wrong-will-take-sustained

Lane, D. (2018). 'The International Context: Russia, Ukraine and the Drift to East-West Confrontation' in: B. Kagarlitsky, R. Desai, and A. Freeman eds. *Russia, Ukraine and Contemporary Imperialism*. London: Routledge, 135-156.

Latimore, J. (2018). 'It's convenient to say Aboriginal people support Australia Day. But it's not true,' *The Guardian*, 21 January 2018. https://www.theguardian.com/australia-news/2018/jan/22/its-convenient-to-say-aboriginal-people-support-australia-day-but-its-not-true

Laruelle, M. (2014a). 'The "Russian Idea" on the Small Screen: Staging National Identity on Russia's TV,' *Demokratizatsiya: The Journal of Post-Soviet Democratization*, 22 (2): 313-333.

Laruelle, M. (2014b). 'Alexei Navalny and the challenge of reconciling "nationalism" and "liberalism,"' *Post-Soviet Affairs*, 30 (4): 276-297.

Laruelle, M. (2015). 'Russia as a "Divided Nation," from Compatriots to Crimea: A Contribution to the Discussion on Nationalism and Foreign Policy,' *Problems of Post-Communism*, 62 (2): 88-97.

Laruelle, M. (2016a). 'The three colors of Novorossiya, or the Russian nationalist mythmaking of the Ukrainian crisis,' *Post-Soviet Affairs*, 32 (1): 55-74.

Laruelle, M. (2016b). 'Misinterpreting Nationalism. Why Russkii is Not a Sign of Ethnonationalism,' *Ponars Policy Memos*, 46, January. http://www.ponarseurasia.org/memo/misinterpreting-nationalism-russkii-ethnonationalism

Laruelle, M. (2016c). 'Russia as an anti-liberal European civilisation' in: Kolsto, P. and Blakkisrud H. eds., *The New Russian Nationalism. Imperialism, Ethnicity, and Authoritarianism*. Edinburgh: Edinburgh University Press, 275-297.

Laruelle, M. (2017a). 'Is Nationalism a Force for Change in Russia?' *Daedalus*, 146 (2): 89-100.

Laruelle, M. (2017b). 'In Search of Putin's Philosopher,' *Intersection*, 3 March. https://www.ponarseurasia.org/article/search-putins-philosopher

Laruelle, M. (2020a). 'Making Sense of Russia's Illiberalism,' *Journal of Democracy*, vol. 31 (3): 115-129.

Laruelle, M. (2020b). 'Ideological Complimentarity or Competition? The Kremlin, the Church, and the Monarchist Idea,' *Slavic Review*, 79 (2): 345-364.

Laughlin, J.M. (2001). *Reimagining the Nation-State. The Contested Terrains of Nation-Building*. London: Pluto Press.

Lavrov, S. (2014). 'It is not Russia that is destabilising Ukraine,' *The Guardian*, 7 April. https://www.theguardian.com/commentisfree/2014/apr/07/sergei-lavrov-russia-stabilise-ukraine-west

Lawrence, J. (1969). *A History of Russia* (New York: New American Library.

Leshchenko, N. (1998). 'The National Ideology and the Basis of the Lukashenka Regime in Belarus,' *Europe-Asia Studies*, 60 (8): 1419-1433.

Leshchenko, S. (2014). *Mezhyhirsky Syndrom. Diahnoz vladi Viktora Yanukovych.* Kyiv: Bright Star publishers.

Likhachev, V. (2016). *The Far Right in the Conflict between Russia and Ukraine*. Paris: Instytut Francais Relations Internationales. https://www.ifri.org/en/publications/notes-de-lifri/russieneivisions/far-right-conflict-between-russia-and-ukraine

Longworth, P. (2006). *Russia: the once and future empire from pre-history to Putin*. New York: St. Martin's Press.

Lozhkin, B. (2016). *The Fourth Republic. Why Europe Needs Ukraine and Why Ukraine Needs Europe*. Kyiv: Novyy Druk.

Magocsi, P.R. (1996). *A History of Ukraine.* Toronto: University of Toronto Press

Magocsi, P.R. (2007). *Istoriya Ukrayiny*. Kyiv: Krytyka.

Magocsi, P.R. (2010). *A History of Ukraine. The Land and Its Peoples, Second Edition.* Toronto: University of Toronto Press

Magocsi, P.R. (2012). *Ukrayina. Istoriya yiyi zemel ta narodiv.* Uzhorod: Padzyak publishing house.

Magocsi, P.R. (2014a). *This Blessed Land. Crimea and the Crimean Tatars.* Toronto: University of Toronto.

Magocsi, P.R. (2014b). 'Crimea is not Russian: History of Crimea, Ukraine.' https://www.youtube.com/watch?v=jYd_-1hP3uA

Magocsi, P.R. (2018). *Historia Ukrainy. Ziemia i ludzie* (Warsaw: Ksiegarnia Akademicka).

Maiorova, A., ed. (2017). *Donbas in Flames. Guide to the Conflict Zone.* Kyiv: Research Centre "Prometheus" NGO. https://prometheus.ngo/wpcontent/uploads/2017/04/Donbas_v_Ogni_ENG_web_1-4.pdf

Mann, M. (1993). 'Nation-States in Europe and other Continents: Diversifying, Developing, Not Dying,' *Daedalus*, 122 (3): 115-140.

Martin, J. L. (1996). *Medieval Russia 980-1584.* Cambridge: Cambridge University Press.

Matveeva, A. (2016). 'No Moscow Stooges: identity polarization and guerrilla movements in Donbass,' *Southeastern European Black Sea Studies*, 16 (1): 25-50.

Matveeva, A. (2018). *Through Times of Trouble. Conflict in Southeastern Ukraine Explained From Within.* Lanham, MA: Lexington Books.

Mazour, A.G. (1975). *Modern Russian Historiography.* Westport, CO and London: Greenwood Press.

MacMaster, N. (2000). ''Black Jew-White Negro'. Anti-Semitism and the Construction of Cross-Racial Stereotypes,' *Nationalism and Ethnic Politics*, 6 (4): 65-82.

Mearsheimer, J. J. (2014). 'Why the Ukraine Crisis is the West's Fault: The Liberal Delusions That Provoked Putin,' *Foreign Affairs*, 93 (5): 77-89. https://www.foreignaffairs.com/articles/russia-fsu/2014-08-18/why-ukraine-crisis-west-s-fault

Medvedev, D. (2009). 'V otnosheniyakh Rossii i Ukrainy dolzhny nastupyt' novye vremena,' 11 August. http://blog.da-medvedev.ru/post/30

Medvedev, Z. A. and Medvedev, R.A. eds., (1976). *The Secret Speech. N. S. Krushchev.* Nottingham: Spokesman Books and Bertrand Russell Peace Foundation.

Menon, R. and Rumer, E. (2015). *Conflict in Ukraine. The Unwinding of the Post-Cold War Order*. Cambridge, MA, MIT Press.

Melnyk, O. 2020. '"From the "Russian Spring" to the Armed Insurrection: Russia, Ukraine and Political Communities in the Donbas and Southern Ukraine,' *The Soviet and Post-Soviet Review*, 47 (1): 3-38.

Merry, W. W. (2016). 'The Origins of Russia's War in Ukraine: The Clash of Russian and European 'Civilizational Choices' for Ukraine' in E. A. Wood, W. E. Pomerantz, W. W. Merry and M. Trudolyubov, *Roots of Russia's War in Ukraine*. Washington DC: Woodrow Wilson Centre, 27-50.

Minchenia, A., Tornquist-Plewa B., and Yurchuk Y. (2018). 'Humour as a Mode of Hegemonic Control: Comic Representations of Belarusian and Ukrainian Leaders in Official Russian Media' in: N. Bernsand and B. Tornquist-Plewa eds., *Cultural and Political Imaginaries in Putin's Russia*. Leiden and Boston: Brill Academic Publishers, 211-231.

Mishchenko, M. (2018). 'Ukrayina ta Rosiysa - Kinets braterstva,' *Ukrayinskyy Interes*, 23 April. https://uain.press/articles/kinets-braterstva-797169

Molchanov, M. A. (2016). 'Choosing Europe over Russia: what has Ukraine gained?' *European Politics and Society*, 17 (4): 522-537.

Molchanov, M. A. (2018). 'A Squeezed Country: Ukraine between Europe and Eurasia' in: G. Besier and K. Stoklosa eds., *Neighbourhood Perceptions of the Ukraine Crisis From the Soviet Union into Eurasia?* London: Routledge, 69-82.

Moore, M. (1997). 'On National Self-Determination,' *Political Studies*, XLV (5): 900-913.

Motyl, A.J. (1990). 'The Myth of Russian Nationalism' in: A.J. Motyl, *Sovietology, Rationality, Nationality. Coming to Grips with Nationalism in the USSR*. New York: Columbia University Press, 161-173.

Motyl, A. J. (1999a). *Revolutions, Nations, Empires. Conceptual Limits on Theoretical Possibilities*. New York: Columbia University Press.

Motyl, A. J. (1999b). 'Why Empires Reemerge: Imperial Collapse and Imperial Revival in Comparative Perspective,' *Comparative Politics*, 31 (2): 127-146.

Motyl, A.J. (2015). 'Ukraine's Donbas is Like America's South,' *Huffington Post*, 5 January. http://www.huffingtonpost.com/alexander-motyl/alexander-motyl_b_6414802.html

Naryshkin, S. (2020). 'Zelensky vse glubzhe pogruzhayetsia v ideyu ukrainskogo natsionalyzma,' *Tass*, 28 January. https://tass.ru/politika/7621843?fbclid=IwAR3Sz Rh-y9k2FBIRkY1sJv-PdmblCMx4ajG7VRnMkvEFtTHMBBRP3fJgWww

National Security and Defence Council. (2016). 'Stenohrama zasidannya RNBO Ukrayiny u zvyazku z pochatkom Rosiyskoyii ahresii v Krymu,' 22 February. https://www.pravda.com.ua/articles/2016/02/22/7099911/

Na terrritorii Donetskoy oblasty deystvovaly voyennye lagerya DNR s polnym vooruzheniyem s 2009 goda. (2014). 20 July. http://novosti.dn.ua/details/230206/

Navalnyi (2012a). 'Navalnyi: Ukraintsy i russkiye – odyn I tot zhe narod,' 11 February. https://censor.net.ua/news/197005/navalnyyi_ukraintsy_i_russkie_odin_i_tot_je_narod

Navalnyi, (2012b). 'Navalnyi: ya bolshe ukrainets po svoim korniam i genetyke,' 11 February. https://lb.ua/news/2012/02/11/136390_navalniy_ya_bolshe_ukrainets_po_svoim.html

Nedozhogina, O. (2019). 'A Bitter Divorce: Narratives of Crimean Annexation and their Relation to Larger State Identifications,' *Europe-Asia Studies*, 71 (7): 1069-1090.

Observations of Public Attitudes in Donbas. (2020). Changes After the Elections in 2019, Emerging Risks amid the War and COVID-19 Pandemic, Democratic Initiatives Foundation, 15 May. https://dif.org.ua/en/article/observations-of-public-attitudes-in-donbas-changes-after-the-elections-in-2019-emerging-risks-amid-the-war-and-covid-19-pandemic

O komplekse mer po vovlecheniyu Ukrainy v evraziiskii integratsionyi protsess. (2013). *Zerkalo Nedeli*, 18 August. https://zn.ua/internal/o-komplekse-mer-po-vovlecheniyu-ukrainy-v-evraziyskiy-integracionnyy-process-_.html

Nimmo, B., Francois, Eib, C.S., Ronzaud, L., Ferreira, R., Hernon, C., and Kostelancik, T. *Exposing Secondary Infektion. Forgeries, interference, and attacks on Kremlin critics across six years and 300 sites and platforms*. Washington DC: Graphika. https://secondaryinfektion.org/downloads/secondary-infektion-report.pdf

Olearchyk, R. (2019). 'Ukraine's workers abroad fuel property boom back home,' *Financial Times*, 26 August. https://www.ft.com/content/762a17b2-c3f0-11e9-a8e9-296ca66511c9

O'Loughlin, J., Toal, G. and Kolosov, V. (2016). 'Who identifies with the "Russian World"? Geopolitical attitudes in southeastern Ukraine, Crimea, Abkhazia, South Ossetia, and Transnistria,' *Eurasian Geography and Economics*, 57 (6): 745-778.

O'Loughlin, J., Toal, G., and Kolosov, V. (2017). 'The rise and fall of "Novorossiya": examining support for a separatist geopolitical imaginary in southeast Ukraine,' *Post-Soviet Affairs*, 33 (2): 124-144.

O'Loughlin, J. and Toal, G., (2020) 'Does War Change Geopolitical Attitudes? A Comparative Analysis of 2014 Surveys in Southeast Ukraine,' *Problems of Post-Communism*, 67 (3): 303-318.

Ongoing Violations of International Law and Defiance of OSCE Principles and Commitments by the Russian Federation in Ukraine. (2018). Vienna: U.S. Mission to Organisation for Security and Cooperation in Europe, 1 February. https://osce.usmission.gov/on-russias-ongoing-violations-in-ukraine-14/

Onuch, O. (2014). 'Who were the Protestors?' *Journal of Democracy*, 25 (3): 44-51.

Onuch, O. and Hale, H. E. (2018). 'Capturing ethnicity: the case of Ukraine,' *Post-Soviet Affairs*, 34 (2-3): 84-106.

Onuch, O. and Sasse, G. (2018). 'The Maidan in Movement: Diversity and the Cycles of Protest' in: D. Averre and K. Wolczuk eds., *The Ukraine Conflict. Security, Identity and Politics in the Wider Europe*. London and New York: Routledge, 6-37.

Operation Armageddon. (2015). Cyber Espionage as a Strategic Component of Russian Modern Warfare. *Lookingglass Cyber Threat Intelligence Group*, CTIG-20150428-01, 28 April. https://www.lookingglasscyber.com/wp-content/uploads/2015/08/Operation_Armageddon_Final.pdf

Osnovni Zasady ta Shlyakhy Formuvannya Spilnoyi Identychnosti Hromadyan Ukrayiny. (2017). Razumkov Centre for Economic and Political Studies, *Natsionalna Bezpeka i Oborona*, 1–2. http://razumkov.org.ua/uploads/journal/ukr/NSD169-170_2017_ukr.pdf

Osipan, A. (2015). 'History, Myths, Enemy Images, and Regional Identity in the Donbas Insurgency,' *Journal of Soviet and Post-Soviet Politics and Society*, 1 (1): 109-140.

Paasi, A. (1995). 'Constructed Territory, Boundaries and Regional Identities' in: T. Forsberg ed., *Contested Territory. Border Disputes at the Edge of the Former Soviet Empire*. Aldershot: Edward Elgar, 42-61.

Pain, E. (2014). 'The imperial syndrome and its influence on Russian nationalism' in: P. Kolsto and H. Blakkisrud eds., (2016) *The New Russian Nationalism. Imperialism, Ethnicity, and Authoritarianism*. Edinburgh: Edinburgh University Press, 46-74.

Paton, C. (2015). 'Letter. Let's talk to Russia,' *The Times*, 1 January. https://www.thetimes.co.uk/article/lets-talk-to-russia-7wwc8gz0970

Paxman, J. (1999). *The English. A Portrait.* London: Penguin Books.

Perspektyvy Ukrayinsko-Rosiyskykh Vidnosyn. (2015). Razumkov Centre for Economic and Political Studies, *Natsionalna Bezpeka i Oborona*, 8-9. http://razumkov.org.ua/uploads/journal/ukr/NSD157-158_2015_ukr.pdf

Peterson, (2014). 'A Ukrainian murder mystery ensnares a church in former rebel stronghold,' *Christian Science Monitor*, 12 August. https://www.csmonitor.com/World/Europe/2014/0812/A-Ukrainian-murder-mystery-ensnares-a-church-in-former-rebel-stronghold

Petro, N. N. (2015). 'Understanding the other Ukraine: Identity and allegiance in Russophone Ukraine' in: A. Pikulicka-Wilczewska and R. Sakwa eds., *Ukraine and Russia: People, Politics, Propaganda and Perspectives.* Bristol: E-International Relations Publishing, 19-35. http://www.e-ir.info/wp-content/uploads/2015/03/Ukraine-and-Russia-E-IR.pdf

Petro, N. N. (2016). 'Why Ukraine and Russia Need Each Other,' *Russian Politics*, 1 (2): 184-202.

Petro, N. N. (2018). 'How the West Lost Russia: Explaining the Conservative Turn in Russian Foreign Policy,' *Russian Politics*, 3 (3): 305-332.

Petrushev, N. (2016). 'Myrovoye soobshchestvo dolzhno skazat na spasybo za Krym,' *Moskovskyj Komsomolets*, 26 January. https://www.mk.ru/politics/2016/01/26/nikolay-patrushev-mirovoe-soobshhestvo-dolzhno-skazat-nam-spasibo-za-krym.html

Pidsumky-2018: hromadska dumka. (2018). Democratic Initiatives Foundation, 28 December. https://dif.org.ua/article/pidsumki-2018-gromadska-dumka

Pijl, V. der (2018). *Flight MH17, Ukraine and the New Cold War. Prism of Disaster.* Manchester: Manchester University Press.

Ploeg, C. de. (2017). *Ukraine in the Crossfire.* Atlanta, GA: Clarity Press.

Plokhy, S. (1996). 'Book Review,' *Journal of Ukrainian Studies*, 21 (1–2): 342–345.

Plokhy, S. (2000). 'The City of Glory: Sevastopol in Russian Historical Mythology,' *Journal of Contemporary History*, 35 (3): 369-383.

Plokhy, S. (2015). *The Gates of Europe. A History of Ukraine.* London and New York: Allen Lane and Basic Books.

Plokhy, S. (2016). *Brama Yevropy. Istoriya Ukrayiny vid skifskykh voyen do nezalezhnosti*. Kharkiv: Knyzhkovyy Klub 'Klub Simeynoho Dozvillya.'

Plokhy, S. (2017). *Lost Kingdom. A History of Russian Nationalism from Ivan the Great to Vladimir Putin*. London: Penguin Books.

Pop-Eleches, G. and Robertson, G.B. (2018). 'Identity and political preferences in Ukraine – before and after the Euromaidan,' *Post-Soviet Affairs*, 34 (2-3): 107-118.

Poroshenko, P. (2017). 'Pro rishennya Rady natsionalnoyi bezpeky i oborony Ukrayiny vid 28 kvitnya 2017 roku 'Pro zastosuvannya personalnykh spetsial□nykh ekonomichnykh ta inshykh obmezhuvalnykh zakhodiv (sanktsiy),' Presidential Decree 133/2017, 15 May. https://www.president.gov.ua/documents/1332017-21850

Poroshenko, P. (2018). 'Zvernennya Prezydenta Ukrayiny do Vselenskoho Patriarkha Varfolomiya,' 19 April. https://www.president.gov.ua/administration/zvernennya-prezidenta-ukrayini-do-vselenskogo-patriarha-varf-438

Poshuky Shlyakhiv Vidnovlennya Suverenitetu Ukrayiny Nad Okupovanym Donbasom: Stan Hromadskoyii Dumky Naperedodni Prezydentskykh Vyboriv. (2019) Democratic Initiatives Foundation, 13 February. https://dif.org.ua/article/poshuki-shlyakhiv-vidnovlennya-suverenitetu-ukraini-nad-okupovanim-donbasom-stan-gromadskoi-dumki-naperedodni-prezidentskikh-viboriv

Prina, F. (2016). *National Minorities in Putin's Russia. Diversity and assimilation*. London and New York: Routledge.

Pritsak, O. and Reshetar, J.S. (1963). 'The Ukraine and the Dialectics of Nation-Building,' *Slavic Review*, 22 (2): 224-255.

Prizel, T. (1998). *National Identity and Foreign Policy. Nationalism and Leadership in Poland, Russia, and Ukraine*. Cambridge: Cambridge University Press.

Procyk, A. (1995). *Russian Nationalism and Ukraine: The Nationality Policy of the Volunteer Army During the Civil War During the Civil War*. Edmonton: Canadian Institute of Ukrainian Studies.

Public Opinion in Donbas a Year After Presidential Elections. (2020). Democratic Initiatives Foundation, 9 April. https://dif.org.ua/en/article/public-opinion-in-donbas-a-year-after-presidential-elections

Putin, V. (2008). 'Text of Putin's speech at NATO Summit (Bucharest, 2 April 2008).' https://www.unian.info/world/111033-text-of-putins-speech-at-nato-summit-bucharest-april-2-2008.html.

Putin, V. (2014a). 'Address by President of the Russian Federation,' 18 March. http://en.kremlin.ru/events/president/news/20603

Putin, V. (2014b). 'Direct line with Vladimir Putin,' 17 April. http://en.kremlin.ru/events/president/news/20796

Putin, V. (2015a). 'Rossiia i Ukraina "obrechenyi" na sovmestnoye budushchee,' *RIA Novosti*, 19 June. https://ria.ru/20150619/1079341748.html

Putin, V. (2015b). 'Ukraina – samaya blyzkaya k nam strana,' *Tass*, 29 September. https://tass.ru/interviews/2298160

Putin, V. (2017). 'Speech to the Valdai Club,' 25 October. https://www.youtube.com/watch?v=GvY184FQsiA

Putin, V. (2019). 'Putin fears second "Srebrenica" if Kiev gets control over border in Donbass,' *Tass*, 10 December. https://tass.com/world/1097897

Putin, V. (2020a). Vladimir Putin rasskazal o "podarkakh" russkogo naroda respublykam, vyshedshym iz sostava Sovetskogo Soyuza,' *Nika TV*, 22 June. https://nikatv.ru/news/obshestvo/vladimir-putin-rasskazal-opodarkah-russkogo-naroda-respublikam-vyshedshim-izsostava-sovetskogo-soyuza

Putin, V. (2020b). 'Twenty questions with Vladimir Putin. Putin on Ukraine,' *Tass*, 18 March. https://putin.tass.ru/en

Putin, V. (2000c). 'Putin said that the deterioration of relations between Russia and Ukraine is not connected with the accession of Crimea,' *Tass*, 12 July. https://tass.ru/politika/8945395

Reagan, P. M. (2000). *Civil Wars and Foreign Powers: Interventions and Intrastate Conflicts*. Ann Arbor, MI: University of Michigan.

Rehionalni Osoblyvosti Ideyno-Politychnykh Orientatsiy Hromadyan Ukrayiny v Konteksti Vyborchoyi Kampanii. (2006). Razumkov Centre for Economic and Political Studies, *Natsionalna Bezpeka i Oborona*, 1. http://razumkov.org.ua/uploads/journal/ukr/NSD73_2006_ukr.pdf

Report on the human rights situation in Ukraine. (2014). Office of the United Nations High Commissioner for Human Rights, 15 April. https://www.ohchr.org/EN/Countries/ENACARegion/Pages/UAReports.aspx

Riabchuk, M. (2016). 'Ukrainians as Russia's Negative 'Other': History Comes Full Circle,' *Communist and Post-Communist Studies*, 49 (1): 75-85.

Riasanovsky, N. V. (1977). *A History of Russia*. Oxford and New York: Oxford University Press.

Rik diyalnosti Prezydenta Volodymyra Zelenskoho: zdobutky i prorakhunky. (2020). Kyiv: Razumkov Centre for Economic and Political Studies. http://razumkov.org.ua/uploads/article/2020_Rik_diyalnosti_Prezydenta.pdf

Robinson, N. (2020). 'Putin and the Incompleteness of Putinism,' *Russian Politics*, 5 (3): 283-300.

Roth, A. 2014. 'From Russia, 'Tourists' Stir the Protests,' *New York Times*, 3 March. https://www.nytimes.com/2014/03/04/world/europe/russias-hand-can-be-seen-in-the-protests.html

Roth, A. (2019). 'Ukraine's ex-president Viktor Yanukovych found guilty of treason,' *The Guardian*, 25 January. https://www.theguardian.com/world/2019/jan/25/ukraine-ex-president-viktor-yanukovych-found-guilty-of-treason

Rowley, D.G. (2000). 'Imperial versus national discourse: the case of Russia,' *Nations and Nationalism,* 6 (1): 23-42.

Russia's 'Hybrid' War – Challenge and Threat for Europe. (2016). Razumkov Centre for Economic and Political Studies, *National Security and Defence*, 9-10, http://razumkov.org.ua/uploads/journal/eng/NSD167-168_2016_eng.pdf

Russian Patriots. (1971). 'A Nation Speaks,' *Survey*, 17 (3): 191-199.

Russian 'road map' for annexing eastern Ukraine. (2015). *Kyiv Post*, 25 February. https://www.kyivpost.com/article/content/ukraine-politics/roadmap-for-annexing-easternukraine-leaked-from-putins-office-381811.html

Russian-Ukrainian Conflict. Prospects and Parameters of UN Peacekeeping Mission in Donbas. (2018). Kyiv: Razumkov Centre for Economic and Political Studies, August. http://razumkov.org.ua/uploads/article/2018_Russian-Ukrainian_Conflict_ru_en.pdf

Said, E. (1994). *Culture and Imperialism*. London. Vintage.

Said, E. (1995). *Orientalism. Western Conceptions of the Orient*. London: Penguin.

Sakwa, R. (2015). *Frontline Ukraine. Crisis in the Borderlands*. London: I.B. Tauris.

Sakwa, R. 2016. 'Back to the Wall: Myths and Mistakes that Once Again Divide Europe,' *Russian Politics*, 1 (1): 1-26.

Sakwa, R. (2017a). *Russia Against the Rest. The Post-Cold War Crisis of World Order*. Cambridge: Cambridge University Press.

Sakwa R. (2017b). 'The Ukraine Syndrome and Europe: Between Norms and Space,' *The Soviet and Post-Soviet Review*, 44: 9-31.

Sakwa, R. (2020a). 'Greater Russia: Is Moscow out to subvert the West?' *International Politics*. https://doi.org/10.1057/s41311-020-00258-0

Sakwa, R. (2020b). 'Is Putin an Ism,' *Russian Politics*, 5 (3): 255-282.

Sambanis, N. (2002). 'A Review of Recent Advances and Future Directions in the Quantitative Literature on Civil War,' *Defence and Peace Economics*, 13 (3): 215-243.

Sambanis, N., Skaperdas, S. and Wohlforth, W. (2017). 'External Intervention, Identity, and Civil War,' *SSRN Research Library*, 17 August. https://papers.ssrn.com/sol3/papers.cfm?abstract_id=3019206

Sasse, G. and Lackner, A. (2018). 'War and identity: the case of the Donbas in Ukraine,' *Post-Soviet Affairs*, 34 (2-3)139-157.

Saunders, D. (1993). 'What Makes a Nation a Nation? Ukrainians Since 1600,' *Ethnic Groups,* 10: 101-124.

Saunders, D. (1995a). 'Russia and Ukraine under Alexander II: The Valuev Edict of 1863,' *The International History Review*, XV11 (1): 23–50.

Saunders, D. (1995b). 'Russia's Ukrainian Policy (1847–1903): A Demographic Approach,' *European History Quarterly*, 25 (2): 181–208.

Schwartz, M. (2018). 'Who Killed the Kiev Protesters? A 3-D Model Holds the Clues,' *New York Times*, 30 May. https://www.nytimes.com/2018/05/30/magazine/ukraine-protest-video.html

Seton-Watson, H. (1967). *The Russian Empire, 1801-1917*. Oxford: Oxford University Press.

Seton-Watson, H. (1971). *The New Imperialism. Revised Edition*. London and Toronto: The Bodley Head.

Shandra, A. and Seely, R. (2019). *The Surkov Leaks. The Inner Workings of Russia's Hybrid War in Ukraine*. London: Royal United Services Institute. https://rusi.org/publication/occasional-papers/surkov-leaks-inner-workings-russias-hybrid-war-ukraine

Shekhovtsov, A. (2014). 'Neo-Nazi Russian National Unity in Eastern Ukraine,' *Shekhovtsov blog*, 14 August. http://anton-shekhovtsov.blogspot.com/2014/08/neo-nazi-russian-national-unity-in.html

Shekhovtsov, A. (2016). 'How Alexander Dugin's Neo-Eurasianists geared up for the Russian-Ukrainian War in 2005-2013,' *Shekhovtsov blog*, 25 January. https://anton-shekhovtsov.blogspot.com/2016/01/how-alexander-dugins-neo-eurasianists.html

Shekhovtsov, A. (2017). 'Aleksandr Dugin's New Eurasianism and the Russia-Ukraine War' in: M. Bassin and G. Pozo-Martin eds., *The Politics of Eurasia: Identity, Popular Culture and Russia's Foreign Policy*. London: Towman and Littlefield, 185-204.

Shekhovtsov, A. (2018). *Russia and the Western Far Right. Tango Noir*. London: Routledge.

Shkandrij, M. (2001). *Russia and Ukraine. Literature and the Discourse of Empire from Napoleonic to Post-Colonial Times*. Montreal and Kingston.: McGill-Queens University Press.

Shkandrij, M. (2011). 'Colonial, Anti-Colonial and Postcolonial in Ukrainian literature' in: Jaroslav Rozumnyj ed., *Twenty Century Ukrainian Literature. Essays in honour of Dmytro Shtohryn*. Kyiv: Mohyla Academy Publishing House, 282-297.

Shostyy rik dekomunizatsii: stavlennya naselennya do zaborony symboliv totalitarnoho mynuloho. (2020). Democratic Initiatives Foundation, 16 July. https://dif.org.ua/article/shostiy-rik-dekomunizatsii-stavlennya-naselennya-do-zaboroni-simvoliv-totalitarnogo-minulogo

Shpiker, M. (2016). 'Is There a war going on between Russia and Ukraine,' Kyiv International Institute of Sociology, 15 March. https://kiis.com.ua/?lang=eng&cat=reports&id=609&page=1

Sindelar, D. (2015) 'We're nothing more than bargaining chips. What it means to be Ukrainian in wartime,' *The Guardian*, January 23. https://www.theguardian.com/world/2015/jan/23/-sp-ukraine-russia-identity-wartime

Situation of human rights in the temporarily occupied Autonomous Republic of Crimea and the city of Sevastopol (Ukraine). (2014). Office of the United Nations High Commissioner for Human Rights. http://www.ohchr.org/Documents/Countries/UA/Crimea2014_2017_EN.pdf

Skrypnyk, O. ed., (2019). *Peninsula of Fear: Five Years of Unfreedom in Crimea*. Kyiv: Zmina Human Rights Centre, Crimean Human Rights Group, Ukrainian Helsinki Human Rights Union, May. https://ccl.org.ua/wp-content/uploads/2020/04/poluostrov-straha-angl-book_en.pdf

Smart, P. (1992). 'Mill and Nationalism. National Character, Social Progress and the Spirit of Achievement,' *History of European Ideas*, 15 (4-6): 527-534.

Smith, A.D. (1981). 'War and Ethnicity: the role of warfare in the formation, self-image and cohesion of ethnic communities,' *Ethnic and Racial Studies*, 4(4): 375-397.

Snyder, T. (2018). 'Ivan Ilyin, Putin's Philosopher of Russian Fascism,' *New York Review of Books*, 5 April. https://www.nybooks.com/daily/2018/03/16/ivan-ilyin-putins-philosopher-of-russian-fascism/

Socor, V. (2020a). 'Putin and Ukraine's Black Sea Lands: Another Iteration of New Russia?' *Eurasia Daily Monitor*, 17 (2). https://jamestown.org/program/putin-and-ukraines-black-sea-lands-another-iteration-of-novorossiya/

Socor, V. (2020b). 'Ukraine Designates Legitimate Representatives of Donetsk and Luhansk in the Minsk Process. Parts 1 and 2,' *Eurasia Daily Monitor*, 17 (85, 87). https://jamestown.org/program/ukraine-designates-legitimate-representatives-of-donetsk-and-luhansk-in-the-minsk-process/ and https://jamestown.org/program/ukraine-designates-legitimate-representatives-of-donetsk-and-luhansk-in-the-minsk-process-part-two/

Sokolov, B. 'Kogty uvyazly,' *Grani.ru*, 12 April. https://grani-ru-org.appspot.com/War/m.275929.html

Solzhenitsyn, A. (1990). 'Kak Nam Obustroit Rossiu? Posilnye soobrazheniia.' http://www.solzhenitsyn.ru/proizvedeniya/publizistika/stati_i_rechi/v_izgnanii/kak_nam_obustroit_rossiyu.pdf.

Stavlennya Naselennya Ukrayny do Postati Stalina, (2019). Kyiv International Institute of Sociology, 11 July. https://www.kiis.com.ua/?lang=ukr&cat=reports&id=872&page=6

Sotsialno-politychna sytuatsiya v Ukrayini, (2020). Razumkov Centre for Economic and Political Studies and Sotsis Centre, 21-28 July. http://razumkov.org.ua/napriamky/sotsiologichni-doslidzhennia/sotsialnopolitychna-sytuatsiia-v-ukraini-lypen-2020r

Sukhankin, S. (2020). 'The Dark Side of Russia's Youth Military-Patriotic Upbringing,' *Eurasia Daily Monitor*, 17 (119), 12 August. https://jamestown.org/program/the-dark-side-of-russias-youth-military-patriotic-upbringing/

Stein J. ed., (2010). *Russia*. New York: H.W. Wilson Co.

Subtelny, O. (1988, 1994, 2000, 2009). *Ukraine. A History. Four editions*. Toronto: University of Toronto Press.

Subtelny, O. (1991). *Ukrayina. Istoriya.* Kyiv: Lybid.

Subtelny, O. (1994). *Ukraina, Istoria.* Kyiv: Lybid.

Subtelny, O. (1994). 'American Sovietology's Great Blunder: The Marginalization of the Nationality Issue,' *Nationalities Papers*, 22 (1): 141-155.

Sumner, B. H. (1947). *Survey of Russian History.* London: Duckworth.

Surkov, V. (2020). 'Mne interesno deystvovat protyv realnosty,' *Aktualnye Kommentarii*, 26 February. http://actualcomment.ru/surkov-mne-interesno-deystvovat-protiv-realnosti-2002260855.html

Suslov, M. (2018). '"Russian World" Concept: Post-Soviet Geopolitical Ideology and the Logic of "Spheres of Influence",' *Geopolitics*, 23 (2): 330-353.

Svoboda, K. (2019). 'On the Road to Maidan: Russia's Economic Statecraft Towards Ukraine in 2013,' *Europe-Asia Studies*, 71 (10): 1685-1704.

Szporluk, R. (1997). 'Ukraine: From an Imperial Periphery to a Sovereign State,' *Daedalus,* 126 (3): 85-119.

Teper, Y. (2016). 'Official Russian identity discourse in light of the annexation of Crimea: national or imperial,' *Post-Soviet Affairs*, 32 (4): 378-396.

The hardest word. 1997. *The Economist*, 9 September. https://www.economist.com/asia/1999/09/09/the-hardest-word

The Views and Opinions of South-Eastern Regions Residents of Ukraine. (2014). Kyiv International Institute of Sociology, April. https://www.kiis.com.ua/?lang=ukr&cat=reports&id=302&y=2014&m=4&page=1

Tillet, L.R. (1964). 'Soviet Second Thoughts on Tsarist Colonialism,' *Foreign Affairs*, 42 (2): 309-319.

Tillet, L.R. (1967). 'Nationalism and History,' *Problems of Communism,* XVI (5): 36-45.

Tillet, L.R. (1969). *The Great Friendship. Soviet Historians on the Non-Russian Nationalities*. Chapel Hill, NC: University of North Carolina Press.

Toal, G. (2017). *Near Abroad. Putin, The West, and the Contest over Ukraine and the Caucasus.* New York: Oxford University Press.

Tolz, V. (1998a). 'Forging the Nation: National Identity and Nation-Building in Post-Communist Russia,' *Europe-Asia Studies*, 50 (6): 993–1022.

Tolz, V. (1998b) 'Homeland Myths' and Nation-State Building in Postcommunist Russia,' *Slavic Review*, 57 (2): 267–294.

Torbakov, I. (2020). 'Examining the Origins of Russia's Superiority Complex vis-à-vis Ukraine,' *Eurasianet*, 26 May 26. https://eurasianet.org/perspectives-examining-the-origins-of-russians-superiority-complex-vis-a-vis-ukrainians

Tottle, D. (1987). *Fraud, Famine and Fascism: The Ukrainian Genocide Myth from Hitler to Harvard.* Toronto: Progress Books.

Treuer, D. (2020). 'This Land Is Not Your Land. The Ethnic Cleansing of Native Americans,' *Foreign Affairs*, July-August, 99 (4): 171-175.

Trudolybov, M. (2016). 'More Than a War of Words,' *New York Times*, 3 February. https://www.nytimes.com/2016/02/04/opinion/more-than-a-war-of-words.html

Tuminez, A. (1997). 'Russia in Search of Itself: Nationalism and the Future of the Russian State,' *Ponars Policy Memos*, 20, October. https://www.ponarseurasia.org/sites/default/files/policy-memos-pdf/pm_0020.pdf

Tytykalo, (2020). 'Rol Medvedchuka: Yuriy Lytvyn i Vasyl Stus maly odnoho advokata ta zahynuly v odnomu tabori,' *Istorychna Pravda*, 9 July. https://www.istpravda.com.ua/articles/2020/07/9/157794/

Ukraine: The Russia Factor in Crimea – Ukraine's "Soft Underbelly?" (2006). US Embassy Kyiv, 17 December. http://wikileaks.org/cable/2006/12/06KYIV4489.html.

Ukraine: Crimea Update – Less Tense Than in 2006: Interethnic, Russia, Land Factors Remain Central (2007). US Embassy Kyiv, 8 June. http://wikileaks.org/cable/2007/06/07KYIV1418.html

Ukraine: ad hoc visit of the Advisory Committee on the Framework Convention for the Protection of National Minorities (2014). Council of Europe, 20 March. https://www.coe.int/en/web/minorities/news/-/asset_publisher/d4ZbHbFMMxCR/content/ukraine-ad-hoc-visit-of-the-advisory-committee-on-the-framework-convention-for-the-protection-of-national-minorities?inheritRedirect=false

Ukraine's Fight Against Corruption: The Economic Front. Economic Assessment of Anticorruption Measures Implemented 2014–2018. (2018). Kyiv: Institute of Economic Research and Policy Consulting. http://www.ier.com.ua/files/publications/Policy_papers/IER/2018/Anticorruption_Report_EN.pdf

Ukrayinska mova: shlyakh u nezalezhniy Ukrayini. (2020). Democratic Initiatives Foundation, 10 September. https://dif.org.ua/article/ukrainska-mova-shlyakh-u-nezalezhniy-ukraini

Ukrainian Parliament. (2015a). 'Pro vyznannya henotsydu krymskotatarskoho narodu,' 12 November. https://zakon.rada.gov.ua/laws/show/792-19#Text

Ukrainian Parliament. (2015b). 'Pro pravovyy status ta vshanuvannya pamyati bortsiv za nezalezhnist Ukrayiny u XX stolitti,' 9 April. http://www.golos.com.ua/article/254977

Ukrainian Parliament. (2015c). 'Pro uvivchennya peremohy nad natsyzmom u Druhiy svitoviy viyni 1939-1945 rokiv,' 9 April. http://www.golos.com.ua/article/254978

Ukrainian Parliament. (2015d). 'Pro dostup do arkhiviv represyvnykh orhaniv komunistychnoho totalitarnoho rezhymu 1917-1991 rokiv,' http://www.golos.com.ua/article/254979

Ukrainian Parliament. (2015de). 'Pro zasudzhennya komunistychnoho ta national-sotsialistychnoho (natsystkoho) totalitarnykh rezymiv v Ukrayiny ta zaboronu propahandy yikhnoii symvol,' http://www.golos.com.ua/article/254980

Ukrainian Parliament. (2016a). 'Proekt Zakonu pro vnesennya zmin do Zakonu Ukrayiny 'Pro kinematohrafiyu' (shchodo filmiv derzhavy-ahresora),' 29 March. http://w1.c1.rada.gov.ua/pls/zweb2/webproc4_1?pf3511=56877

Ukrainian Parliament. (2016b). 'Zayava Komitetu z pytan prav lyudyny, natsionalnykh i menshyn i mizhnatsionalnykh vidnosyn u zvyazku z vshanuvannyam 18 travnya v Ukrayini 72-x rokovyn deportatsii krymskotatarskoho narodu 1944 roku,' 18 May. https://zakon.rada.gov.ua/laws/show/792-19#Text

Ukrainian Parliament. (2016c). 'Zvernennya Verkhovnoii Rady Ukrayiny do Yoho Vsesvyatosti Varfolomiya, Arkhiyepyskopa Konstantynopoliya I Novoho Rymu, Vselenskoho Patriarkha shchodonadannya avtokefalii Pravloslavnoyiy Tserkvi v Ukrayini,' 16 June. https://zakon.rada.gov.ua/laws/show/1422-19#n9

Ukrainian Parliament. (2018). 'Pro pidtrymku zvernennya Prezydenta Ukrayiny do Vselenskoho Patriarkha Varfolomiya pro nadannya Tomosu pro avtokefaliyu Pravloslavnoyii Tserkvy v Ukrayini,' 19 April. https://zakon.rada.gov.ua/laws/show/2410-19#Text

Ukrainian State Film Agency. (2014). 'Natsrada oprylyudnyla spysok rosiys☐kykh kanaliv, zaboronenykh v Ukrayini,' *Ukrayinska Pravda*, 9 September. https://www.pravda.com.ua/news/2014/09/9/7037233/

Ukrainian State Film Agency. (2016). 'Perelik filmiv, na yaki skasovuyet☐sya derzhavna reyestratsiya ta vyznayutsya nediysnymy prokatni posvidchennya,' 25 April. http://dergkino.gov.ua/ua/news/show/744/perelik_filmiv_na_yaki_skasovuietsya_derzhavna_reiestratsiya_ta_viznayutsya_nediysnimi_prokatni_posvidchen.html

Ukraine versus Russia. (2018). Case Concerning Application of the International Convention on the Elimination of All Forms of Racial Discrimination and International Convention of the Suppression of the Financing of Terrorism Submitted by Ukraine 12 June 2018. The Hague: International Court of Justice. https://www.icj-cij.org/files/case-related/166/166-20180612-WRI-01-00-EN.pdf

Ukraine versus Russia. (2019). Written Statement of Observations and Submissions on the Preliminary Objections of the Russian Federation Submitted by Ukraine 14 January 2019. The Hague: International Court of Justice. https://www.icj-cij.org/files/case-related/166/166-20190114-WRI-01-00-EN.pdf

Ukrayina Pislya Vyboriv: Suspilni Ochikuvannya, Politychni Priorytety, Perspektyvy Rozvytku. (2019). Kyiv: Razumkov Centre for Economic and Political Studies. http://razumkov.org.ua/uploads/article/2019_Koalits_Ugoda.pdf

Umland, A. (2016). 'The Glazyev Tapes: Getting to the root of the conflict in Ukraine,' European Council on Foreign Relations, 1 November. https://www.ecfr.eu/article/commentary_the_glazyev_tapes_getting_to_the_root_of_the_conflict_in_7165

Vatchagaev. M. (2015). 'Two Chechen Battalions Are Fighting in Ukraine on Kyiv's Side.' *Eurasia Daily Monitor*, 12 (153). https://jamestown.org/program/two-chechen-battalions-are-fighting-in-ukraine-on-kyivs-side/#.VdLmEfmqpBd

Velychenko, S. (1991). 'Perestroika and Interpretation of Russian-Ukrainian Relations,' *Journal of Soviet Nationalities*, 2 (2): 35-51.

Velychenko, S. (1992). *National History as Cultural Process. A Survey of the Interpretations of Ukraine's Past in Polish, Russian, and Ukrainian Historical Writing from the Earliest Times to 1914*. Edmonton-Toronto: Canadian Institute of Ukrainian Studies.

Velychenko, S. (1993). *Shaping Identity in Eastern Europe and Russia*. New York: St Martin's Press.

Velychenko, S. (1994a). 'Restructuring and the Non-Russian Past,' *Nationalities Papers,* 22 (2): 325-335.

Velychenko, S. (1994b). 'National History and the "History of the USSR": The Persistence and Impact of Categories' in: D.V. Schwartz and R. Panosian eds., *Nationalism and History. The Politics of Nation-Building in Post-Soviet Armenia, Azerbaidzhan and Georgia*. Toronto: University of Toronto, 23-47.

Velychenko, S. (2004). 'Post-Colonialism and Ukrainian History,' *Ab Imperio* (1): 391-404.

Verkhovskyj, A. (2014). *Rossiya – ne Ukraina: sovremennyje aktsenty natsionalizma*. Moscow: SOVA Centre. https://www.sova-center.ru/files/books/ru14-text.pdf

Violations of human rights and international crimes during the war in the Donbass. (2018). Kyiv: Centre for Civil Liberties, Coalition of Human Rights Organizations and the Justice for Peace in the Donbass initiatives. https://drive.google.com/file/d/1lPfUNjusOPhndAqB5oPLjjdWkyaIffnQ/view

Viyna na Donbasi: Realii i Perspektyvy Vrehulyuvannya. (2019). Razumkov Centre for Economic and Political Studies, *Natsionalna Bezpeka i Oborona*, 8-9. http://razumkov.org.ua/uploads/journal/ukr/NSD177-178_2019_ukr.pdf

Volkoff, V. (1984). *Vladimir the Russian Viking*. N.P: Honeyglen Publishing.

Vorobyev, S. (2020). 'Comparison of Russian Neo-Nazis and Putin's Statements About Ukraine,' 12 April. https://www.youtube.com/watch?v=ZD62ackWGFg

Vyatrovych, V. et al. (2018). *Donbas: Pereprochytannya Obrazu*. Kyiv: Ukrainian Institute of National Memory. https://uinp.gov.ua/elektronni-vydannya/broshura-donbas-pereprochytannya-obrazu.

Wawrzonek, M. (2014). 'Ukraine in the "Gray Zone": Between the "Russkiy Mir" and Europe,' *East European Politics and Society*, 28 (4): 758-780.

Weeks, T. R. (1996). *Nation and State in Late Imperial Russia. Nationalism and Russification on the Western Frontier, 1863-1914*. De Kalb, IL: Northern Illinois University Press.

Weight, R. (2000). *Patriots. National Identity in Britain 1940-2000*. London: Pan Macmillan.

Williams, C. and Smith., A.D. (1983). 'The national construction of social space,' *Progress in Human Geography*, 7(4): 502-518.

Williams, B. G. (2015). *The Crimean Tatars: From Soviet Genocide to Putin's Conquest*. London: Hurst.

Wilson, A. (1995). 'The Donbas between Ukraine and Russia: The Use of History in Political Disputes,' *Journal of Contemporary History*, 30 (2): 265-289.

Wilson, A. (2014). *Ukraine Crisis. What it Means for the West*. New Haven, CT: Yale University Press.

Wilson, A. (2016). 'The Donbas in 2014: Explaining Civil Conflict Perhaps, but not Civil War,' *Europe-Asia Studies*, 68 (4): 631-652.

Wolkonsky, A. (1920). *The Ukraine Question. The Historic Truth Versus The Separatist Propaganda*. Rome: Ditta E. Armani.

Wong, E. (2006). 'A Matter of Definition: What Makes a Civil War and Who Declares It So?' *New York Times*, 28 November. https://www.nytimes.com/2006/11/26/world/middleeast/26war.html

Wu, J. C. (2018). 'Disciplining Native Masculinities: Colonial Violence in Malaya, 'Land of the Pirate and the Amok' in: P. Dwyer and A. Nettlebeck eds., *Violence, Colonialism, and Empire in the Modern World*. New York and London: Palgrave and Macmillan, 175-196.

Yekelchyk, S. (2004). *Stalin's Empire of Memory. Russian-Ukrainian Relations in the Soviet Historical Imagination*. Toronto: University of Toronto Press.

Yekelchyk, S. (2019). 'The Crimean Exception: Modern Politics as Hostage of the Imperial Past,' *The Soviet and Post-Soviet Review*, 46 (3): 304-323.

Yermolenko, Y. ed., (2019). *Re-Vision of History. Russian Historical Propaganda and Ukraine*. Kyiv: K.I.S., Internews, Ukraine World. https://ukraineworld.org/storage/app/media/Re_vision_2019_block%20eng.pdf

Yushchenko, V. (2008). 'Pro Den khreshchennya Kyivskoyii Rusi-Ukrayiny,' Presidential Decree 668/2008, 25 July. https://www.president.gov.ua/documents/6682008-7760

Zakem, V., Saunders, P., and Antoun, D., (2015). Mobilizing Compatriots: Russia's Strategy, Tactics, and Influence in the Former Soviet Union. *CAN Analysis and Solutions*, November. https://www.cna.org/CNA_files/PDF/DOP-2015-U-011689-1Rev.pdf

Zarembo, K. (2017) ed., *Ukrayinske Pokolinnya Z: tsinnosti ta orientyry*. Kyiv: New Europe Centre. http://neweurope.org.ua/en/analytics/ukrayinske-pokolinnya-z-tsinnosti-ta-oriyentyry/

Zatulin, K. F. (2012). ed., *Yazykovoye ravnopraviye na Ukraine: problemyi i vozmozhnosty*. Moscow: Institute for CIS Countries. http://www.materik.ru/upload/iblock/c84/c84a9f6cc6ede9f5ce5442211e80bca5.pdf

Zelenskyy, V. (2020). 'Pro rishennya Rady natsionalnoyi bezpeky i oborony Ukrayiny vid 14 travnya 2020 roku 'Pro zastosuvannya personalnykh spetsial☐nykh ekonomichnykh ta inshykh obmezhuvalnykh zakhodiv (sanktsiy).' Presidential Decree 184/2020, 14 May. https://www.president.gov.ua/documents/1842020-33629

Zhuk, S. (2014). 'Ukrainian Maidan as the Last Anti-Soviet Revolution, or the Methodological Dangers of Soviet Nostalgia (Notes of an American Ukrainian Historian from Inside the Field of Russian Studies in the United States),' *Ab Imperio*, 3: 195-208.

Zhurzhenko, T. (2015). 'Ukraine's Eastern Borderlands: The End of Ambiguity' in: A. Wilson ed., *What Does Ukraine Think?* London: European Council on Foreign Relations, 45-52. https://www.ecfr.eu/publications/summary/what_does_ukraine_think3026

Zolotukhin, D. Yu. Ed., (2018). *Bila Knyha. Spetsialnykh Informatsiynykh Operatsiy Proty Ukrayiny 2014-2018*. Kyiv: Mega-Press Hrup. http://mip.gov.ua/files/pdf/white_book_2018_mip.pdf?fbclid=IwAR1oloK5UbxY5fyxRJLbnnd7FxcBPs6zEiNdqG89Rx7c23uLqriJ-ZVAYLY

Zygar, M. 2016. *All the Kremlin's Men. Inside the Court of Vladimir Putin*. New York: Public Affairs.

Note on Indexing

E-IR's publications do not feature indexes. If you are reading this book in paperback and want to find a particular word or phrase you can do so by downloading a free PDF version of this book from the E-International Relations website.

View the e-book in any standard PDF reader such as Adobe Acrobat Reader (pc) or Preview (mac) and enter your search terms in the search box. You can then navigate through the search results and find what you are looking for. In practice, this method can prove much more targeted and effective than consulting an index.

If you are using apps (or devices) to read our e-books, you should also find word search functionality in those.

You can find all of our e-books at: http://www.e-ir.info/publications

www.ingramcontent.com/pod-product-compliance
Lightning Source LLC
Chambersburg PA
CBHW071732080526
44588CB00013B/2003